Breaking into Television

Proven Advice from Veterans and Interns

**Dan Weaver and
Jason Siegel**

Peterson's

Princeton, New Jersey

About Peterson's

Peterson's is the country's largest educational information/communications company, providing the academic, consumer, and professional communities with books, software, and online services in support of lifelong education access and career choice. Well-known references include Peterson's annual guides to private schools, summer programs, colleges and universities, graduate and professional programs, financial aid, international study, adult learning, and career guidance. Peterson's Web site at petersons.com is the only comprehensive—and most heavily traveled—education resource on the Internet. The site carries all of Peterson's fully searchable major databases and includes financial aid sources, test-prep help, job postings, direct inquiry and application features, and specially created Virtual Campuses for every accredited academic institution and summer program in the U.S. and Canada that offers in-depth narratives, announcements, and multimedia features.

Visit Peterson's Education Center on the Internet (World Wide Web) at www.petersons.com

Copyright © 1998 by Peterson's

Library of Congress Cataloging-in-Publication Data

Weaver, Dan, 1957–
    Breaking into television : proven advice from veterans and
        interns / Dan Weaver and Jason Siegel.
    p.   cm.
  Includes index.
  ISBN 0-7689-0121-9 (pbk.)
  1. Television broadcasting—Study and teaching (Internship)—United States.
I. Siegel, Jason. II. Title.
PN1992.45.W43 1998
791.45'071'55—dc21   98-28763
                                                        CIP

Printed in the United States of America

10 9 8 7 6 5 4 3 2 1

dedication

to my dad, Ralph, who took me to my first television studio.

To my mom, Joanne, who typed my first television paper.

To Jane Temple and Carol Story, who took in a stray intern and gave me my wings.

To my sisters, Stephanie, Cindy, and Randi, and my brother Mike, who have always fueled my television journey.

And to Lee, who has given me my greatest internship in life.

—Dan Weaver

To my friends who became my family and my family who became my friends.

To my mom and dad, who always had faith in me: my debt to you is more than financial.

To Eric, Amy, and Snowflake for putting up with me.

To my "oh captain, my captain," George Rodman for never letting me do any less than my best.

To the memory of Bob Gresh and Loomis Irish: your influence on my life cannot be overstated.

—Jason Siegel

contents

foreword

at age 8, I built an entire *Price is Right* set out of cardboard. Neighborhood friends would gather in our wood-paneled basement, and I'd produce my make-believe show. New cars were given away on a daily basis.

At age 11, I built a lagoon in the woods behind our house. You guessed it: the neighborhood clan was now cast in daily after-school episodes of *Gilligan's Island*. My younger brother resented playing Skipper; Alan Hale's work was never fully appreciated.

When I was 17, we loaded up the Galaxy 500 and embarked on the proverbial family vacation to—where else—California. My parents secured tickets to a television taping at Metromedia Studios at the intersection of the Hollywood Freeway and Sunset Boulevard. Stage 6. 7 p.m.

For 4 hours, I sat mesmerized while countless actors, writers, camera people, and stage managers made Episode #126 of *Mama's Family* (you know, Vicki Lawrence, again underappreciated in a fine character role). Alas, I knew what I wanted to do with my life.

Maybe this sounds silly but if you are reading this book, most likely you can relate. Have you always dreamed of working in TV? Are you moved by the magic? If so, this book could change your life.

Here's an absolute fact: Every powerful executive, producer, director, or writer working in television started as an intern. The cliché is true—getting your foot in the door is the hardest part. This book will tell you how. It will tell you how to research internships, choose the right one, and how to ace the interview. It will reveal how to make the most of your internship and, most importantly, how to turn that internship into a real career in television.

Personally, I had no "connections." I grew up in a small midwestern town 2,000 miles from Hollywood. We knew farmers, not moguls. I desperately needed guidance from somebody on the "inside." This book is powerful because it contains very practical "inside" advice from over 100 successful television professionals, former interns themselves, including the executive producer of *Star Trek: Voyager*, David Letterman's personnel manager, talk show host Leeza Gibbons, and many others. Authors Dan Weaver and Jason Siegel, with whom I've made many hours of television, do an amazing job of navigating through the maze of television internships. I'm also honored that they have chosen me to be the first person inducted into the "TV Intern Hall of Fame."

When I eventually landed my internship, I delivered packages, made copies, poured cup after cup of coffee, and even picked up the dry cleaning. Luckily my mentor (Stephen Tao, now president of the USA Network) also took time to teach, actively involving me in the production of a pilot. The pilot was for a long-shot show called *Cops*, one that would eventually put a little upstart network, Fox, on the map.

Within eighteen months of my getting my internship, I had a real job and the opportunity to create and develop my own show. Believe it or not, in March 1991, I found myself back at Metromedia (now Fox Television) Studios—on Stage 6, the same sound stage I had visited ten years before.

Now I was on the studio floor, applying what I had learned as an intern, calling the shots. That night, as cameras rolled on Episode 101 of my first television hit series *Studs*, I couldn't help but wonder, "Was someone sitting in the audience dreaming of a career in television?"

Today, I head up programming for MTV and continue to consult as an original producer of *South Park*. In a typical week, I might preview Madonna's latest video, brainstorm hosts for the Video Music Awards, fly to Jamaica to oversee a shoot for *Spring Break*, or talk to *Newsweek* magazine about Cartman.

Supposedly, this is a job. But the ride is far too much fun to be called "work." I am living my dream; so can you. Read this book. Get your foot in the door. Make it happen. I have no doubt you'll succeed.

—Brian Graden
Executive Vice President, MTV
Developer, *South Park*
June 1998

acknowledgments

We have many Emmys to award when it comes to supporting players for this book. Extra special honors to our literary agent, Paige Wheeler, and our editor, Erika Heilman, who directed us well in our book debut.

Lifetime achievement trophies to Tisi Aylward, Diane Eaton, Adora English, Brian Graden, Chuck Lioi, and Jan Landis who were there from the beginning, birthing this book.

Thanks to Christian Walker for his incredible Web illustrations. Chris, the best artist award goes to you. Best writing award to Dane Hall. Also, kudos to Antony Beilensohn, George Severson, Craig Martinelli, and Herbie J. Pilato for their contributions.

Special thanks from Jason to Valerie Chiovetti, Kysha Mounia, Marni Joy Schmidt, Gregory Kestin, Steve Kalty, Katie Sweat, Elizabeth Behm, Heidi Smookler, Jason Kalan, Christine Webster, and Megan Stone and the rest of the University of Arizona students who gave a helping hand as the midnight oil burned. Thanks also to the University of Arizona Communication Department, the Brooklyn College TV/Radio Department, and Ami Hoffman, the Nagi family, the Kish family, Kish, Gina Caccesse, Jenna Messina, Bari Granowsky, Anthony Scire, Adam Kurnitz, Dave Ginsberg, David Tedeschi, Mikki Knudsen, Mike Dobbs, Leah Polcar, and Wendy Layne for their unconditional support.

Special thanks from Dan to Marlaine Selip, Bill Reardin, Glenn Meehan, Marla Kell Brown, and Marilyn Kagan, for all of their support. To my "other" brother, Jamie Huysman, to my "other father" John Kelly, and to my "other mothers" Barbara Zara and Helen Moore, thanks for all of your cheerleading. And gratitude to Brad Bessey, Jill Mullikin-Bates, Chuck Lioi, Kac Young, Edward Boyd, Barbara Hunter, Jack Forrestel, and John Zak. My thanks go to the wonderful cast of friends, co-workers, professors, mentors, and interns I've been fortunate enough to meet along this yellow brick road. You are too numerous to mention, but without your contributions, this project would not have come to life.

introduction

from CNN's breaking news to Oprah's hour of talk—from the Simpsons' spin on American life to David Letterman's Top Ten Lists—television shapes our thoughts, our dreams, our culture. It's no wonder that careers in the industry are among the most sought-after in America. Having your name flashed on the screen to millions of viewers—whether as a producer, writer, editor, or set designer—is an exciting prospect to many. And now with a menu of opportunities to choose from, including The Food Channel, ESPN, HBO, and Comedy Central, the industry has become a virtual sea of job possibilities, with shiploads of people racing to fill these positions.

Over the last decade, the number of students graduating with communication degrees has soared almost 500 percent. This translates to keen competition for the limited number of available television jobs. If you are a relative of Rupert Murdock or were high school pals with Jerry Seinfeld, you've got a good shot at your name being on the TV payroll. But what if you don't have that automatic foot-in-the-door? How can you still make the dream come true? In a word . . . intern.

DAN'S STORY:

I am celebrating twenty years this month being an intern. I say "being," because once you become one, you are always part of this special brotherhood and sisterhood. Like so many former-interns-turned-TV-success stories you're about to meet in the book, it was my internship that granted admission to TV Fantasyland and helped so many of my childhood dreams come true.

As a 5-year-old boy in Meadville, Pennsylvania, I was mesmerized by "Captain Penny," a show host from a children's program out of Cleveland. I wanted to live in the Captain's Comedy Clubhouse. How fitting that fifteen years later, I'd end up in that very studio, doing my internship and beginning my TV magic carpet ride on the *Morning Exchange*, the nation's number one locally produced morning show. Amazingly, that was only the beginning of the fulfillment of my childhood fantasies.

Another TV idol of mine was "Captain Kangaroo." Years later, it was awesome to produce his segment on *The Pat Sajak Show* and to actually "slip on" "Mr. Moose" and "Bunny Rabbit" and to shake the hand of the puppeteer who gave them life.

Growing up, I was also "bewitched" by Elizabeth Montgomery. How meaningful it was to eventually meet her and then to ultimately produce a minitribute about her for *Entertainment Tonight* after her death.

The soaps were another passion of mine. Thirty years ago, I watched *General Hospital* with my mom, back when the show still had organ music and well before Luke and Laura. How proud I was years later to be able to arrange for my sister Cindy to meet Nurse Bobbie and get a special tour of Port Charles!

I also loved watching Geraldo Rivera in high school. He would try anything on *20/20*. Years later, what a kick I got out of helping him "gain" 100 pounds for a show on weight loss and convincing him to have the fat sucked out of him for another show. What a great man and a great sport!

But it was while producing *Kelly and Company*, a live morning talk show in Detroit, that I discovered the real magical power of television. I did a segment on Sudden Infant Death Syndrome (SIDS) with a mother who had lost her child to this baffling condition. Two weeks later, a viewer wrote us saying how much she had learned from that show. She went on to say that she never dreamed that the following week, she would find her own infant dead from SIDS. "My life is a living hell now," she wrote, "but somehow I keep remembering that mother on your show. If she can make it, so can I." Truly, TV can change and even save lives.

I have always tried to use television as a teacher. When I was a producer on *Donahue*, Phil and I went to a hospital and talked with people in their final stages of AIDS. It was the most difficult, yet most memorable, hour of television I have ever done.

My proudest moment in TV has been creating the first talk show "Aftercare" program with Geraldo, executive producer Marty Berman, and psychiatric social worker Jamie Huysman. Through this program, more than fifty guests have received thousands of dollars' worth of free treatment—and new lives because of it.

Everything I have done on the tube relates back to that internship at WEWS-TV 5. Throughout my career, I have done everything I can to help students get the most out of their internships. This desire to help interns learn the tricks of the trade was the motivation for this book. It wasn't until recently, however, that the final inspiration came to me. About three years ago, while I was a development executive at Fox, I was introduced to a young man who had just left his friends, family, and true love to travel 2,500 miles to pursue an internship in Hollywood. Jason, who had the gleam in his eye that many of you probably have right now, became the greatest intern I have ever seen. In less than six months, he was a producer who hired and supervised all interns on a show I created, *Jim J. and Tammy Faye*.

Together, we want our experience to be put to good use. What are your dreams? I hope our words help you on your journey to achieving them.

JASON'S STORY:

My eight-week internship felt like eight days—it came and went without a blink. Looking back at what I knew before I walked in the doors, I can't believe how much I learned. The decisions I helped make had an effect on the television shows the entire country was watching.

How did it all happen? Two months before graduation, one of my professors announced that a Fox producer, Steve Ridgeway, a Brooklyn College alum, was coming to give a talk. This was a blessing in disguise because up until then I had no idea what I was going to do after graduation. When Steve came to give his presentation, I made sure that I brought a resume with me. After he was done, I gave it to him and told him I would love to work in the TV industry. Being close to many of my professors, I had no problem asking them to casually bring up my name a few hundred times when they saw Steve at the weekend reunion. On Monday, one of my professors gave me Steve's card. Immediately, I called him with all the anticipation and enthusiasm in the world. He told me that he couldn't offer me pay but I was welcome to come and intern in LA. The thought blew my mind. I couldn't picture myself working in this imaginary place . . . TV Land. Without thinking, I said, "Okay," and I was off to chase my dream.

Two months later, a week after graduation, I said good-bye to my best friends, my family, my girlfriend, and my doggie and hopped on a plane. It was a great feeling . . . I was on my way—Hollywood here I come! Too bad that when I got off the plane that excitement turned into gut-wrenching fear. Before I left New York, I figured if I ever stopped to really think about what I was doing there would be a chance fear would get the best of me. So, I didn't think about my trip whatsoever. No plans, no place to stay, no clue in the world.

I got a rental car and drove around Hollywood for hours looking for somewhere to live. After seeing that Hollywood Boulevard isn't as pretty in person as one might think and realizing that not every street in LA is filled with movie stars and limousines, I began to panic. Figuring I was never going to make it out of this situation alive, I began to wonder who would go to my funeral. My home for my first glorious Hollywood night turned out to be a room at the Sunset Palms Motel. Placing every movable piece of furniture against the door for safety, I tried to get some sleep. It didn't work. The next day, Steve helped me find a nicer place in Burbank. Still shaking from my night on Sunset, I kept badgering the landlord with questions of safety. He said, "Kid, you're from New York. What are you worried about?" He comforted me by saying that the apartment was next to a church. From there, the internship began.

Having no friends in LA was probably the best thing that happened to me. Since I knew nobody and had no place to go, I ended up hanging out at the station after all of the other interns went home. It was during those hours that I realized that the best way to get a good assignment was by default. If a producer needed a fresh set of eyes to read a script and no one else was in the building, I got the task. That is, of course, if the janitor was too busy. Before long I was staying late almost every night learning more and more about the industry and the staff. Within about a week, I had earned the respect and trust of many people on staff such that I was given the responsibility of looking after other interns. I was taken out to dinner, played golf cart derby on the fifth-floor parking garage, and had access to the boss's ranch, including the exterior hot tub located directly under every star in the sky.

This was not to say that my job was all fun and games. I was lonely, scared, and I missed my family and friends back home. Having no clue whether or not I'd be offered a job at the end of the internship didn't help either. I found myself having 4 a.m. anxiety attacks thinking of what my future would hold. Would I get a job? Would I be successful? Would I be able to survive next week as my money slowly dwindled? These thoughts rolled through my mind constantly.

I still remember sitting up the night after my internship ended. As sappy as it is, this what I wrote in my journal that night:

8/22/95

"So, it's finally over. Two months of insane hours and hundreds of dollars in savings spent, but it was all so worth it. Granted, I'm broke, and I've missed Jenna something fierce, but I did it. Tomorrow I'll wake up as an employee of the industry that I've spent the last four years studying and the last twenty-two years watching. I never thought I'd actually make it."

Once I got my first position, I began working twice as hard. I went from being an intern, to a production assistant, to an executive assistant, to an associate producer, to a producer, to a coordinating producer—all in the span of a year. I really had no clue what I was doing right, but I figured with hard work and a good attitude I would continue to succeed. By the two-year anniversary of my internship, I was being flown out to Minneapolis to do consulting work for UPN.

Looking back at my interning days, I remember being scared, lonely, and extremely overwhelmed. I lost my money and my girlfriend and spent plenty of time in a cold sweat trying to figure out what my future would hold. I also remember those days as some of the best in my life. It was like being a kid in Toys R Us. I couldn't believe I was part of the TV process. It was like a fairy tale. There's nothing I wouldn't give to go through that experience again.

You will definitely feel overwhelmed as you embark on your internship journey, but hang in there. Dreams do come true!

WHY SHOULD YOU INTERN?

As we started researching for this text, we realized more and more how important internships are becoming in every industry:

> *"More than ever, employers are looking for work experience and internships as evidence of a student's initiative."*
> —USA Today

> *"If you want a job after college, get an internship . . . It's the most bankable credential you can put on a resume."*
> —Maury Hanigan, President of Hanigan Consulting Group NYC

Considering the intense competition for a career in television, an internship in this field is close to essential. But what does an intern do, anyway? Like a doctor completing a "residency" in medicine, an "intern" is working as an apprentice for a television show, station, or newsroom in exchange for college or high school credit. Most are not paid, but what interns receive is greater than any salary.

Where else can you gain invaluable knowledge while sitting side-by-side with an editor racing to get a piece cut for *20/20*? How else will you have the opportunity to join a writer's meeting and contribute dialogue to an episode of *Friends*? While the thought of becoming a news director, creating your own series, or programming NBC's Thursday night line-up might seem like a mere pipe dream, it is very much achievable.

> *"I grew up in a place where the only people I knew were either farmers, bankers, or ex-football heroes. I always knew that someone must create the television programs I watched, but it just seemed sort of unreachable or untouchable."*
> —Brian Graden, Executive Vice President, MTV; Developer, *South Park*; and a former intern

From your first day you'll be making friends and contacts that will be your lifeblood once you're inside the business. You may find yourself doing some grunt work . . .

> *"The Executive Producer insisted that there were to be no bubbles in his coffee. If coffee is stirred too much, bubbles form on top. Whoever brought her coffee had to make sure it was bubbleless. It was a very serious thing."*
>
> —Chuck Lioi, Post Production Supervisor, *Sunset Beach*, and a former intern

. . . but, you'll acquire skills and experience to surpass any of those classmates who never left campus.

> *"Looking back at the graduating class, out of all those people who majored in TV, radio, or film, there are maybe fifteen of us working in the industry, and we're all people who had internships."*
>
> —Diane Eaton, *Wheel of Fortune*, *Rescue 911*, and *The Pat Sajak Show*, and a former intern

THE ONLY RULE IS THAT EVERYTHING IS THE EXCEPTION

By no means can we even attempt to claim that this book will give you perfect guidance for every situation. No book could possibly prepare you for every predicament that you will encounter on your journey. What one boss loves, the other boss will hate—that's just the way it is. We knew that in order to create a book that would truly give readers the knowledge they need to make it, the best thing we could do was combine our knowledge and experience with the advice and opinions of over 100 working members of the television industry. From the Executive Vice President of MTV, to the Supervising Producer of *The Bold and the Beautiful* (the world's most watched drama), to the Executive Director of Publicity and Promotion at Walt Disney Television, to Producers on *Good Morning America* and *Today*, you'll get firsthand thoughts from former interns who are now ruling the TV world.

Of course, not every one interviewed has their key to the executive washroom. Some have just finished their internships, some are still interning, some have been in the field for a couple of years and are still a little wet behind the ears, and others decided that the industry was not in their future.

We asked all of our TV players dozens of questions, such as:

What do you look for when you're sizing up an intern?
What should an intern know before the first day even begins?

What can an intern do to get himself or herself hired when the
    internship is over?

If you could do your internship over again, what would you do
    differently?

What is the most important thing for an intern to know?

These interns, former interns, and industry leaders are here to teach you
what their experience has taught them. Sometimes these employees of the
TV world will agree, other times they'll disagree completely. In either case:

Learn from Their Advice

*"A good intern is enthusiastic and happy to be a member of the team.
An even better intern helps anyone who asks at any time and adds to
the creative process with ideas of his or her own. A great intern doesn't
have to be asked to help out; great interns figure out what needs to be
done and get it taken care of."*

    —Charlie Cook, Supervising Producer, *Donny and Marie*, and a former
    Capitol Hill intern

Heed Their Warnings

*"I definitely know now far more than I ever did before about interning and
how to make it. But I got lucky when I interned. The competition wasn't as
fierce as it is now. You have to be prepared or you'll be crushed."*

    —Don Wells, News Director, KGTV San Diego, and a former intern

Follow In Their Footsteps

*"The lack of sleep had a major effect on me, but basically as soon as I
graduated I ended up being hired. I've worked ever since, and I owe
each paycheck to my internship."*

    —Tisi Aylward, Director, Talent, E! Entertainment Television, and a
    former intern

In addition, this book will induct the first twelve former interns into the
first-ever "TV Intern Hall of Fame." To make the "Hall," you don't have to
be Aaron Spelling. You just have to be someone who had a TV dream and
made it happen through interning.

    At the end of each "channel" you'll be treated to a personal tale from
one of our "famers." They'll tell you in their own words how they went from
TV viewer to TV intern to TV employee. You'll also benefit from

"Commercial Breaks," stories designed to provide some comic relief while offering some insight into how the business works. "Flashbacks" will also be found throughout this text. This is our way of telling stories of our experiences, from our worst fears to our greatest triumphs.

HOW SHOULD YOU READ THIS BOOK?

Read the text all the way through. First we'll help you figure out which part of the industry is right for you, then we'll help you set up the interview and score the starring role. Once you're in the door, this book will help you get to the top of the intern ladder and give you advice on how to turn your internship greatness into a paycheck.

After reading the entire book (yes, you do have to read the appendix and the glossary as well) take the book channel by channel doing the research, the leg work, and recommended soul-searching. To get the most out of this book, you must really dedicate yourself to your journey. Just reading the book, without doing the recommended work, will not get you where you want to go. For example, thinking about the lifestyle associated with your dream job isn't enough. You must make the calls, analyze the field, and be the one to make it happen. If you are not willing to truly commit yourself to your career, there will unquestionably be "super interns" who will crush you as they head for success.

These chapters offer a recommended pathway to success, but the element to remember is to use your own creativity and ambition to further your goals. Yes, heed the warnings but devise your own ideas for making your mark so that you don't come off as being formulaic. This is our story and we're pleased to share it with you.

Lastly, if you are looking for more information on TV internships, have a great internship story to share, or just want to get in touch with us, visit our Web site at **www.tvintern.com**.

Best of luck!

Dan Weaver and Jason Siegel

FADE TO BLACK
ROLL "TV INTERN HALL OF FAME" PACKAGE

••

THE TV INTERN HALL OF FAME SALUTES

Brannon Braga
Executive Producer, *Star Trek: Voyager,* and a former intern

I know what you're thinking. He's going to use Star Trek catch-phrases to get his point across. "Boldly go where no intern has gone before!" "Beam yourself to success!" "A galaxy of opportunity awaits!" You're right.

Before the Big Bang (in this case, my internship), my universe was small. I was a 6-year-old boy tapping at a plastic typewriter, creating little stories for my mother to read. One writer with an audience of one.

My universe expanded when I discovered television. By age 10, I realized that television had more impact than my stories. TV caused an immediate reaction in the viewer that you could see with your own two eyes. So I started writing screenplays. But like most writers, I had no idea how to become a "Hollywood professional."

I devoured every book I could find on the subject. I bought a Super-8 camera and convinced my teachers to let me make movies instead of doing homework. I went to film school at University of California, Santa Cruz. But more important, I kept on writing—every day, all the time. I knew an opportunity to break into show business might arise one day, and I wanted to be prepared. As it turned out, that opportunity was—you guessed it—an internship.

It was the summer of 1989. A year away from college graduation, I still had no idea how to get my foot in the door. On a whim, I applied for an internship—and a very good one at that. Each year, the Academy of Television Arts and Sciences offers twenty-six internships in categories ranging from directing to casting to network programming. I picked scriptwriting. But I didn't get the internship.

I applied again the following year and, this time, I succeeded. I was placed at Paramount Pictures on a popular TV show called *Star Trek: The Next Generation.* I'd never watched *Star Trek* in my entire life. In fact, I didn't really like science fiction. How was I going to fit in?

Eight years later, I'm still here only now I am the head writer and Executive Producer on *Star Trek: Voyager.* You might be wondering how my career went into warp drive. First of all, there was my internship: the Big Bang. During those two months, I saw how television worked. I had the honor of observing professionals in action. They took a gamble and gave me a script to write. It turns out I did a decent job and eventually they hired me as a staff writer. I wrote a few good episodes and they promoted me to Story Editor. The Executive Producer became my mentor and before long he was grooming me to take the job.

I was blessed. Important people took an interest in my career and helped me every step of the way. But it wasn't all good fortune. I'd been polishing my writing abilities for many years. When the internship came along, I had enough talent and skill to turn it into something more. The lesson: Be ready!

It's been a wild, wonderful ride. I've written over fifty *Star Trek* episodes and two *Star Trek* movies. Recently, I signed a multiyear deal with Paramount Pictures to develop my own television series. To my surprise, I won a Hugo Award for my writing and was nominated for an Emmy.

And the people I've met! Prince Charles, Ronald Reagan, the Shuttle astronauts, to name a few. I've even worked with some of the writers and directors I admired as a child. I still can't believe it.

But the best part of the job is remembering that little plastic typewriter. One writer but now I have an audience of millions. I haven't changed. My universe just got a whole lot bigger.

channel 1

Preparing for Prime Time Success

What do Spike Lee, Jodie Foster, JFK Jr., and President Clinton all have in common? They all began their road to success with a college internship. Throughout this book, we'll be introducing you to many people from our "TV Intern Hall of Fame." Some have just begun their trek toward success in the television industry, while others are well on their way. A few have even arrived at their television dream job. Now it is time for you to join the ranks of the successful and, as we mentioned in the Introduction, the best way to break in to this exclusive profession is to secure an internship. To do so requires a lot of hard work, so let the countdown begin:

THREE . . .

"Regardless of whether you want to become a director, writer, camera operator, or do any of the hundreds of other TV jobs on a local or national level, your first career break will most likely come while you're still in school. From the smallest TV and cable stations to the largest studios, thousands of students each year are finding that internships are an entrée to their first job."

> —Price Hicks, Director, Educational Programs and Services, The Academy of Television Arts and Sciences

TWO . . .

"Here's the thing they never taught me in school. I could spend six weeks writing copy and coordinating designs to create the perfect campaign. Then the client sits down, listens to the tag line, and hates it! There isn't any college class that will prepare you for what to say for the next hour of that presentation. Trust me. You can spend four years in college and two for your master's, but the only course of action that will ever really matter is your internship."

> —Ellen Fruchtman, President, Fruchtman Marketing in Toledo, and a former intern

ONE . . .

"In the past, you were special if you did an internship. It was rarely done. A producer would go down to the corner, kidnap someone, and say, "Hey, do you want to work in TV?" Now everyone's doing it. You have to do more than one internship to get noticed. Interns are everywhere. There are hundreds, thousands of these worker bees. They have become the lifeblood of television."

—Tisi Aylward, Director, Talent, E! Entertainment Television, and a former intern

AND ACTION!

THE STARTING POINT—READY, SET, GO!

Before you start your intern engines, know that this TV journey will probably be the most incredible voyage that you've ever taken, but it will also be one tough trip. Try to have faith in your abilities, and most important, keep your eye on the finish line: Your TV dream job!

This channel begins by asking you to dream about that perfect TV job. This is the fun part. Who doesn't love to imagine their Emmy speech? Who will present your trophy—Katie Couric, perhaps, or Oprah? In your "thank-you speech," will your dog, Shakespeare, come before or after your mom? We'll put you to the test (literally) to find out what TV intern program is best for you. Later, you'll get recommendations on how many times to intern, when to intern, and tips on how to have the most effective experience. If you can't follow all the advice because of financial or personal reasons, that's okay. There is plenty of information in this book to lead you from TV intern to TV mogul. So as Arsenio Hall would say, "Let's get busy!"

R-E-S-P-E-C-T

Be aware that you will probably get mixed reviews about your internship endeavors. Some people will respect your tenacity, others will make fun of you. If you get a little teasing, don't be discouraged. Years from now, you may hit the local diner for a quick burger and discover a former communication classmate behind the counter! Don't be surprised if the one who used to tease you about making coffee is now asking you, "Would you like fries with your shake?" Never underestimate the power of your TV internship, and also give yourself a large dose of credit for taking the initiative. That's exactly the kind of behavior and drive that'll set you apart from the rest!

> *"Ed Burns, the hot writer, director, and actor, was once an intern at Entertainment Tonight. I will never forget the day he drove the van like a rocket ship through New York traffic to get me to an interview on time. He was always humble and took his internship seriously. I'm always nice to interns because I know I'll be working for them someday."*
> —Leeza Gibbons, Talk Show Host and a former intern

WHERE TO BEGIN?

The first step is figuring out where you'd like to plant yourself in this huge field of television. Think back to what it was that inspired you to enter television in the first place. Did you grow up picturing yourself penning your own *Seinfeld* episode? Have you ever yelled at the director of *General Hospital* to get a close up when she held the two-shot too long? Ever go to bed dreaming about covering a breaking story for *World News Tonight* and then tossing it back to Peter Jennings? "YOUR NAME HERE, ABC News, London."

It's essential to click the remote control in your mind and really analyze what buttons TV has pushed inside your soul. What did you daydream about while growing up?

- Going in for a close-up on Heather Locklear's face as a director?
- Briefing Larry King between breaks as a producer?
- Plotting NBC's Thursday night line-up as a programming executive?
- Covering the Democratic primary as a reporter?
- Writing and creating the next hit sitcom as a development executive?
- Doing play-by-play on *Monday Night Football* as a sports anchor?
- Deciding which beach chairs look better on *The Bold and the Beautiful* as a set decorator?
- Deciding how the series finale of *The Simpsons* will end?
- Cutting a CBS *Movie of the Week* as an editor?
- Doing Mimi's eye shadow on *The Drew Carey Show* as head make-up artist?

Sit back and ponder these questions:

What Emmy award do I want to win?
What kind of TV job is really going to make me happy?
How can I make a positive difference?

Despite what the naysayers would like to have you believe, television is an extraordinarily powerful medium with an unparalleled ability to affect people's lives. One well-produced program can speak to millions in a way no other form of media can. Think about it.

Start with "The Trades"

Still coming up with nothing but static when deciding which part of the biz is for you? Here's a simple test. Go to your local newsstand and track down "the trades." The trades are daily/weekly papers published specifically for the TV industry. These magazines and newspapers contain all of the latest entertainment news, casting deals, planned projects, overnight ratings, and even births and deaths in the industry. They are the bibles of the business, read religiously by professionals. Most college libraries carry them, and you can go on line for them too. Here's a money-saving tip: Start asking your parents or relatives to buy you subscriptions to these vital magazines in place of birthday or holiday gifts. While the latest CD might be great, the information you'll receive month after month from a trade journal could very well prove invaluable.

Variety, Broadcasting and Cable, Hollywood Reporter, and *Electronic Media* are among the leading trade publications. The calendar section of the *Los Angeles Times* and the "Living Arts" section of the *New York Times* are also valuable sources of information. Page through them and see which articles

"ON SPECIAL ASSIGNMENT" #1

List all the jobs you have ever dreamed about having. Don't forget to list which genre you'd like to work in as well. If you want to be a producer, is it in sitcoms or in news? If you want to be an editor, is it cutting for sports events or soaps? Dial in on your TV desires and be "REEL" specific . . .

1. _____

2. _____

3. _____

4. _____

5. _____

catch your eye. Did you automatically jump to the items about news, programming, sales, development, syndication, or production? Consider browsing the classified section to pique your interest in areas you've never considered before. Does any ad whet your career whistle? Even if you're not sure about your ultimate dream job, it's a start. If you're passionate about any facet of the industry, let that passion be your guide. Those TV trenches are going to get pretty murky at times, and passion is often your only companion.

If you are already browsing the trades, you've got a great head start. If you haven't been, it's time to catch up. On the average, 100,000 industry insiders read the *Hollywood Reporter* daily. You should make it 100,001. Start now. What if you're totally bored reading the trades? You may want to question if you have enough passion to be in TV. To make it, you are going to need to live and breathe this business. If you don't, the other job-hungry interns reading this book are going to eat you alive.

Are You Entering the Industry for the Right Reasons?

A TV career will make you the hit of your high school reunion. Whether you're working with the local weatherman or David Letterman, people can never hear enough about the business. A survey in the *Journalism Educator* found that, "the most satisfying dimension of work within the media industries is the prestige." You'll be the life of the party, but is that the only reason you're entering the industry? If so, you are in for a bumpy ride. The television obstacle course requires much training. Does the idea of devouring the trades with your morning cereal bore you? How do you feel about taking as many as three different internships? Are you ready to give up a lot of sleep and partying with your friends?

Television is about sacrifice. Sure, it's possible you'll find an ideal 9-to-5 television job right in your hometown. However, more than likely, as will be discussed later in this channel, you'll have to move to a different part of the country and work long hours to make it in broadcasting.

"I interned at a TV station in Cleveland. Talk about sacrifices—up every morning at 4:30 a.m. to be to work at 6 for our 8 a.m. live show. I rarely saw daylight. It didn't leave any time for partying. But it was worth it . . . I was hired the very next day after graduation."
—Debbi Casini, Pittsburgh TV Producer and a former intern

As stated in the *American Journalism Review*, "The truth is, of course, that life is not a tidy black-and-white drama. Real reporters don't really score headline-grabbing scoops every week." Working in broadcasting is not like living on an episode of *Murphy Brown* or *The Mary Tyler Moore Show*. Unfortunately, too many people enter the industry with that false hope. Take some time and really ponder your reasons for wanting to get inside the tube. Are you truly interested in covering news story after news story? If no one ever knew you worked on a hit TV show, would you still want to do it? What if you had the opportunity to work on your favorite show, but you wouldn't be able to meet any of the cast members? Still interested? In other words, answering yes to these questions most likely indicates that you're entering the profession for the appropriate reason.

What is it about this industry that gets you excited? Remember: Editors love the art of cutting the film or video just perfectly; camera people are known to get chills when they catch just the right shot; producers feel they are on top of the world when everything comes together perfectly; comedy writers thrive on the laughter of the studio audience; news reporters live for breaking that once-in-a-lifetime story; development executives dream about getting their show on prime time; salespersons fantasize about getting their syndicated show sold to New York, LA, and Chicago; advertisers pray for the moment when their commercial is played during the Super Bowl.

Are you going into the industry because you truly love the work itself, not the image associated with the work? If you're sure, prepare for greatness. Find the nearest phone booth and change into your costume to become SUPER INTERN!

DOING THE DETECTIVE WORK ON TV JOBS

If you are sure you're here for the right reasons, then it's time to research the responsibilities and duties of your dream job. Very few people would walk into a final exam without studying for it, and yet way too many people choose a potential TV career totally on impulse. Round up the bloodhounds, grab your magnifying glass, and prepare for the most important investigation of your life.

Many people think they know which part of TV is for them, only to be sadly disappointed. Don't let this happen to you. Most likely you'll end up working over 200 hours for free in hopes of landing a job. Doesn't it make sense to spend at least 20 hours doing research to be sure you'd want to take the job if it's offered to you?

"A student should figure out what he or she wants to specialize in, like a doctor does. Is it telefilms, drama, news, comedies, programming, sales, or sitcoms that gets you the most excited? Pursue that field. Like a

medical student, you don't want to choose proctology over podiatry because you didn't know the difference."

—Kac Young, Vice President, Television Production and Development, Universal Studios Hollywood, and a former intern

Television jobs differ greatly, and it's essential that you know all the types and areas. The duties depend on the genre, the size of a company, your geographical location, the show or station's budget, and a dozen other factors.

Your internship will be a great way to narrow down your search for your ultimate position. Nevertheless, if you can fine-tune your interests now and get an internship in that area, all the better. When researching the aspects of the TV industry, the lifestyle associated with many TV jobs is often overlooked.

TAKE TIME TO PONDER

The Lifestyle of Working in TV

While it's crucial to know the responsibilities that go with your potential dream job, you must also be aware of the effect your career will have on your personal life. Spend time now to consider the sacrifices; you may save yourself a lot of time and misery. It's not uncommon for people to leave the industry, wanting more stability, better hours, or a safer and saner existence:

> *"I loved my job as a news reporter in one of the ten biggest markets in the country. But when my son was born I realized the danger in it. They wanted me to go cover the Rodney King trial, but as a black reporter I felt vulnerable, I felt the tension. I looked at my wife and son. There were too many family functions I had to back out of because of a breaking story. Should I go to my son's baptism or cover the LA riots? It wasn't fair to say 'no' to my wife or my job. And suddenly it wasn't fair to me to always be in this situation. So I decided to leave. Today I sell life insurance, and, while I do miss news, I am very happy."*
>
> —Darryl Savage, former News Reporter and a former intern

Here's another brutally honest piece of information about working in TV: More often than not, industry employees don't have families and the divorce rate is high. Producing television and raising children can work, but it requires a great deal of effort.

Stephan Reynolds, a reporter from one of the top ten markets, has had major challenges juggling family and career. After his show was canceled, he had to uproot his wife and two kids to a new city because of a job offer. "The lack of security in this business puts a strain on a marriage. My wife is wonderfully understanding, but there are certainly days she wishes I were selling life insurance instead." But despite all the rejection, the periods of unemployment, and the insecurity, Stephan still loves his work. "There are still those days when I am shocked that actually I get paid to work in the greatest playground: The TV studio!"

Former news intern Brian Anderson has just moved out to LA to work in TV. He has found out that his TV experience in the number eight market doesn't mean beans in Tinseltown. He has been pounding a lot of pavement and doors for the last three months. Recently he was one of 300 applicants for a low-paying production assistant job on an infomercial. For now, he is waiting tables at Applebee's, but he has not lost his passion for the business. However, looking back, he would have charted his TV course differently: "I needed to take my internship more seriously, focus my direction, and develop contacts sooner. As I now think about settling down and getting married, I don't even know if becoming a sportscaster is all that practical. On the same note, even as I see my savings account shrink, I can't imagine myself in any other field. I just should have been a better planner while in college."

Moving, Again?

Are you willing to move to Timbuktu? Very often, especially in news, the industry forces people to relocate. You're usually not going to start reporting in New York or Los Angeles; Fargo is much more likely. What happens if you've just put the kids in school in Erie and you get an offer in Atlanta? Would you uproot? Keep location, finances, and job security in mind when weighing your career options.

Out of Work Again?

Can you handle being unemployed? Is it possible that you'll have the same job for life? Maybe, but highly doubtful. The bigger the market you're in, the less chance of getting a job for life. It is not uncommon to be working 100 hours one week, raking in big bucks, and then be unemployed for several months. The Screen Actors Guild says only about 2 percent of Hollywood actors are employed at any given time. The rest of the TV industry often doesn't fare much better. TV people are often put on a financial and emotional roller coaster. Can you handle it?

How Long Are You Willing to Wait?

Although an internship will steer you toward your dream job, especially if you follow the advice in this book, it still may be several years away. Can you hold out?

> *"Five years after an internship in market #140, I'm still waiting to set foot into a high-powered newsroom."*
> —Sheila Brummer, News Anchor, WAOW-TV, Wausau, Wisconsin, and a former intern

Associate Producer and Researcher Wayne Hopkins has had a staggering thirteen jobs in two years since finishing his internship. As he points out, "That's production!" While he's gone back and forth from being overworked to penniless, he remains very optimistic that his dream job is out there. "And along the way I have gotten to work with everybody from Jerry Lewis and Dick Clark to Sinbad. If I wanted security, I would have been a shoe salesman!" Do *you* have the drive to get your foot in the TV door?

Some Other Options

Keep in mind there are jobs that will allow you to have a very sane 45-hour work week. A Human Resource Executive with one of the world's largest entertainment companies told us that positions in promotions, computer graphics, sales, etc., aren't difficult to find, and they offer a solid pay check with a solid lifestyle for the right individual. You may wish to consider working on the "edges" of the television world by pursuing one of these more traditional professions within the industry.

The Final Jeopardy Bonus Question

What are you willing to sacrifice to get into this industry? Don't let this channel scare you away from your dream. Let it be a wake-up call and help you better prepare for this highly competitive business. Sure, we'd rather be able to say "Everyone's going to make it and live happily ever after," but if the goal of this book is to help get you working in television, then it is also our responsibility to make you aware of some of its potential downfalls. On the same note, keep in mind, they are just *potential* downfalls. There are many people who make it all work; it is possible! Just walk in to the TV screen with your eyes wide open. All these questions might be giving you a headache, but they must be considered!

COMMERCIAL BREAK:

"I arrived in LA with my life savings of $3,000, and one of the first things I did was go to a taping of *Family Ties*. While there, I went up and talked to a page about what he did and how he got in. 'It doesn't pay anything, the hours stink, and the work isn't filled with the glamour you might expect,' he offered. I was still interested, and he got me an interview. As a tour guide, I must have had 100 people a day tell me how they wanted my job. I loved it. I still can't believe what I was exposed to. As an NBC page, I found myself backstage on the set of *Family Ties*, *The Golden Girls*, and *Wheel of Fortune*. I helped coordinate an affiliates convention, two network press tours, five Bob Hope Specials, the Democratic Presidential Debates, and the Emmys. I joked with hot comedians, lunched with network executives, and passed out tickets for *Scrabble*. Don't forget to consider page programs when researching internships."

—Herbie J. Pilato, TV Historian, Author, and a former NBC page

MONEY, MONEY, MONEY

The salary scale varies considerably in TV. The 1997 *Forbes* 400 lists Michael Eisner, CEO of Disney, as being worth about $760 million while listing Oprah Winfrey as the wealthiest on-air personality, having already banked an estimated $550 million. Now that's something to talk about! According to *Advertising Age*, the "total compensation" for some top TV execs in 1995 was as follows:

1. Gerald M. Levin, Chairman/CEO Time Warner—**$5,310,969**
2. Herbert J. Siegel, Chairman/President Chris-Craft Industries—**$4,532,219**
3. Leonard Tow, Chairman/CEO Century Communications Corp.—**$3,973,733**.

Even Murray the dog from the NBC program *Mad About You* reportedly fetches $3,000 a week. When you start out, you may be eating Murray's dog food to get by. Entry-level positions, such as runners, production assistants, and pages (those behind-the-scene people who escort audience members to their seats) in large markets earn around $300–$700 per week. In smaller markets, it can go as low as $200 a week. It takes time for the big bucks to come in, and for many it never happens. What is the least you can live on now, and what do you hope to be making in five years? Salaries range greatly in this industry, and it's vital to find out what your dream job pays. For a breakdown of salaries for a variety of positions in different parts of the industry, tune in to the Glossary at the end of this book.

The Variables
Your salary will depend on several variables:

1. *The size of the market.*

According to a 1996 Radio-Television News Directors Association survey, a News Director in a Top 25 market makes an average of $107,500, whereas a News Director in a 101–150 market makes about $45,000. A News Producer averages $36,000 in the larger markets and $19,500 in the smaller ones.

> *"It really floored me that it took four years as a reporter in the #15 market to surpass what I was making in LA as a production assistant!"*
> —Darryl Savage, former News Reporter and a former intern

Is the show national or local? A producer for a show only seen in St. Louis will not make nearly as much as one working on a show with a national audience. Also, salaries are usually larger on syndicated shows. These are shows sold to individual stations around the country, such as *Oprah* or *Entertainment Tonight*, as opposed to network shows, where an outlet like ABC or Fox creates its own programming, like *Good Morning America*.

2. *The position.*

The National Association of Broadcasters and the Broadcast Financial Management Association did a survey in 1990: News Anchors' salaries averaged $52,000/year, ranging from $27,000 in the smaller markets to $129,000 in larger ones. Weathercasters averaged $43,000/year, ranging from $25,000 to $98,000, again depending on market size. Do you want to be a sportscaster? The average is $40,000/year, $23,000 in smaller cities, $109,000 in larger ones. What job can you afford?

> *"I had been a weekday producer for a station in El Paso. This was my dream job right out of college. But what really angered me was finding out that after doing this two years and being their top producer putting on two shows a night, I was still making less than a rookie reporter hired there [LA] straight out of college!"*
> —Richard Ayoub, Executive Producer, *KABC Morning News* in LA, and a former intern

3. *The size of the staff.*

In 1996, if you were a News Anchor at a station with a staff of 51+, the RTNDA survey reports you would have made $117,000 versus $30,000 at a station with a staff of 11–20. An independent station in Boston would most likely have a much smaller staff than a network-owned station in the same market.

4. *The station or the network.*

Some places just pay their staff more. E! Entertainment Television is much lower on the pay scale than a dinosaur like Paramount TV. In general, cable networks like CNN, the Discovery Channel, and A&E pay less than syndicators like King World, Tribune Entertainment, or MCA Universal for the same kind of position. Just remember that money isn't the only thing that talks in television. A good working environment and a chance for advancement are important, too. Cable networks have seen incredible growth the last few years. According to recent information from the National Cable Television Association, the top ten biggest networks (by subscribers) are:

1. ESPN
2. CNN
3. TBS
4. USA
5. DISCOVERY
6. TNT
7. C-SPAN
8. MTV
9. A&E
10. TNN

Staying Power

Make sure you check out the prognosis for various professions over the next few years. Technology has changed the demand for certain positions. Some news stations don't even have camera-people anymore; cameras are robotic, run by remote control. Be sure to scan the trades for a weather forecast of your desired profession. Are thunderstorms fast approaching?

> *"The TV sales market is exploding and there are wonderful job opportunities. Sales execs can sell cable services to consumers, sell time to local stations, cable companies, and networks. There are many*

options. In sales you are well compensated, unlike other areas of the business. You are rewarded for a big sale. Consider sales if you are looking for a lucrative area in TV."

—Lou Dennig, Senior Vice President of Programming, Worldvision Enterprises, and a former intern

Sales jobs are selling well in TV. What are some other areas? In the June 1997 issue of *U.S.News & World Report*, a "computer animator" in entertainment made the "20 Hot Job Tracks List."

U.S.News & World Report Online considered the creation of thirty new 24-hour cable news stations when they selected the position of "TV news producer" as their "Hot-Track Runner Up."

According to an established Human Resource Executive in the industry, jobs in ". . . software technology, computer generated graphics, stop animation, and all kinds of engineering are huge explosive areas." People cannot be hired fast enough in these areas. You can become an entertainment producer for CD-ROMs. The industry is changing dramatically; it is much more technically driven than it ever was. Don't forget big international career opportunities!

Plan a trip to the library to see what other jobs hold the hottest tickets in television.

Take the list of jobs you wrote in *"On Special Assignment" #1* and track down the responsibilities and lifestyle associated with each—don't start shortening the list just to avoid work.

When researching, get as specific as possible. Investigate not only your desired position but the responsibilities of that position in different genres as well. For example, read the following testimonials to understand the range of opportunities that producers have in the industry.

Producer of a Game Show

"As a producer of Price, I was under a deadline to have the show ready to tape on a given date. We shot two shows on Mondays, Tuesdays, and Wednesdays. If there was a problem on stage, I would have to stop tape, analyze the situation, and report to the Executive Producer. I would sit with Bob Barker and let him know of anything unusual coming up. I'd sort through prize information sheets and coordinate them with Contestant Awards. Each show needs about fifty prizes, and you try not to repeat them more than every two weeks. I oversaw scripts, staging

---

"ON SPECIAL ASSIGNMENT" #2

Answer the following questions as best as you can:

How much money do you need to make?

_____

How many hours are you willing to work?

_____

Are you willing to relocate?

_____

How much stress can you deal with on a daily basis?

_____

How do you see yourself in ten years? Married? Married with children?

_____

What would you do if you were in the middle of your kid's first birthday party when a huge news story broke? Would you leave to get the scoop?

_____

---

sheets, and graphics. On Fridays, producers would work in the 'War Room,' where you'd map out six shows for a coming week. It was grueling."

    —Barbara Hunter, Director of Daytime Programs, CBS

Producer of a Talk Show

"Being a Leeza producer means being part detective, part 'artiste,' and part therapist. Shows that rate the highest for us are news-reactive, so we spend a great amount of time going after breaking stories (the detective part). Every talk producer has his war stories of booking guests, flying to a news scene, scoring a guest at a party, or hitting the streets . . . but I'd say 90 percent of a producer's day is spent on the phones. The standards for guests here are high; they need to be articulate, passionate, friendly, and presentable. You often have to talk a guest into doing the show (the therapist part). Once you've done the *bookings, the pre-interviews, and the research, then comes the creative (the 'artiste') part. You figure out a provocative way of laying out the show and writing the script."*

　　—Jill Mullikin-Bates, Supervising Producer, *Leeza*, and a former intern

Producer of a Sitcom

"When I was Supervising Producer of In the House, *I was very involved in running the writer's table, casting, working out stories. I'd try to help an Executive Producer without appearing to want to take over the show. My job is mainly to serve as a crossing guard and try to make sure the 'baby' gets across the street without getting hit by a bus. This attitude has worked well for me, with the exception of one pair of EPs whose own incompetence sent the poor baby out to play in the middle of traffic and left all the writers on the curb to just yell, 'Watch out!'"*

　　—Jeffrey Duteil, Executive Producer, *The Steve Harvey Show*; Emmy-nominated writer, *The Golden Girls*

Producer of Daytime Drama

"A good producer has involvement in all aspects of the show. It's our responsibility to have the final say on the show's various production values (set design and decorating, lighting, costumes, hair/makeup, etc.). When we walk into the booth each day, we have to evaluate each area to be sure the look is appropriate for the scenes that day, for continuity, and for anything special that may be upcoming. We are the final word on production needs and changes. We are also responsible for guiding each day's performances. This is the most difficult area and the one that really takes the time and patience and the commitment to being 'inside the characters.' As producers, we have to be comfortable that we know the reasons for each action and word, and if things aren't working, we have to be able to make adjustments quickly. Add the various problems of staff, cast and crew, editing of shows, scheduling the week's shooting, and generally putting out all kinds of production brushfires, and that's the job."

　　—Deveney Kelly, Producer/Director, *The Bold and the Beautiful*

Producer of a News Program

"News producers combine a journalist's sense of what's a good story with the knowledge of what makes good TV. They look every day for

what's significant, what's visually exciting, and sometimes combine the two. The ability to write with special clarity and creativity, familiarity with journalistic standards, ethics, and the law—all combined with a certain amount of technical knowledge and the ability to time a live broadcast—are an unusual combination of skills for a difficult job, done behind the scenes and often without recognition!"

—Dana Benson, News Director, KMSP-TV, and a former intern

Producer of a Sports Program

"Basically, producers are responsible for coordinating all aspects of a show. They make sure the host/anchors are set and have everything they need. They schedule guests. Producers select the stories or pieces that are going to run and where. They do write some of the stories and/or introductions and check the ones that they don't write. And they have to make sure the show is the proper length, if it involves a timeslot."

—Jonathan C. Kilb, Coordinating Producer, New England Cable News, Videographer Boston Bruins/Celtics, and a former intern

EXPLORING ALL THE OPTIONS

Reading the Glossary may give you some help in narrowing down your search for the perfect job, but it is not a substitute for hard-core investigating.

Here's how to find out the necessary information about your "dream job:"

1. *Quiz your professors and fellow students about every job on your list.*

They probably researched various areas, or may even know people who've held these positions.

2. *Track down alumni.*

Many schools have College Directories that give career updates on school graduates. Find this book and seek out the alums who hold jobs that interest you. They'll be helpful. The college bond will always bind you, and they may become a great contact.

"Contact people from your college. You immediately have something in common. If you're reading your local paper and you find out that

somebody who went to your high school is now working in a certain place, track that person down. They'll be flattered and ready to help you."

> —Adora English, Producer, *KTLA Morning News* in LA, and a former intern

3. *Go to the library.*

There are dozens of books breaking down every kind of career option. For starters, check out the *Occupational Outlook Handbook* (http://stats.bls.gov/oco/ocohome.htm). *Careers for Film Buffs & Other Hollywood Types* (VGM Horizons, 1996) is a book that offers an encyclopedia of TV positions available.

4. *Hop on the Web.*

You can get additional help and/or information by contacting TV organizations like the Broadcast Education Association (www.usu.edu/'bea/main.html), the Radio-Television News Directors Association (www.rtnda.org/rtnda/), the Society of Professional Journalists (http://spj.org), and the Academy of Television Arts and Sciences (www.emmys.org). Also check out the Communications Roundtable (www.roundtable.org/siteoverview.html).

5. *Contact some stations.*

If your professors, fellow students, the Web, and the library can't answer all of your questions, it's time to hit the TV station in your area.

Call some program managers, introduce yourself, and ask if you can come and hang around with them at work. You might be saying, "Oh yeah, I'll just call Rupert Murdock, the head of Fox, and we'll chat about life." Mr. Murdock may not take your call, but a local news director or assistant program director probably will.

> *"I highly recommend going on an informational interview by calling a station Executive Producer or News Director. What EP doesn't like talking about herself or himself?"*
>
> —Shannon Keenan, Producer, Live Events, E! Entertainment Television, and a former intern

This might be harder to do in larger markets. If you're in New York, you may want to try one of the smaller cable stations.

How do you track down the phone numbers of program managers? Often TV stations are listed in the front of a phone book or in the TV section of your newspaper. If you have access to the Web, look up the "Ultimate TV" Web site (www.ultimatetv.com/tv/us/stations1.html). This site will give you the call letters of any station in the country. Did you know that the call letters for the Fox affiliate in Dothan, Alabama, is WDAU? Cable stations are on this site as well.

Just remember, persistence is key—don't give up. Sooner or later someone will talk to you. After you make contact and get as much information as possible, be sure to write down each contact's name and add it to your growing Rolodex. Many people will tell you over the years how small the business is; they're right. Now list all the jobs that still seem up your alley. It's time to take your research one step further.

THE NEXT STEP

Now that you've done your digging and know which TV job you'd like to claim, it's time to map out the best plan of internship attack. Here are important things to consider.

How Many Times Should You Intern?

You should try, if at all possible, to intern on three different occasions. Why three?

1. *Practice makes perfect.*

"ON SPECIAL ASSIGNMENT" #3

List all the jobs that, after researching the duties and lifestyle, still pique your interest:

1. _____

2. _____

3. _____

4. _____

5. _____

As television news veteran Adora English says, "the more you intern, the better you get." She started her "intern career" as a junior and three internships later found herself with real job value, a whole lot of experience, and "well ahead of the graduation pack." By planning on doing more than one, you will become much more marketable than your competition.

Taking three internships is ideal. Your first internship will be a great baptism, but you'll make mistakes; you're human. In your second, you'll be wiser and come across as more seasoned. They'll be ready to build a shrine around you during your third one. By then, you'll be experienced, knowledgeable, and confident about your career choice.

2. *Having a previous internship on your resume will give you an edge when going for the more competitive internships.*

How many students will be graduating with three different career-related experiences on their resume? Tim Mancinelli, Associate Director for *The Late, Late Show with Tom Snyder*, says run, don't walk, to your nearest internship. "It will not only help your resume, but you'll build a good contact base for when you finish school. Internships will give you that 'edge' over other applicants applying for the same job."

> *"My internship at WNEV in Boston helped me get my BBC Internship. Both aided me in landing my first job at ABC Network. Employers care more about where you've been than what college you graduated from. Intern Power!"*
> —Randi Kaye, New York News Reporter and a former intern

3. *Everyone makes mistakes.*

What happens if you put all of your internship eggs in one basket and hate it? By deciding to do only one internship, you might be putting yourself in a bad situation.

If nothing else, you'll find out what you don't want to do. CBS Soap Producer/Director Deveney Kelly remembers her first production job as a writer's secretary on *Welcome Back, Kotter* all too well. "After just three weeks, it was clear to me that the job I never wanted to have was being an associate producer. It was a no-win situation." It's better to find out that you don't like a position during your internship as opposed to after you have relocated 3,000 miles and spent your life savings for your "dream job."

4. *You can never have too many contacts.*

In an industry where "who you know" is as important as anything else, doesn't it make sense to get as many internship contacts as possible? Why not walk away from your internships with your own fan club?

> *"Looking back, I wished I had taken an internship every quarter. My first one was in the research department at CBS, where I learned all about ratings and audience testing. My second was with* The Price is Right. *It was there I met my mentor, Barbara Hunter. She is now the Director of Daytime for CBS. You can't believe the base of people in this business who were interns. The more you do, the broader your base."*
> —Bob Boden, Vice President, Development and Production, FX Networks

FLASHBACK

"I definitely know the feeling of waking up in the middle of the night with cold sweat dripping down my forehead. I think it's called pre-graduation syndrome. I was a month away from graduation without the slightest clue about what I was going to do. I would spend hours pondering the past four years of my college life, trying to figure out what I could have done differently, wondering where I went wrong. I panicked for weeks, I was sick for days on end, but when it came down to it, it worked out. The funny thing is, the more people I talked to, the more I realized my situation wasn't unusual. Not only do most people wait for the end of their senior year to start interning, many wait until a year after graduation to begin the journey. If only someone could have told me that everything was going to work out before the panic attacks, I would have slept much better my senior year."
—Jason

When Should You Start Interning?
Like many subjects discussed in this book, there is no "best way." Opinions differ depending on whom you ask:

> *"I think college students should intern as soon and as often as they can afford to. They should look for colleges with good internship programs and be willing to go anywhere for experience where they REALLY learn."*
> —Gail Frank, Director of Primetime Programming, CNBC

"Look at an internship as your dress rehearsal to getting that TV job—do it late in your college program and use it to transition into the workplace."

> —Scott Storey, Emmy award-winning Hollywood Set Designer and Art
> Director

Many overzealous college students are all set and ready to take over a major network during their freshman year. This is not advised. Many colleges won't even allow students to take internships unless they are in their third year. Many executives feel that younger students lack knowledge and life experience.

Politically Incorrect's Carole Chouinard feels strongly that juniors, seniors, and graduate students make the best interns. "Freshmen and sophomores are too young and immature. They want the experience of being away from school but are less likely to have a good work ethic." Also, by the time underclassmen graduate, their intern experience is already two or three years old, and their contacts might have dried up, or the production they worked on may have gone into the TV black hole along with the pilot program that never made it.

Ideally, you want to start interning during the second half of your junior year. Your second internship should be at the start of your senior year, and then your "finale" internship close to graduation. You'll have more maturity and more experience and be really ready to take your first job in television. If your school only allows you to take one internship, then wait until your senior year.

"Intern during your junior and senior years. Prior to that you are still learning so much about yourself and where your interests lay. You should use your freshman and sophomore years to study hard and excel in a variety of courses—get a broad-based education. Then, as a junior, you should begin focusing on your major and find an internship that will complement your course of study plus give you firsthand field experience."

> —Tisi Aylward, Director, Talent, E! Entertainment Television, and a
> former intern

The important thing to do, especially if you're currently a senior, is to stay calm. Don't panic. Even if you're about to graduate, you can still make it; many people have.

COMMERCIAL BREAK:

"It was a fascinating period to work in a broadcast newsroom. I heard the first bulletin bells on the AP and UPI machines with the Kent State shootings. My time at the station continued through the Watergate scandal, Nixon's resignation, and the end of the Vietnam War. I can honestly say that the greater part of my education during those years occurred during the afternoons and evenings at the station, as opposed to my mornings in the classroom. One day we were reading a quote in class about a famous radio broadcaster, Quincy Howe. What a privilege it was for me to actually be working with him later in the day at my internship! Right after I graduated, Geraldo Rivera was looking for someone to write and produce for him. He saw 'commentaries' on my resume and called me in to write four samples. I was hired the next day. That was twenty-two years ago and I'm still proudly working for Geraldo."

—*Steve North*
Senior Producer, CNBC's Rivera Live!, *and a former intern*

BEING ABLE AND AVAILABLE

If you are going to take three internships, it's okay to work only two or three days a week for your first two. You'll be learning, but you'll be able to still take the necessary number of credits to graduate. However, during your third internship, clear your schedule; it's time to hit the home run.

News Producer John Michael had three internships. The first two were during the summer and consisted of observing the newsroom a couple days a week. Then for his last one, he kicked into high gear. "I had cleared my schedule and worked five days a week doing everything from shooting to editing and writing. This led right into a job as a general assignment reporter."

Do all you can to clear your calendar, and your mind, when going into an internship. Don't just date your internship, be married to it. It's not uncommon to work 12- or 15-hour days. Working around classes and a part-time job is a hard juggling act. Avoid it if you can. Of course, if you can't—don't despair. Maximize the time you are available for your internship and make them miss you when you're not around. If you're interning three or four days a week, your boss will quickly learn to dread your absence.

If you are interning five days a week, the employees will come to count on you. You will become the golden savior of the office, as critical an element as the coffeepot and the salvation found within. If you are only interning a couple of times a week, you're limiting your time to impress your boss, and you're less likely to get assignments because you don't have full-time follow through.

Remember, you'll be competing against other interns for any positions that may open up. If the staff spends five days a week with one intern and only two days a week with the other, and they're equal in competence, who do you think will be first on their minds for employment? Your boss will love penciling you in for an entire week of work! You will also get the best assignments and have the best shot at being the boss's pet. Aim to be an understudy who is always there waiting in the wings and ready for the starring role.

"Most jobs in television are not 9-to-5, so don't be a clock-watcher unless you are timing something for your boss! Hours vary widely depending on your category and placement. You might go nonstop for long, long hours, or you might have more down time than you expected. Just go with the schedule."

—Price Hicks, Director, Educational Programs and Services, The Academy of Television Arts and Sciences

By interning five days a week, and by staying as late as possible, the staff will become so dependent on you, they'll have no choice but to hire you. You'll read more in Channel 4 about how the best intern opportunities often happen after hours.

GIVE YOURSELF SOME CREDIT

How will you ever intern five days a week while going to school? You must plan ahead. Sign up for summer or night classes, so you can take off a semester. Will you have to sacrifice some beach time during break? Yes, but in the long run it will be well worth it.

"The biggest sacrifice I had to make for my first internship was having to take off my first semester of my senior year. This short hiatus caused me to graduate one semester later than all of my friends. Coming back to school after the semester off was certainly not the smoothest transition. It sort of felt like when you leave a movie theater to get something to eat and when you return, you just know you've missed something. I never

regretted the decision I made to do my internship when I did, though. The pluses definitely outweighed the minuses."

—Timothy P. Cavanaugh, LA Talent Agent

Since it's difficult to take a whole semester off, many utilize their summer to get their foot in the internship door. The thought of spending the summer interning makes even the most dedicated wonder what they'll be missing.

Sure, you may miss some summer excitement . . .

"The summer that I was planning on interning was when all my friends were heading to Florida to party. I wanted to go so badly, but I knew I had to do an internship. While my friends partied away, I was dubbing tapes."

but, in addition to avoiding sunburn, the investment can pay off big time.

". . . the great part is that when they came home from Florida they were starting their job search and I was already employed."

—Darnell Jones, Script Coordinator, P. J.'s; former Writer's Assistant, *Hangin' With Mr. Cooper*; and a former intern

Boston sports producer Jonathan Kilb joined the "summer camp," too. He points out it would have been too hard to keep those kind of long hours while juggling classes. "I gave up a great paying summer job for this internship. It was a struggle to save enough money for school and support myself at the same time, but it worked out well."

"It was a big sacrifice making no money the summer I interned. But the payoff was a job offer at the end of that summer. I made the internship successful by showing a complete willingness to do anything. That summer my boss was producing the Clio Awards, and tapes of winning commercials were streaming in and not organized. I stayed late, logged them, categorized them creatively, and made it look effortless. I scored big bonus points with my boss."

—Brian Graden, Executive Vice President, MTV; Developer, *South Park*; and a former intern

Are there disadvantages to summer interning? Sure. Many more students will be swimming in the intern sea. Also, many shows are on hiatus. Words of advice: If your only option is spending a summer answering phones in an empty production office, take the job at the local pizza palace and save your money.

CAN YOU AFFORD IT?

"Due to the amount of time put in the internship, it was impossible to hold down another job to make money. Because money is tight for most college students, it is important to bank some cash before your internship begins."
—Brad Faust, Toledo High School Dean and former Detroit TV intern

Unless you are lucky enough to get a paid internship, such as the highly recommended Academy of Television Arts and Sciences' Internship Program, you must begin as early as possible to fill your piggy bank. Save, save, save. Instead of going to the movies at night, go to a matinee. When they say "Would you like fries with that?" you say "No!"

"I had to cut back on my paid hours in retail to work free at a local TV station. But all of the scrimping was so worth it."
—Jill Mullikin-Bates, Supervising Producer, *Leeza*, and a former intern

FLASHBACK

"I will never forget checking in at the YMCA in the seedier part of town. The night I moved in they literally found a man who had been dead in his room for four days. It was only $11 a night, but would I live to tell about my internship? My food budget was a tight $10 a day, so I had to eat as much as possible of the free food being prepared by guest chefs for our show. For Christmas, my whole family got books off the show's shelves. I was broke, but in many ways it was one of the richest times of my life."
—Dan

Low-Budget Living
If you didn't have a chance to save up much, you can still get by, but your lifestyle will have to change. It may be tough, but you'll have to accept it.

"Handle your money issues privately. Don't be going to the accounting department asking for an advance to pay your rent. Live within your means. Take care of yourself financially and don't always run out of money. You are in a low-paying (if not no-paying) position. You can't compete with other paid employees who go out to eat every night, party, and throw dollars away like they print money at home. Bring your lunch."
—Kac Young, Vice President, Television Production and Development, Universal Studios Hollywood, and a former intern

Throughout the book, there will be suggestions made about "dressing the part" and taking staffers out for a bite to eat. These ideas are helpful, but not everyone can afford to follow those suggestions. Don't panic! While some of the suggestions in this text do require a pretty penny or two, many are toll-free. Having money is always helpful, but by no means is it a necessity.

If you're interning too far away to be able to get free housing from mom and/or dad, keep your eyes posted on the bulletin board at work. There are usually plenty of rental ads. Housesitting is another good option; spread the word you are looking for a place. You may want to room with other interns to really save. Make the sacrifice; it'll be worth it in the end. You must cultivate an ability to see into and believe in your future. Things will not always stay this way. You have to know *and believe* that.

To Get Paid or Not to Get Paid—That Is the Question

"Don't expect to get paid much. Some of my internships I worked for free, but I didn't let my attitude reflect that."
—Julie Johnson, Associate Producer, *Oprah*, and a former intern

Keep in mind that an internship is a temporary stage of life. Soak up everything, and don't wonder if you are being adequately compensated. As intern-turned-MTV-President Brian Graden reminds students, "You will be cheating yourself out of something valuable if your attitude gets the best of you."

Can you find a paid internship? Yes. The TV Academy, regularly voted one of the top ten internship programs in the country, has students interning everywhere from *Home Improvement* to *Star Trek*. They receive compensation as well. As stated in the *Los Angeles Times*, "The two-month internship pays a meager $1,600, but it's worth its weight in gold to hungry college graduates vying for a shot at a full-time job working behind the scenes with actors, writers, and directors." Don't expect to find many internships set up like the Academy; it's definitely an industry exception.

When thinking about an internship, it's vital to remember your goal is not just to get an internship, your goal is to get a job that you enjoy! It doesn't make sense to take an internship just because it pays $5 an hour when it can leave you unemployed for an unlimited amount of time after you graduate. Find the perfect one for you. If it pays . . . great! If it doesn't . . . do it anyway. If you do find a paid internship, you have to be extra careful you'll be receiving a quality opportunity. Some companies feel if they pay you, they don't have to give you any industry training and they can make you stuff envelopes all day long. Be careful!

THE "POSTGRADUATION" OPTION

Sometimes, it is possible to intern after you graduate. This depends on the policy of your school and the desired place of "internment." This may be a life-saving option if you only did one internship prior to graduation and it was unsuccessful. There are some positive aspects of a "postgraduation" internship. For one, you'll be all set to take any job offer that comes your way. You'll have no finals to worry about; your internship will be your only focus. However, don't let this be your first internship; it's too risky.

Although many success stories have followed the "after graduation plan," not all places will allow it. As producing veteran Diane Eaton points out, "When I was at CBS they didn't allow students to take internships unless they would be returning to school after the program was completed." Don't just assume you'll be able to get your dream internship after graduation—do the research!

As you'll hear stated throughout the book, you really must be up on all the rules and regulations that apply to your school and desired place of employment. But, if you're graduating and you haven't scored a job in the industry, don't give up. A postgraduation internship may be just your ticket into television.

I'VE BEEN OUT OF COLLEGE FOR YEARS!

FLASH BACK

"There was a 40-year-old woman who interned at a local station where I was producing. We all knew how much guts this took and we all respected her for it. She ran around with the college students, stuffed envelopes, sent out tickets, and pitched segment ideas. I was really impressed that she made this commitment. Given that the show was targeted at stay-at-home moms, she was miles ahead of all of us in life experience. Since then I have heard so many executives say 'Why can't we find any new moms with producing experience?' That intern now is probably running Lifetime TV."
—Dan

According to Labor Department statistics, the average person will have 3.5 different careers in a lifetime. The Bureau of Labor Statistics states that 11.9 percent of workers in 1991 who were between the ages of 25 and 34 switched occupations. Although TV is often a young person's ballgame, it is by no means off-limits to the over-40 crowd.

> *"My favorite intern of all time was the one who just pestered the heck out of me. Most internships require college credit or they must be paid. Well, when I was executive producer of a syndicated news project, at the Cyber Guy, we couldn't afford to pay anyone. This woman called and wanted to intern. I said, 'We cannot pay you, you have to get college credit.' She said 'okay.' She called back and said she had taken several internships and her professor wouldn't let her do any more. I had to say 'Sorry, but you must get credit to intern.' She persisted. Finally, I thought to myself, she wants to work for free. She wants to learn. And bureaucracy is standing in the way. I decided to let her work and she turned out to be magnificent. She was an older student, about 40. She was self-motivated and really helped me a lot. I eventually recommended her for a production assistant job at Good Morning America."*
>
> —Richard J. Ayoub, Executive Producer, *KABC-TV Morning News,* and a former intern

Changing careers midstream isn't easy but it can be done. Maybe you worked in a business office for years and regret the fact you gave up your childhood dream. Well, regret no longer.

Call up your local college and find out how to land an internship. Go for it! Many executives hold an automatic respect for people with the courage to try something new. Considering the demographics many local programmers and national executives are going for, your life experience and maturity will be an asset to you and the show.

Depending on where you live, you may need to get college credit to intern. In many states, you can't get an internship unless you are getting money or credit. If a station, news room, production house, studio, etc., allows you to intern without getting credit, they may be breaking the law. Additional internship laws are discussed in Channel 3.

WHAT IF I DIDN'T MAJOR IN TV OR RADIO?

Although the majority of people working in the industry did study television in college, many employers value a different kind of education experience.

> *"When I graduated, I knew everything about every film that was ever made, every radio personality, the history of every TV show. But I knew*

nothing about world politics or math. I didn't realize until I was in the industry how knowledgeable you had to be about the world outside of TV. If I could do it again I'd major in English or something other than TV, Radio, and Film."

—Adora English, Producer, *KTLA Morning News* in LA, and a former intern

"It is good if an intern has had basic communication courses, like editing and production, and even more advanced courses. This is all very helpful. However, a good liberal arts background is equally important. When producing news or talk shows, or any show that has any significant content, one needs to know general government structure, current news stories, current trends, books, music, magazines, how to do research, and a few phrases in French and Spanish."

—Jane Temple, Cleveland TV Producer

FINAL THOUGHTS . . .

This channel was not meant to discourage you but to help you start planning ahead. It's okay to feel a little overwhelmed now. Take a break, talk to a friend, and revisit the dreams that pointed you in this direction in the first place. Most readers of this book will do anything to get into the industry. Are you one of them? There are a thousand-and-one examples of people who made it in television starting from exactly the spot you're in now. You just have to do it.

(ROLL VTR)

"I was a miserable intern. I lasted two weeks before bailing out and deciding there must be easier ways to get 2 college credits. I hated being slave labor and was bored and disillusioned. But the lesson I have learned since then is that an internship should be your FIRST TV job. It requires real patience and a willingness to tackle small tasks tirelessly. It can seem thankless, but if you're the intern who does all the crummy stuff the other interns weasel out of, you'll make yourself indispensable and first in line for a real job!"

—Bob Bates, Former Producer, E! Entertainment Television, and a former intern

```
AND CUT!
CUE ANNOUNCER TEASE:
```

"And coming up next: Resumes and cover letters that would get a thumbs-up from both Siskel and Ebert, scoring the internship interview that would make even Barbara Walters jealous, and New York vs. Hooterville—which market is best for you?"

```
FADE TO BLACK
ROLL "TV INTERN HALL OF FAME" PACKAGE
```
••

Barbara Koster
Field Producer, *20/20* and *Good Morning America,*
and a former intern

I did my internship in 1979 during the last semester of my senior year. It was the right time to do it, because if a job were to open at WXYZ-TV Detroit I'd be ready to accept it—no pressing decisions about whether or not to forego a semester or two at college.

I was assigned to the documentary–special projects unit reporting to an amazing producer, Harvey Ovshinsky. It was an internship particularly recommended by an AP already employed by the station.

As internships go, mine was fairly routine. Around the office an intern hears "go-fer," "go to," and, when job time comes around, "go away" unless you have managed to make yourself unforgettable and indispensable. My mission was clear!

Fetching coffee, answering the phones, and delivering messages were among the least glamorous tasks I performed. And truthfully they were also among the most glamorous tasks, since interns don't usually get the most desirable jobs. At the time, I didn't see how doing these duties could possibly lead to a career of any stature. The transcribing was endless and often boring. On many occasions, I had to hang back at the office while my producer was doing the real business of making TV, but I did it all with a positive attitude and an open mind, absorbing the subtleties of TV production that Harvey never realized he was teaching me.

This would be a much longer story if I were to trace the track of my career to where I am today: working as a field producer for ABC news on *Good Morning America.* But day after day, story after story, the experiences of that internship are the very basis of my current standing as a producer.

Making a few phone calls to arrange travel to a shoot is a no-brainer on the surface, but logistics, logistics, and more logistics are critical as I discovered in 1992 when I had to get myself into Mogadishu, Somalia, to cover the human tragedy of the famine. Anarchy had demolished the country's infrastructure, and there was no commercial transportation into the hell Somalia had become. I was alone and responsible for my own arrangements. I was grateful that so many years ago I had overheard Harvey "charmingly and sincerely" manage to talk people into doing things they really didn't want to or weren't authorized to do. After a bit of persuasive cajoling over the phone, I had smooth-talked my way on to a cargo plane waltzing in front of a line of journalists waving $100 bills and hoping to buy their way on to a flight.

Field producing for TV has taken me places I never dreamed I would go. I have camped at the North Pole and hunted elephant in South Africa. I have cried with war refugees in Croatia and rejoiced with Olympic champions. On location, I have worked for a solid week with no more than an hour or two of sleep to break up the workdays, but I have also managed to squeeze in a day or two of R&R in some of the most exquisite places. My passports and photo albums are jammed with experiences and memories not even the most experienced traveler could arrange.

The tangibles from my internships are difficult to enumerate. In my day, it was the intern's job to make the producer's life easier, but while most producers made some effort to give interns a variety of experiences, helping us to develop a career was not a priority. At that time I wasn't sure what logging a tape or booking an audience was preparing me to do. I spent a lot of time in the background hovering to meet the needs of those who were busy doing TV. I observed and learned—keeping my eyes open, my mouth shut. It is amazing the access one has when working on a TV station. I wasn't sure what I wanted to do when I grew up—I am not sure that those answers are ever really clear—but I did find that a TV internship provided a unique vantage point from which to imagine the possibilities!

channel 2

Landing the Audition and Scoring the Starring Role

Now that you have a better idea of the television job that has your name on it, it's time to take the next step. The resume, the cover letter, and all the bare essentials of bagging your dream internship will be covered in this channel.

THREE . . .

"My cover letter should have knocked me out of the Arsenio internship. Oprah was my first choice, but I figured I had nothing to lose by applying to Arsenio. I was so lazy that I didn't even rewrite the Oprah cover letter. I sent a letter to Arsenio and didn't even mention him! Amazingly, they took all my Oprah praise and equated it with the courage to stick to my dreams and have a strong black role model. It then got passed on to a woman who just happened to be from my home state. I was lucky . . . very lucky!"

—Darnell Jones, Script Coordinator, P. J.'s; former Writer's Assistant, *Hangin' With Mr. Cooper*; and a former intern

TWO . . .

"Scoring an internship at Primetime Live was an incredible journey. First, I called the Internship Coordinator and asked for an information packet. Then, I had to write two essays, each on a different social issue with global ramifications. I must have revised those essays about a million times. After writing my resume and cover letter, my application was sent off. About a month later I got a call from the assistant. 'Congrats, you did it. You're going to be a Primetime Live intern.' What a feeling!"

—Greg Kestin, former intern, *Primetime Live*

ONE . . .

"We are gathered here today, and I speak to you as a comrade, an old soldier who sixteen years ago survived her first internship. Love it unconditionally. Your rewards will be many if you look to find them. Live through your frustrations. Listen, observe, and respect the process, and you will see the magic appear. And when you first see YOUR NAME on the credits rolling quickly at the end of a show, freeze frame that picture in your mind, that excitement in your heart. If you work very hard, sixteen years from today you will have the pleasure of passing on this very speech as it was passed on to me."

—Jill Coughlan, San Francisco TV Producer and a former intern

AND ACTION!

TAKING THE INTERNSHIP VOWS

Before you take another step toward the golden Emmy, you must make a promise to yourself! Pledge that you will see this internship through to the end, even if you discover that the television business is not for you. You'll be scared, anxious, nervous, and even depressed; don't let it stop you from committing fully to your internship.

The anxiety of trying to set up an internship can be overwhelming. Sometimes it causes people to turn back. Don't! So what if you don't get the internship? Will you be physically harmed?

"In surviving the pressure cooker of shooting for a TV career and an internship and being a student, it's important to surround yourself with two types of people: Those who are 'into' what you're trying to do, and those with whom you can do something completely different. Do have some other interests that make you forget your television 'tunnel vision' occasionally."

—Marilyn Kagan, Radio and Television Psychotherapist

Keep these thoughts in mind as you continue your journey:

1. It's human nature to be afraid of the unknown. Accept that you'll be scared.
2. Stay positive. It is *the* most important and attractive quality you can possess.

3. Be your own best friend. Have absolute faith in your abilities and character.

4. Believe you will be both an incredible intern *and* an incredible TV veteran, too!

5. Above all, enjoy the ride. *Savor the journey, not the destination.*

BEGIN THE INTERNSHIP SEARCH — STEP #1

Make Contacts, As Many As You Can

Your contacts will be the most important part of your television career. Even the most talented person in the industry is nothing without names and numbers. Talk to every friend you have. Do they know anyone in the industry? Don't discount mom. Does she work with the cousin of the accountant of the gardener who works for Barbara Walters? Don't leave any friend or family stone unturned.

> *"If you know someone that I know or that I owe a favor to, call them. I have more of an investment to help you. Everybody is connected to someone in TV somehow. My mother essentially got me the page job at CBS because of a next-door neighbor."*
>
> —Lou Dennig, Senior Vice President of Programming, Worldvision Enterprises, and a former intern

The good news is that many TV people remember where they've been and love giving breaks to hopeful interns. One of those is *CBS This Morning* Planning Producer Carol Story. She says that she constantly talks with young people who are friends of friends. "I'll also call people out of the blue that I don't know. Why? Many people gave me breaks early on, and in a cosmic way, I feel you have to give back." Look for those helping hands. Someday you will also be able to help an intern who has that same gleam in his eye that you now have.

Did you bond with any college alumni when researching your dream job? Ring them up.

> *"When I was at Harvard, there was a list of alumni who were willing to take calls from students wanting to get into TV. I asked ALL of them, 'If you don't have an internship for me, could you give me one other name to call?' I ended up talking with twenty different people before I landed my Fox internship."*
>
> —Brian Graden, Executive Vice President, MTV; Developer, *South Park*; and a former intern

Go back to your high school and talk to teachers who might remember you. Maybe they know someone. Call your old piano teacher, your dad's mechanic, and even the dog's veterinarian. Call anyone you might know and everyone who might know you. One contact can make a career of difference.

After you've gone on your hunt for contacts, write up a concise list of every industry professional you know and how you know them, but *don't* contact these names just yet. Why? You will use them, but for now, see what kind of inroads you can make on your own. Call in those favors later. It'll take a while for your friends to contact their friends and for the word to spread. Use this time to start pounding the pavement yourself.

FLASHBACK

"I had no clue where I was going to intern. I had some offers, but none in development, my top choice. Then, one day a former Brooklyn College student came and spoke to our class. This graduate was a Development Executive for the Fox network. I spoke to him, and he signed me up for an internship that day. One week later, I was on a plane to Hollywood. That simple. Plenty of people were trying to intern there, but because I went to Brooklyn College, I had the in."
—Jason

"Steve Ridgeway, whom I worked with in development at Fox, and I had often talked about how great our internships were and how they got us in the door. I thought it was cool when he told me he'd been invited back to his school to talk about breaking into the business. Little did I know, he was about to hook a student there who would have a profound effect on my life. Jason became an awesome intern, an incredible assistant, a development researcher, and a producer. We were destined to be together. It is sort of like an episode out of 'Touched by an Intern,' and I owe it all to Steve."
—Dan

What If You Can't Find a Contact?

If you can't find a contact, look harder. If you still can't find a contact, don't panic. As you saw in the Flashback, sometimes contacts appear out of the blue. Don't depend on one falling from the sky, but you never know.

"I once met a prospective intern at a department store. A producer friend of mine, Barry Poznick, got his internship by meeting a stranger at an airport. He turned out to be a VP at MTV!"
—Marilyn Kagan, Radio and Television Psychotherapist

"I met my employer while I was working as a Sales Associate at Pottery Barn. She came in frazzled, looking for a wedding gift. She said she was in a rush because the President was in town, and she had to get back to work immediately. I asked her what she did, and she told me she was the Executive Producer at KTVK. I asked if she was hiring, and she told me to send her a resume. Two weeks later, I had the job."

—Heather Lovett, Producer, NBC News Affiliate

By the way, you should be writing down names of people quoted in this book. You automatically have 100 contacts in your back pocket. "I read your quote in the internship book and was curious about . . ."

BEGIN THE INTERNSHIP SEARCH—STEP #2

"The most important thing is to work for a company you respect. Find out what kind of stuff they produce before you go sell your soul to them. It's much easier to clean the ear wax from a head you respect than one you don't."

—Scott St. John, former Fox Television Development Executive

The first step: Create a dream list of places where you'd like to intern. If *Sabrina the Teenage Witch* could conjure up your perfect TV gig, where would her magic take you?

Before you go one step further, there are two vital thoughts that you must not forget as you search for your internship home.

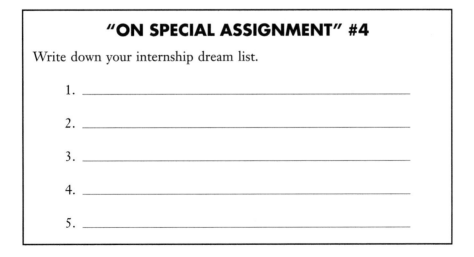

"ON SPECIAL ASSIGNMENT" #4

Write down your internship dream list.

1. _____

2. _____

3. _____

4. _____

5. _____

If You Want to Be the Next Tom Brokaw, Don't Intern for *Friends*.

"Do your research. We once had a color-blind applicant for an art director internship on our soap opera—not a good career choice."

— Jack Forrestel, Five-Time Emmy award–winning Art Director, *The Bold and the Beautiful*, and a former Academy intern

Do you dream about being a news director in New York? Then don't intern for a situation comedy. It will give you bragging rights and probably a date for Saturday night, but if you want breaking news to be your beat, it won't get you a job. TV executives with years of experience will tell you how tough it is to transition from one area to another. Go where you eventually want to work. If you're torn between a few careers, that's okay. Your internships will help you narrow down your choices, but the more focused you can be now, the better off you will be later on.

More Popular Doesn't Always Mean Better

Never intern at a show just because it's popular. Sometimes programs with big budgets and big audiences are big problems. It is very easy to get lost in the Hollywood shuffle. Do an internship for the experience, not for your ego. Also, some high-profile shows have been rumored to turn interns into errand boys and girls. The bottom line: Go to a place that gives you the most bang for your buck, not just a glamour title. A network credit isn't always the best experience.

"The interns we have at Today often have a miserable life. If they don't take some initiative, they will find themselves only making VHS dubs. That's the problem about doing an internship at a network level. While it seems cool to work at Today or Dateline, I think an intern can do a lot more and get more out of an internship at a local station or cable network."

— Jason Raff, Producer, NBC's *Today*, and a former intern

Of course, the *Today* show has led many interns to amazing careers; just be sure you select an internship for the right reasons.

BEGIN THE INTERNSHIP SEARCH—STEP #3

Now that you won't be interning on *Barney* with hopes of nailing a *Nightline* post, it's time to go to the next level. The first step is to contact your college and find out about their internship programs. Often, colleges have ongoing relationships with local TV stations and production houses. Are you currently a high school student? Talk to your teachers. Some places do accept high school students. Look at the TV menu closely.

> *"A few years back, my school, Southern Illinois University, began the Hollywood Studies Program, taking students out of the cornfield and bringing them to Hollywood. They can get their feet wet and work on shows like* The Young and the Restless, Dr. Quinn, Medicine Woman, *and* Entertainment Tonight. *Ithaca and Emerson Colleges have similar kinds of curriculum."*
>
> —Diane Eaton, *Wheel of Fortune, The Pat Sajak Show*, and *Rescue 911*

As you will see shortly, finding an internship already set up by your college has its advantages. But if none of them is right for you, there are other options.

FLASHBACK

"None of the school's internship programs seemed quite right for me. What did I do? I transferred to a different college! In doing some research, I discovered that I could transfer to a school in my hometown and create my own internship! After I enrolled, I went before a board and proposed an internship with the ABC affiliate in Cleveland. Then I had to do a similar pitch to the station. I became their first out-of-state and first paid intern. I was hired the day after graduation."
  —Dan

1. Call up all the other colleges in your area. Ask them for their list of internships. Do any of them pique your interest?
2. If the other colleges aren't any help, do your own investigative report.

Do you want to start in local news? Call up your area news stations and ask if they take interns? Maybe you want to be a set designer. Call the graphics companies in your city or the big Hollywood Studios. But remember, you are only inquiring if a company takes interns, not applying for one yet. Save your laundry list of questions for later.

> *"I decided on my internship after watching lots of TV. I surfed the channels to find programs I liked and wrote down the names of the*

production companies listed in the credits. Soon, I had sixteen shows. I went through fifteen unsuccessful calls before scoring my first internship."

—Loren Ruch, Producer, *Good Day LA*, and a former intern

NARROWING YOUR SCOPE—STEP #4

Now the real work begins. You've narrowed your list to about six places that, at least on paper, sound like solid sites to intern, but which one will land you that great job? Go straight to the horse's mouth. Track down former students who can tell you what the program was like. This is one major advantage to selecting an internship already set up by your college. If you can't find former students, ask your professors for some help. When you *do* find someone, ask:

1. How would you rate this internship?
2. How worthwhile was it? What were your daily responsibilities?

> *"Make sure you get a job description. Some involve too much personal stuff. My first day, I had to get a rectal thermometer for the producer's dog!"*
>
> —Glenn Meehan, Managing Editor, *Entertainment Tonight*, and a former intern

3. How much hands-on experience was there? Were you given more things to do if proven responsible?
4. How structured was the program?

> *"Look for one that is not 100 percent structured, where you can go in different directions. Prove yourself to your bosses and show you want to experience many areas. Don't get stuck answering phones 8 hours a day."*
>
> —Chuck Lioi, Post Production Supervisor, *Sunset Beach*, and a former intern

5. How much of the industry were you exposed to?

> *"Choose a company that is active in several areas of the business, like development and production. It increases your chances of a job after the internship."*
>
> —Patrick Jarvis, Development Executive, Tribune Entertainment, and a former intern

6. If you had to do it again, would you?

Push your contacts on why it worked or didn't work for them. The reasons why they loved their internship may be the reasons why you would hate it. Look at the responsibilities they had. Do any of these interest you? Quiz as many people as you can.

If everything seems to check out, you may be one step closer to having a hit internship on your hands. But with all of your reporting, what is the $64,000 question that needs to be answered? Do they hire interns?

A Few Words of Wisdom
Remember, your ultimate goal is a job, not an internship. Don't end up at a place that has never hired an intern. Avoid any place that bars interns from future full-time employment. What if you want to serve somewhere that has a bad track record for hiring? If this is your first internship and you really think you can learn something there, go for it. But if you're a senior about to graduate, steer clear.

If you can't find anyone at your school who has interned at your first choice, call a nearby college to see if they have any such students. If your desired internship comes from your college list but you can't find anyone from your college who worked at this place, be highly suspicious about this choice. It's possible that this is the first year the station or show is offering internship opportunities, or they may have scared every intern away.

What if they never had interns before but are more than willing to take you on? Be careful. Often, first-time recruits wind up in a tornado with no direction. However, if no systems are in place, you can also become the hero and give birth to a brand new program. If you're aggressive and take risks, go for it. If you're more passive, go for well-oiled internships.

"If you have to transfer to the middle of Antarctica and live in a hut to get the right internship, do it. You'll reap the rewards of your determination for the rest of your life."
—Shannon Keenan, Producer, Live Events, E! Entertainment Television, and a former intern

"Tele"–Visualize Your Success
At this point, you might be wondering if all this internship homework is worth it. Why not just take any internship and worry about everything else later? That would be pretty easy to do, but picture this:

It's graduation time, and two students are standing next to each other. One spent a ton of time, anxiety, and frustration seeking out the perfect internship. This student also ended up with an amazing internship and can't wait to start work at this station right after she is handed her diploma. The other student avoided all the aggravation and took the first internship she found. No stress, no worry, no research. This student also spent a semester doing nothing but stuffing envelopes, and the only company that would hire her now is Hallmark. Which student would you rather be?

Now, let's get back to work. It's time to go city shopping and find the market where you'll make your mark.

Big Cities vs. Local Markets

Some of your picks may be right in your own backyard. Others may be in a big city seven states away. Where should you hang your intern shingle? Here's what some folks from our "Intern Hall of Fame" have to say:

"Whether you're in New York City or Idaho, you have the same opportunities to make it the best internship it can be. Be enthusiastic, be curious, and ask questions. You can learn more on the job than in a classroom."

—Tisi Aylward, Director, Talent, E! Entertainment Television, and a former intern

"Go for a smaller market. Because of unions in bigger markets, interns can't do as much. There's a union for photographers, so you can't shoot; a union for writers, so you can't write. You get stuck doing busywork, like logging videotape and making copies. It's very limiting in the big markets. Sometimes, you're lucky if you can go out on a story. Smaller markets let you do more. You can actually touch equipment, write, and in some cases, report."

—Richard Ayoub, Executive Producer, *KABC Morning News* in LA, and a former intern

"If you want to be a talent booker, aim for the biggest shows you can. Work with the best in the business. You'll get to know the people they work with, the publicists and agents for the hottest stars. If you do your homework, you'll leave your internship knowing who all the important players are in the biz."

—Janice Penino, Personnel Manager, *The Late Show with David Letterman*, and a former intern

"If not a small city, at least a smaller station. You can do more and learn more in that environment. In a large operation, unless the internship program is highly structured and managed, it's easy to be pushed aside and overlooked."

    —Dana Benson, UPN News Director and a former intern

"Reach for the top. Experience the big city. Play with the big kids. The bigger the sand box, the bigger the toys!"

    —Jason Gurskis, Producer, Discovery Channel, and a former intern

"City size isn't important, but I'd suggest an internship at a small company or a small division of a larger company. I think it gives you a better chance at building personal relationships and really being a star and getting noticed."

    —Michael Seligman, Associate Producer, E! Entertainment Television, and a former intern

As you can see, it's a mixed bag when talking about market size. Here is what we suggest:

If at all possible, do one internship in a smaller market and one in a larger market. Use the smaller market to learn the ropes, then the spotlight will really shine on you in the big city. If you live in a large market, then consider interning first at a local cable station. Having both kinds of experience under your belt is best. Let's weigh both sides.

Smaller Market
Advantages:

1. More hands-on experience. Most larger markets are unionized, and you'd be restricted in the amount and type of work you perform.
2. There are fewer people to do more jobs. You'll have a chance to try out many different areas.
3. The cost of living is cheaper.
4. Even if you want to be the head of a network, it's to your benefit to know how a smaller market works.

Disadvantages:

1. If you want to work in the big leagues, many executives would say small markets do little for a resume.

2. Fewer positions are open in smaller markets. Someone usually has to die or retire for a position to open. There are more jobs in a big city.
3. You are more limited in your opportunities. If you want to work on a soap, for instance, you have to hit the East or West Coasts.

Larger Market
Advantages:

1. Your resume will sing. National shows catch attention.
2. The range of contacts is unlimited. The way people jump from New York to LA, you'd never know the two cities are 2,800 miles away from each other. Your Rolodex will swell with cross-country connections.
3. Potential employers will constantly be put in your path. A big-city internship means something anywhere.
4. It's the ultimate life experience. You'll be in the eye of the storm.

Disadvantages:

1. The cost of living. Ouch! Can you afford it?
2. The stakes are much higher. Even as an intern, the stress and hours may get to you.
3. You will not get the hands-on experience that the small town will grant you.
4. Your internship will be more limited, with less chance to venture off into other TV areas.

The Bottom Line
Do one of each. If you can only do one, think big! Remember, if your dream is to work on a sitcom, you need to be laughing it up in LA. Making an impression on the set of *Friends* will very possibly get you a job on the show, whereas working your tail off at a small station probably won't. Breaking barriers in Hollywood or New York is difficult.

HIT THE GROUND RUNNING—STEP #5

You have a bed of contacts and know exactly where you'd like to intern. Now, pick up the phone and get your internship, right? Not quite. You still have a resume to write.

Resume Writing
The resume is your passport into the world of television. Why is it essential to have your resume before you phone? Anytime you call anyone in

television, there's a good chance you'll hear, "fax me your resume." If you have to scramble to get it done, you might miss your golden opportunity. Give yourself the right amount of time for resume construction. First impressions are everything.

There are hundreds of books about resume writing, and they're great for getting down the basics, but what's the best way to sell yourself? It's almost impossible to say. What turns one executive on will turn another off. You may spend eight weeks on a resume and not get called in just because the executive's ex-wife went to your college.

Here are some basic resume rules most executives agree on:

1. Be honest.

When writing a resume in college, it is very common for students to want to embellish previous job experience.

"I hate getting a letter where the student has beefed themselves into something that there's no way they could ever be. If they are not going to be honest on a resume, what's to stop them from lying in front of you? Be real and be who you are."
> —Adora English, Producer, *KTLA Morning News* in LA, and a former intern

The person interviewing you knows you're in college and doesn't expect you to have won an Emmy. An executive doesn't hire an intern based on where they've been but on where the intern is going. If you're honest, you may or may not get the internship; if you lie, you definitely won't. It makes sense to tell the truth.

2. Don't have any spelling errors.

One misspelled word on a resume can kill your internship.

"When I was a news director, I was shocked by the number of letters I'd receive with my name misspelled. I'd send them back with my name circled saying, 'Do you seriously expect me to consider you for a news position when you can't get a simple fact straight like my name?' Do your homework!"
> —Mendes Napoli, President, Napoli Management Group In Los Angeles

Chuck Lioi, the Post Production Supervisor of *Sunset Beach*, agrees completely. He will often throw away resumes with grammatical errors. "I'm tough that way. I expect them to be like me." And you should expect most potential employers to be like Chuck.

3. Make the resume look professional.

When you reproduce your resume, have it done professionally. Kinko's pulls all-nighters every night. Don't run off your resume on an old photocopy machine.

Think crisp. Keep your paragraphs short, and bullet the sentences. Use **bold** sparingly. Make sure all your information is laid out in a readable fashion. Save the flowery thoughts for your next Mother's Day card. Executives have short attention spans. Try the scan test. Do the important aspects stand out? Would you hire the person behind this page?

4. List your accomplishments, not just your titles.

"Many students do not emphasize important skills they've acquired through classes like school yearbook, newspaper, and the AV club. Writing and clerical skills need to be highlighted more than your latest job at Burger King."

—Debbie Casini, Pittsburgh TV Producer and a former intern

If you were President of your local chapter of Alpha Epsilon Rho, don't just list the title, let the potential interviewer know what you accomplished while you held office. Did you increase membership by 50 percent or produce an award-winning promotional piece for your department?

5. Avoid gimmicks unless you are sure they won't backfire.

In television, the only rule is that "everything is the exception." Many interns have gotten hired by being creative with their resume presentation, and others have been banned from the business because of them. Here's a sampling of some out-of-the-ordinary resumes. You decide if they belong in the "TV Intern Hall of Fame."

- A dozen cupcakes with a toothpick in the center of each. Attached to each toothpick was a miniature resume.
- A shoe mailed to an executive with the resume attached. The card read, "Now I got my foot in the door."
- A student who sent his resume on a baseball card in hopes of scoring an ESPN internship.

Unless you are absolutely sure that the executive loves the adventurous approach, don't take the risk. Ask former interns and others before ordering the marching band. Have interns been noticed by resorting to stunts? Of course, but be sure that you don't bomb. Your time is better spent planning strategy for your interview. More on interview etiquette in the next channel. Here are some additional thoughts about resumes to ponder:

"They are always too long and detailed. Give it up—we know you haven't done much; that is why you are interning."

> —Patrick Jarvis, Development Executive, Tribune Entertainment, and a former intern

"See an expert about your resume. Criteria are constantly changing. Be up on what is current. I always see a professional."

> —Julie Johnson, Associate Producer, *Oprah*, and a former intern

"I don't care if you 'aspire to procure a position in the exciting field of TV production and produce award-winning documentaries for the BBC.' I just need someone to organize my shelves. Put your objectives in your cover letter—that is what it's for."

> —Jim Casey, Producer and President, Painless Productions, and a former intern and NBC page

"Put it on a nice stock paper, not bond. Use a heavier-weight gray, parchment, or cream color for example. Everyone gets hundreds of white, gray, and manila envelopes. It's difficult not to open a black envelope. Try sending a resume in one, but don't do it with gold ink and lots of stars and hearts."

> —J. William Reardin, Executive in Charge of Production, *The Geraldo Rivera Show*

Should You Use a Resume Service?

First, try to do it on your own. No one knows you better than you. If it's just too hard, or you don't have access to a computer or quality printer, turn to a service. It could run anywhere from $50 to $300. One that costs only $20 is probably not done by a service but by an entrepreneurial student with a laser printer.

If you go to a service, give them clear guidelines on what you want it to accomplish. Pick a service that has written for the entertainment field before. Getting a job with *20/20* is different than getting one at an average corporation. Be sure the service doesn't oversell; this will turn off an interviewer. Like a well-written play, know the motivation behind every line of your resume. Convey to the writer exactly what you want; content is key. Come off as professional, not slick. Make sure they show you a draft *before* getting out your wallet.

Things Not to Lose Sleep Over

You have a lot to worry about on this intern hunt. Here are a few things you shouldn't sweat.

1. *The color of your paper.*

Years ago, if you sent your resume on colored paper, it stood out. Now, everyone does. Have you ever heard an executive say, "I hired her because her resume was on the most gorgeous shade of blue." It doesn't matter. If you know the executive's favorite color, maybe. Otherwise, let it go.

2. *Whether or not to have an "objective statement."*

For every book that says to have an objective, there is another that says don't. You will be sending your resume with a cover letter; let that explain your objective.

3. *The length of your resume.*

This is another topic that has resume books up in arms. Should you ever have a two-page resume? If—and only if—you have enough information to justify a second page, go for it. Will some think it's too long? Yes. Will some take the time to turn the page and be intrigued? Yes. Go with your gut.

4. *"References available upon request."*

Have a separate list of references ready if asked, but this line is a waste of space.

5. *Following everyone's advice.*

Everyone is going to have different advice about your resume. Some will say your font is too small, others will want you to include the 4-H club you joined. If you reprint your resume every time someone gives you a suggestion, you'll destroy another rain forest. Listen to others' advice, but ultimately be your own TV salesman.

THE COMPANY, THE INDUSTRY, THE WORLD

You've penned your award-winning resume; now check out the sites you could be calling home next semester. How long has the show, newscast, company, or studio been in business? How successful is it? What are its future prospects? You'd be surprised what little attention many students give to their interview search. Once again, 20 hours of research could lead you to a gold watch at your favorite network. Isn't it worth the effort?

Call your prospective internship home. Ask for the media or public relations department and see if they will send you a press kit. Request biographical information on key people at the facility, including the person by whom you will most likely be interviewed. Check out the Web site.

If you haven't tracked down the trades yet, get on it. Do you know the latest mergers, overnights, or Oprah's latest investment? You never know what the interviewer will ask when you make first contact. Hit the library and do a search on your interviewer, too. You can never have too much information!

The Cover Letter

FLASH BACK

"I still shudder when I think of my first cover letter . . . a handwritten letter on notebook paper, with no resume. Having long been a fan of this TV station in Cleveland, I had thought a sincere, casual approach was best. For a third grader writing his teacher, maybe, but not for one of the most powerful women executives in local TV. Luckily, she had a sense of humor and an extreme curiosity. She was dying to find out who had the nerve to send it. Thank you, Jane, for not trashing me or my note!"
—Dan

Do you have to write a cover letter? Absolutely. Some people get so anxious about their letter, they rationalize why *not* to write one. "All my experience is on my resume, what's the point?" The point is: When going for an internship, and especially in this industry, *personality* is as important as *work history*. Your resume will not show your personality.

The purpose of the cover letter is to shout, "Hey, look at me, and let me fill your needs!" The biggest complaint of executives is that "interns are not worth the effort." They frequently have new recruits coming in, getting basic training, earning their stripes, and then being discharged. The executive wants to find an intern who will make his or her life easier. Make sure you convey why you want to be invited and what you can bring to their party. This is why it is key to do the research before writing this cover letter. Strut your stuff!

Tell them you're great at grunt work, believe in paying dues, and want the chance to be a part of their TV picture. The exceptions to the rule are programs like the one for the Academy of Television Arts and Sciences. These internships are highly competitive, and grunt work is virtually nonexistent. A selection committee chooses several interns in various areas, such as Children's Programming and TV Scriptwriting. We'll discuss these in greater detail later. For now, find out what an interviewer's needs are as you're figuring out your own.

Is there one type of cover letter that's guaranteed to win applause? No. What's the best way to get an interview in two or three paragraphs? Be short, direct, and upbeat.

> *"Make the cover letter short, sweet, and to the point. If they run on and have large paragraphs, I lose interest real fast. A lot of times I won't even read them. I'm busy. If you can show me that you've got a personality and can cut to the chase in just a few sentences, I'll be impressed."*
>
> —Chuck Lioi, Post Production Supervisor, *Sunset Beach*, and a former intern

There are plenty of books that give advice on how to write the perfect cover letter. Try to read a few, but be your own author. Producer veteran Adora English notes that it is frustrating to get a letter where it is obvious that the person has been studying the books on how to write a cover letter. Don't ever use "Dear Sir or Madam:" ! Take the time to find out someone's name. Don't send a letter that misspells the name of the show or studio, and don't send a blind cover letter. That is insulting. Adora also advises that "truthfulness is more important than experience."

The cover letter is the perfect place to show off all the research you have done. Don't make it a thesis, just let them know what your goals are and why you want to intern there. Do as much of the advance work for them as possible.

> *"I look for someone who does have an idea of what they want to do. They don't have to have it completely nailed down, but the 'I-will-do-anything approach' doesn't fly with me. I'd rather have*

someone say, 'This is what I'm thinking about doing, and working with your company will allow me to get there.' Tell me why you think the company fits into your future."

—Don Wells, News Director, KGTV San Diego

An important rule to follow is "show, don't tell." Don't *tell* the executive you're reliable; *show* them by giving specific information about what you've accomplished. Anyone can say they're motivated. Prove it!

In general, see the cover letter as you'd like others to see you. Is it clear? Does it have a sense of your personality? Does it show you're a stickler for detail? Does it convey you have pride in your work? Put yourself on the other side of the desk. "What does this student bring to the table?" "What sets him apart from the rest of the herd?"

But wait! Don't drop it in the mail yet! Do a little phone work first. It's also a great opportunity to start your relationship with the assistant:

1. Call the company and ask for the name of the person in charge of hiring the interns. After you get the name of your potential boss, ask for the name of his/her assistant, and then get transferred to the assistant.
2. Be friendly and relaxed but to the point with assistants. They will be flattered when you ask for them by name. Introduce yourself and let them know you're sending a letter inquiring about internships. Ask for proper spellings of names. Treat them with respect, and they'll be on the lookout for your resume—more on the key people in a minute.
3. Send your resume and cover letter in a large folder, not an envelope. It will increase your chances of being noticed, and many executives have pet peeves about resumes wearing creases.
4. Indicate in your letter that you plan to call the supervisor in about a week to follow up.

Every executive will look for something different. A few more cover letter suggestions:

"Keep it short and friendly. But not overly friendly. And save the $100 words to impress your parents. People want to hire a person, not a walking dictionary of ten ways to say something. Less is more. Get to the point!"

—Dane Hall, VH1 Writer and Producer

"Forget the 'Top Ten Reasons to Hire Me.' Believe me, it's already been done."

—Janice Penino, Personnel Manager, *The Late Show with David Letterman*, and a former intern

The More the Merrier

Make sure you send your resume and cover letter to at least three different places. Also, when you go on an interview, it's nice to sincerely say you are considering a couple of other offers! You're marketing yourself. Everyone wants what they can't have.

THE ASSISTANT, YOUR HERO

As you will hear throughout the book, the assistant to the executive can be your ally when it comes to making your mark. He or she has the ear of your potential boss. But amazingly, some assistants are treated badly by would-be interns.

> *"Teryn, my assistant, is my gatekeeper. I am very busy in and out of the office. She prioritizes me. So when someone calls her and is rude, that is a big mistake. She sets up meetings, and I encourage her to tell me how someone has treated her or her observations."*
>
> —Lou Dennig, Senior Vice President of Programming, Worldvision, and a former intern

Like anyone, assistants deserve kindness and respect. These key support people can be your Cliff Notes to learning the office, the procedures, and all the players. They know the inner-office lowdown, who's liked and disliked, and which shows are hiring, and they have the trust of the people you need to reach. Nurture this relationship.

THE ALL-IMPORTANT FIRST CALL

Wait one week after you send your letter (figuring in mail time) before making the first call. When you call, you'll probably speak to the assistant; befriend him or her. Ask them if they've ever interned. Be cordial but sensitive to her time. See if you can set up the meeting, but she'll probably have to get back to you.

If you *are* lucky enough to score the executive on the phone, remind him or her who you are and that you sent your resume and cover letter the week before. Chances are, the executive will not remember you. Don't take it personally. She could have easily received a few dozen resumes in the past week. When on the phone with her, keep these tips in mind:

1. *Be relaxed but focused.*

This is a very important phone call, but try to keep control of your nerves. Be conscious of your pronunciation and your enunciation. Don't talk too fast! If you feel a wave of nerves coming on, pause, take a deep breath, and slowly *and silently* exhale. Remember, they can't see you . . . yet.

2. *Ask the executive, "Is now a good time?"*

Everyone is usually swamped with work. Your future boss will appreciate your offer to reschedule the phone call at another time.

3. *Be warm, but don't ramble.*

Yes, tell the executive how much you appreciate his or her time, but don't go overboard. Thank him or her and move on to the business at hand.

4. *Enlist them, don't assign them.*

Many executives were given their big break and want to give a shot to someone else, but don't hold a gun to your potential employer's head. Subtlety is always best.

5. *Be very aware of the time.*

Executives have no time to see their families, so don't expect them to spend 3 hours on the phone with you. Think *Reader's Digest* version and be the one to end the call.

6. *Be appreciative.*

Whether you get the part or not, the executive just took time to talk to you. Wrap it up with another "thank you"; you may be the only one they get the whole day.

Let's assume everything has gone as planned: You've gotten your package to the executive, befriended their assistant, and have just phoned to set up a meeting. To your surprise, the executive picks up the phone. Here is how your scene might play out:

```
INT. OFFICE—NOON
(OPEN ON JAN, A HIGH-STRUNG EXECUTIVE WHO GETS WORD THAT A
PROSPECTIVE INTERN, WHO HAS JUST WRITTEN HER ABOUT AN
INTERNSHIP, IS ON THE PHONE. CUT TO NERVOUS INTERN ON A
TWO-WAY PHONE FILTER.)
```

YOU

Hi, Ms. Landis. I'm from UCLA and wrote you last week about interning with your company. Am I catching you at a bad time?

JAN

I am a little swamped, but I do have a couple of seconds.

YOU

Well, as I said in my cover letter, I am extremely interested in pursuing a career in news. I know your newscast has been number one for the past two years. Reports like the one your show did on the oil scam really make me want to be part of your team. Plus, in talking with past interns, I know I'd get a lot out of the internship. But most importantly, I have a lot to offer.

JAN

What part of news would you like to go into?

YOU

Right now I'm really interested in research. I know that's also where you started. I worked on NEWSSTAR in school as well as LEXIS-NEXIS, so I'll be able to jump right in and help out in any way possible.

JAN

In that case, let me hand you over to my assistant; she'll set up a meeting. Any other questions?

YOU

Honestly, there are about a million things I'd love to ask you. I know how busy you are, so I'll hold off until we meet to ask some of them. Thanks for agreeing to see me. Getting the right internship is so important to me. I am meeting with two other stations about their programs, but I have heard such great things about yours, and I am very eager to see things firsthand.

JAN

I am a little biased, but we do have the best internship program. I was one myself. Looking forward to meeting you and let me put my assistant back on the phone.

(END ON CUT OF AN EXTREMELY HAPPY STUDENT.)

This call incorporated all the things that have been discussed up until now. Will your call go this well? Maybe. Maybe not. But if you take the time and do all the legwork, it will pay off. You may not have a chance to talk about the executive's past, but you could be asked why you want this particular internship. You don't know how long the call will be, so cover all the bases. This research is needed for your actual interview anyway, so why not get a running start now?

CONTACT YOUR CONTACTS

So, you've gotten your meeting. The countdown to your interview has begun. Now what? It's time to call in the troops. Get out your list of contacts and give them a call. Remember—you haven't asked them for help yet. Why? Sometimes they are hesitant to help out for fear of getting egg on their face. If a contact recommends someone who is incompetent, they end up looking bad. This is why you waited to call your contacts until now. Give them an update on all the legwork you've done and the interview that has been scheduled. Their confidence in you will soar, and they'll be more than willing to help you. You're going to make them look good!

Find out all you can from your contacts about the interviewer. Ask your contacts to put in a good word for you with the executive. This will mean big votes in your campaign. Continue to research. Keep reading the trades and watching the show. Spend a few extra days to get more data. It's not possible to know too much about the show, station, etc.

As you'll hear time and time again, the assistant can easily be your most important contact. Call your friend the assistant and ask if she could fax you a staff list. This will be your own "Who's Who" for everyone involved on the show.

Go through the names and see if you recognize any. If you're in college or high school, go to your friends and professors and see if there are any they know. Hop on the Internet. Go through newspaper archives and see if any of the staff members have been written up. Most colleges have programs that allow you to go through the *New York Times* and *USA Today* archives for free. Go through back issues of all the trades. Leave no *TV Guide* unturned.

What if you can't get your hands on a staff list? Watch the program and record the credits. Play the credits back with a remote control in hand for frequent pausing. Instant staff list!

"By the time I went in for my interview I had memorized the credits. I learned a bit about the personalities of the on-air team just by watching the show. I tried to watch the show as much as possible so that while I

was in my interview I could jump in with, 'Oh remember that newscast last week when you said . . .' I came across informed, not like I was just trying to get 3 easy credits."

—Adora English, Producer, *KTLA Morning News* in LA, and a former intern

What If You Can't Get an Interview Set Up?

If you don't have any luck setting up the interview, call your contacts. Be honest with them. Sometimes it takes your Uncle Vinnie's doorman's grocer to sink the interview puck. Your contact may be able to make one call and have you in at the studio in 2 seconds. Don't be afraid to ask.

What If You Can't Get an Interview and Have No Contacts?

If you can't get an interview at one place, keep calling numbers on your list. If you are told by the assistant or by the executive that they won't grant you an interview, ask them why. Is there anything you can do to get it next semester? (Another reason to intern as a junior!)

What if you're a second-semester senior? Go back to your college list and contact any places you may have overlooked. Don't just run and take any internship. The chances are too great that you'll waste your semester. Watch the credits of the show or newscast for lower-profile people to call. Get in contact with the people on the lower end of the totem pole; they are much more accessible.

```
INT. PRODUCTION OFFICE—3 P.M.
(OPEN ON BRENDA, A PRODUCTION ASSISTANT FOR ESPN, WHO HAS JUST
RECEIVED A CALL FROM RICH, A HOPEFUL INTERN.)

SFX: PHONE RINGS


                         BRENDA
Hello, Rich, how can I help you?


                          RICH
I caught your name on the credits of last week's baseball
special. I am a huge Pirates fan. Do you have a few minutes?


                         BRENDA
Sure . . . even if you do like the Buckos. I'm a Mets woman
myself.
```

                              RICH

I would like any advice you could give me on the business. How
hard was it for you? I am hoping to find an internship.

                             BRENDA

This place hires tons of interns.

                              RICH

Well, I know. I wrote a letter and then called Sharon, the
internship supervisor, but I couldn't even get an interview.

                             BRENDA

I could find out why for you. Sometimes resumes fall through
the cracks here.

                              RICH

That would be great. But even if I can't get an interview, I'd
love to take you out for lunch one day and hear how you did it.
I'd love to have a job like yours someday.

(DISSOLVE TO EXTERIOR OF CONNECTICUT COFFEE SHOP,
WHERE WE FIND BRENDA AND RICH MID-CONVERSATION
OVER LUNCH.)

Will your conversation go this well? Again—maybe, maybe not. If the call
doesn't work, give one of your "target" places a visit. Put on a nice outfit and
your charm. Look for an assistant, tell them your problem, and ask for some
advice. If you don't see an assistant, ask around for the internship supervisor;
maybe you'll be able to convince them. Granted, sometimes stopping by
unannounced is ineffective, but as the clock ticks away, more drastic
measures need to be taken. Don't forget to take several resumes with you,
and be prepared for anything.

   If you still haven't scored the interview, you may want to stop. If it's
this hard to be considered, do you really want to work in this kind of
environment? You don't want to be accepted out of pity and then spend the
semester staring at a coffee machine. Sure, you'll have an internship, but at
graduation, you won't have a job. What's the point?

   Do you want to keep pushing? Here's a way to show your initiative and
research capabilities at the same time: Look on the Internet or go to the
library and track down every article about your desired place of intern. (You
should already have a bunch of these articles from your previous research).
Photocopy the articles and organize them chronologically. Write up a table
of contents and then go to a copy shop and have all the articles bound. You'll

have a nice booklet of articles that will impress all who see it. With the article book, enclose one more final plea.

What else can you do? If you've followed the steps and still haven't obtained a meeting, go after another station or production house. Have people pushed further? Sure. Prospective interns have sent cakes with the message "please interview me" written in icing. This has worked, but it usually doesn't. After you have thrown all the possibilities out to the universe, you should let go. Trust the force and something good will happen.

THE DREAM SCENE

You've followed the advice in this channel. Now sit back and picture the following dream scene:

> You're sitting with your friends. They're talking about dates they hope to have for the weekend, but not you. You're staring at the phone, that wacky combination of metal and plastic that will hopefully deliver the news you've been dreaming about. Suddenly, it rings. Your roommate, hoping it's for him, leaps over you and your fantasy and attempts to grab the phone. "Hello," says your roommate. "Oh, yes, hold on please. Who may I say is calling?" Disappointed, your roommate hands you the phone. "It's some TV place." You're shaking a bit, and your stomach is about to explode as you take the phone and hope to hear those words that rank up there with "I love you," "You've won the lottery," and "There is leftover pizza." You say hello, and then the most beautiful voice in the world says, "Would you like to come in for an interview?" You try not to scream, you try not to pass out, but deep in your heart you know it . . . TV World, here I come.

Take a night off to celebrate. You've done well, and you should be proud.

. . . AND CUT!

CUE ANNOUNCER TEASE:

"And coming up next: Internship interview techniques that'll get you more attention than Ellen's coming-out episode and what to do when the offers start rolling in."

FADE TO BLACK
ROLL "TV INTERN HALL OF FAME" PACKAGE

"WOW! HOW'D THEY DO THAT?!"

Looking back, I can remember asking myself that question, many times out loud, as I lay on the floor with my favorite pillow, watching television. As a kid, I always seemed to be watching TV: I'd race home from the school bus to watch *The Guiding Light* with my mom; I'd sneak home during the summer from the nearby community swimming pool to sit in front of the tube (much to my mother's dismay); and I always chose watching TV instead of playing hide-and-seek with the neighborhood kids.

It came as no surprise to me when I figured out that I wanted to make a career out of television. When I entered the tenth grade, I announced to my family that I planned to major in communications when I enrolled in college three years down the road. My family was thrilled; they thought I aspired to a career with the phone company.

After educating them on what exactly it meant to be a communications major, they were less than thrilled, thinking—I'm sure—that I had lost my mind at such an early age. But then in my junior year of college, I was accepted for an internship with KDKA-TV's *Evening Magazine* in my hometown of Pittsburgh, Pennsylvania.

At the time, KDKA and *Evening Magazine* were both institutions in Pittsburgh. This CBS affiliate has always outshined the other stations in the markets and is actually one of the first TV stations to broadcast in this country. My family was thrilled—even more the first time they saw my name roll by on the credits of the show.

It has been thirteen years since my internship at *Evening Magazine*, and even to this day, I look back to the summer I spent there with fond memories. My internship taught me a lot and prepared me for a fascinating career in television production.

I have some advice for new interns: **Look, listen, learn.** Take in your surroundings, listen to what everyone says, and ask questions. You'll be perceived as someone who's on top of things, and you'll take this newfound knowledge with you into the real world.

Since my internship, I've been the associate producer for ABC's *One Life to Live*, the production manager for *Home and Family* on the Family Channel, and an associate producer for the syndicated talk show, *Scoop with*

Sam and Dorothy. Today, I'm the postproduction supervisor for Aaron Spelling's NBC soap opera *Sunset Beach.* I have a large role in the production of this show, which is seen around the world. I didn't realize it at the time, but my internship prepared me for this role.

Even today, I still say, "Wow!" when I watch TV; but now I don't have to ask, "How'd they do that?!"

channel 3

Rehearsing for the Part of Super Intern

This channel will prepare you for a successful interview as well as for the first day of your new career. Congratulations, you've already accomplished more than many even dream of.

THREE . . .

"Get yourself mentally pumped up. Having an air of confidence and conveying that you will be a dedicated hard worker with a smile on your face will get you the job."

—Dianne Abramms Gotlieb, TV Producer and a former intern

TWO . . .

"After six months of biweekly calls of inquisition, I was drained. 'Who needs this job,' I groveled to myself. 'You do,' I replied. My mother used to say, 'A watched tea kettle never boils.' So I went away for a few days. Just after I returned, I received a call from NBC asking me if I could start Monday!"

—Herbie J. Pilato, Television Historian, Author, and a former NBC page

ONE . . .

"The man who interviewed me asked why I wanted to intern there. I answered, 'Because Baywatch doesn't have any interns!' He laughed, so I guess that was good."

—Dan Zweifler, Technical Recruiter and a former Albany news intern

AND ACTION!

PREPARING FOR THE INTERVIEW

Everything you've done thus far has led up to the vital step known as the interview. In college, you may have occasionally crammed for a final or a midterm, but don't even think of cramming for your interview. Follow these tips when preparing for your big day.

1. *Do more research.*

Find out everything you can about your interviewer and the company. What shows were taped at that studio thirty years ago? When was the last time the company boss was quoted in *Electronic Media?* Did she like *The Munsters* or *The Addams Family* better? Uncover every shred of information and store it in your show files.

> *"If it's a talk/reality show internship you are interviewing for, gather clippings and bring in show ideas. Try to research the producer's past credits for anything you can tie into when they say, 'Tell me a little about yourself.' "*
>
> —Rich Brandt, Post Production Supervisor, *Sightings*

Did any fellow students meet with the interviewer earlier? Hunt them down and find out what their audition was like.

2. *Do a dry run to the studio.*

Know exactly how long it will take you to get to the interview. If two trucks collide in front of you while heading to the studio, how long would it delay you? Find out and give yourself another twenty minutes.

3. *Stay up on their airwaves.*

Keep your eyes glued to the station's or studio's programming before your interview. If their newscast just broke the local equivalent of Watergate the night before, you better be up on it. Not only might you miss a great opening line, you could wind up missing a great internship opportunity.

4. *Be a current events guru.*

Be aware of everything and anything that has recently happened in the world, especially if it happened in your market.

> *"Prospective news interns must be ready for a current events quiz. Make sure you know the names of all your local government officials. A common question is 'If you were the producer of last night's show, what story would you have led with?' Be sure to read every newspaper from that week, especially Sunday's, from cover to cover."*
>
> —Heather Lovett, News Producer, NBC Affiliate, and a former intern

4. *Keep reading the trades.*

If the interviewer starts off the meeting referring to the front page of today's *Variety*, you want to be able to compare the front page of *Variety* to the front page of *The Hollywood Reporter*. Show off your love for the industry.

> *"READ, whether it be industry-related magazines or an insider's look at a particular genre. Learn the lingo of your trade."*
> —Michelle Davis, TV Producer

5. *Rehearse interview questions.*

You should practice answers to the common questions found in interview books, but you don't want to come across like you're reciting a script. You're auditioning for an internship, not a plum part on *Melrose Place*. You'll want to come across warm and sincere and very *you*.

6. *Make sure you have extra copies of your resume and a reference list.*

> *"Know your own resume and be prepared to explain what you did at each job. Don't ever bad mouth another employer; this will only make you look bad. Be prepared to answer questions like 'Why do you want to intern here?' and 'What do you hope to get out of interning?' I've been asked that at every intern interview. Most of all, have a positive attitude, and let them know you're serious about the job."*
> —Tim Mancinelli, Associate Director, *The Late Late Show with Tom Snyder*, and a former intern

7. *Bring a notepad and pen.*

Jot down points. They will be impressed.

8. *Ponder other interviews you've had.*

Where did they go wrong? Learn from your mistakes.

9. *Buy a thank-you card for your interviewer.*

Bring it with you to the interview, but don't fill it out yet. This will be explained later.

Dress for Interview Success

Your dress depends largely on where you're meeting. Know your audience. If you're interviewing at a TV sales department, wearing a suit is necessary.

For a studio crew gig, denim might be right. Geography is also important. New Yorkers usually dress up; Californians, by and large, dress down.

> *"My advice for interview preparation—shower!"*
>
> —Edward Boyd, Producer/Writer, E! Entertainment Television

> *"Although you're a college student and most likely on a tight budget, dress as professionally as possible. Working in TV is more informal than working in a bank, but don't draw unnecessary attention to yourself. Let 'em remember you for your great ideas, not the halter top or nose ring!"*
>
> —Barbara Koster, Field Producer, *20/20* and *Good Morning America*, and a former intern

Take a field trip down to your potential new home and survey the dress code; when in doubt, favor the dressy side. It shows how seriously you take this meeting. Our "Hall of Famers" have some definite advice about wardrobe they think is fitting:

> *"The wrong approach for women would be wearing a three-piece navy blue suit with a tie and a briefcase just for show. The right approach? A pair of dress pants and a sweater. Don't overdress to impress."*
>
> —Adora English, Producer, *KTLA Morning News* in LA, and a former intern

However . . .

> *"I've met people who have walked into my office wearing a ripped T-shirt and torn jeans, looking like they just got in from working on their cars in the garage, grease and all. I may be from a different era, but show some respect."*
>
> —Tisi Aylward, Director, Talent, E! Entertainment Television, and a former intern

It's Okay To Be Nervous

Many people lose a lot of sleep before interviews. Accept it and try to find ways to relax. There is an expression in recovery programs called "act as if." It means that when you face a frightening situation, act as if you've been through this before. Imagine you are Jodie Foster being cast in a new role. Act your part. Soon your feelings will catch up with your actions, and it will become easier.

VH1 Writer/Producer Dane Hall has some great advice for when it comes to those nerve-wracking moments: "If I start to get the jitters, I tell myself, 'Hey, you're not really nervous, you are excited about this opportunity.' Let your excitement take over, not your nerves."

Meditation and exercise are wonderful for butterflies, too. Don't get caught doing push-ups in the hallway, but try to relax. Research has shown a little bit of anxiety is good for one's performance, but too much can be hurtful.

"Don't be afraid. We've all stood where you're standing."
—Jack Forrestel, Five-time Emmy Award–Winning Art Director, *The Bold and the Beautiful*, and a former TV Academy intern

Keep telling yourself, "I will do the best I can. I am proud of myself for getting this far."

Meeting the Assistant

If the boss has an assistant, you have hopefully already bonded over the phone. Say hello and thank him or her for all the help. If you're nervous, share it. Get some last-minute advice for your exclusive interview. Head for the restroom for one final touch-up before you go "on camera."

Know Your Rights

As you are primping and giving yourself one last pep talk, keep in mind there are some legal issues involving your internship. There are laws concerning interns, and you need to be aware of them for your own protection. According to the Fair Labor Standards Act, interns who are not being paid:

- Must be receiving credit for the internship
- Must receive industry training and on-site supervision
- Shouldn't spend more than half of their time doing work that is also done by the paid employees
- Can't be promised employment at the completion of the internship
- Can't do work that results in a layoff or the reduction of hours of a paid employee
- Should not be filling a position that was previously held by a paid employee

It is important to be aware of these rules before your interview. If you're told anything that conflicts with these items, you might try asking the interviewer for clarification on a particular point that illustrates your knowledge of the subject. Alternatively, you might see what course of action your academic adviser recommends. Some places have a reputation for abusing interns and you'll want to know this in advance. Now, one final tuck and its time for . . .

THE BIG MOMENT . . . QUIET ON THE SET

"I never expect students to be experts on the show or on the industry—they're students, and they want the internship in order to learn. I want to see earnestness, enthusiasm, and maturity."

—Carole Chouinard, Segment Producer, *Politically Incorrect*, and Intern Coordinator, *Arsenio*

When you meet the interviewer, let him extend his hand first. Be sure and give a firm grip, but, of course, try to leave all of the interviewer's fingers in working condition. Don't call them by their first name unless they tell you its okay. What else?

1. *Work your contacts into your talk.*

Give your interviewer a frame of reference. "Marlaine sends her regards. She is so excited about her new job producing the Tonys." This opening line should connect you both.

2. *Keep great eye contact.*

This is television. Talk directly to your "viewer."

"When I interviewed for my internship, the last question I was asked was 'Someone calls the desk to report that there's an abortion protest going on; what would you do?' I had no idea. But I took a second to think about it, looked her right in the eye, and answered her quickly and like I knew exactly what to do—no doubts. My interviewer said the way I answered the question clinched the job. She said most candidates look away, say 'I guess I would,' and show no confidence. That's what'll help set you apart."

—Shannon Keenan, Producer, Live Events, E! Entertainment Television, and a former intern

3. *Don't lose your energy!*

Enthusiasm can make all the difference.

"Don't downplay your life experiences. That's what makes you unique. I like to hear about a person's background. But again, remember, less is more. Once you've started droning on, you've lost me."

　　—Dane Hall, VH1 Writer/Producer

Be excited about your past and accomplishments.

"My interviewer loved beauty pageants and noticed on my resume that I had been a Park Princess in Minnesota. I have gotten more jobs from that title!"

　　—Jill Bandemer, Film Development, *Boy Meets World*, and a former intern

Convey your passion for television.

"One of my first questions was always 'What TV shows do you like?' If the answer was 'I watch only PBS,' I knew the person was not right for broadcast TV. If they said, 'I love soaps, Monday Night Football, or reruns of Mary Tyler Moore' and had some sort of reason about the message, presentation, etc., that was the answer I was looking for."

　　—Jane Temple, Cleveland TV Producer

4. *Stay honest.*

If you're nervous, 'fess up. Be real and you become a much more sympathetic character. Don't exaggerate about your accomplishments, either. Be proud but genuine.

5. *Listen.*

This is the most important quality of a reporter or a host. Put on your radar. What are they saying beyond their words? How are they responding to you? Try to read their nonverbal signals as well.

"Preparation isn't as important as keeping your ears open. Listening is key."

　　—Sheila Brummer, News Anchor, WAOW-TV, Wausau, Wisconsin, and a former intern

6. *Convey your reliability and have faith in yourself.*

This is perhaps the most important quality to emphasize during the interview. Most interns can get coffee and run tapes, but you must convince them that they can trust you and count on you, at all costs. The person interviewing you will be putting herself on the line if she hires you. She is telling her staff, "I trust this person." If you don't come across as having faith in yourself, why in the world should the interviewer?

OTHER WAYS TO CLINCH THE DEAL

Keep these additional points in mind—they may come in handy:

1. *Ask for clarification.* If you don't know the answer to a question, admit it. It's better than babbling for 20 minutes. If you're unsure about the question, ask the interviewer to be more specific. "I'm sorry, but I'm not exactly sure what you meant by that question. What did you want to know?" Chances are, his mind is racing with news budgets or technical problems. Help him focus. Also, remember that while a sense of humor is nice, don't go overboard and turn the meeting into an HBO comedy special.

2. *Limit your small talk.* Get conversational, but don't miss the meat of your interview. Hit on the major points in your life that led you to TV. Make sure your story reveals information about your determination and dependability. Instead of just saying, "I've always wanted to be in news," offer that, "I wanted to learn about news so badly that a reporter friend of mine taught me Newsstar and LEXIS-NEXIS afterhours at her station." The executive will expect you to be up on current events as

COMMERCIAL BREAK:

"My first day in New York, I took a train ride with my only friend in the whole state. Those subways scared the death out of me. My friend was nice enough to take the train in with me for my first three days of work, but on the fourth day I was on my own. Being the daring person that I am, I decided to go a different route. I heard it was shorter. I'm sure you can see where this story is going. Picture it, a scared suburban boy from the middle of the country, stuck on some train heading who knows where, already an hour late for his internship. I landed in Queens and then finally made my way back to the city. I was afraid I'd get in trouble, but they were too busy laughing at my adventure."

—*Greg Kestin, former intern, Primetime Live*

well. Work a headline, a study, or an anecdote into the discussion. Show them you are as timely and topical as *20/20*. A current *USA Today*, a trade, and even a tabloid can give you great material.

3. *Be specific about your career goals.* Your specific goals were in your cover letter, but it's best to repeat them. If you are working in a development house, would you rather be part of the writing, editing, or production team? Are you interested in field production? In the game of TV, tell them what position you'd ultimately like to play. "While I'd love helping out anywhere, my main passion is being out in the field."

Utilize your research in expressing your career goals. Instead of saying, "I want your job," a better line may be, "I would love to be in a position similar to yours someday. I know that the road isn't easy. Is it true you really have lived in ten cities before settling here?" If possible, get the interviewer talking about his or her experience. Show genuine interest, but remember that too much enthusiasm may be transparent to them. The interviewer has been in that seat dozens and dozens of times.

> *"If I ask them what they want to do and they reply, 'I want to get in and do whatever,' that's too unfocused for me. I look for someone who really does have a sense of purpose. Most interns who come in without focus end up drifting around, forcing me to pull them in different directions. That is not my job!"*
> —Don Wells, News Director, KGTV-TV San Diego

If you are interested in a highly specialized area, bring it up. Their program might not be as specialized as you desire.

> *"If you want to be an investigative reporter, investigate how closely interns can work at that station's unit. Because of secrecy, hidden camera set-ups, and complicated legal issues, I won't take on interns. But if you really want this, make it your first investigative piece and find a reporter who will. They are out there."*
> —Joel Grover, Investigative Reporter, KCBS-TV LA

"Can I Wear My Bunny Slippers?"

Let the interviewer know your availability, but do it in a way that shows your enthusiasm. If you can work five days a week, definitely work that into the conversation. "I can be here anytime you need me. If there's a problem at 3 a.m., I might come running into the station with my purple bunny slippers on, but I'll be here." This will be music to his ears. Don't worry if you can only work two days a week; put a positive spin on it. "I am only available two days a week, but I can stay as late as needed those days. If there's work to be done until midnight, I will be here. Does the station have a policy against bunny slippers?" Bunny slippers are always a good thing. What if you'll be free five days a week next semester? Work that in as well. "I'm only available two days a week this semester, but I can probably be here five days a week next semester. I'd already know the office and the systems, so I'd have a ton to contribute. And I'll even throw in my bunny slippers!"

"Do You Have Any Questions for Me?"

"Go in with your own questions ready. Not 'Where can I park?' and 'Do you have bagels in the morning?' More like 'If I interned on six of those projects, would I be in line for advancement if you liked my work?' 'Where do you envision the company in five years?' 'Are there plans to expand?'"

—Kac Young, VP, Television Production and Development, Universal Studios, Hollywood, and a former intern

You will be asked if you have any questions. Don't get caught unprepared, and be sure your question reflects well on you.

While panicking isn't a good thing, be aware that one really bad question can cost you the internship. *CBS This Morning* Producer, Carol Story, recounts the time a potential intern asked, "About that 8:30 a.m. start time—is that firm, or could I come in when I get up . . . around 10?" Needless to say, the intern did not get the job. Asking the right questions can also show how much you know. "In checking, I see that this studio handles everything from pilots to postproduction. While my main interest is being in the field, will I have a chance to help out in post?"

"I look for a willingness to learn EVERYTHING and for someone to check their attitude at the door. It's great that a 20 year old wants to be a director, but it's important to learn other jobs, too. All knowledge makes you a wiser worker."

—Michelle Davis, TV Producer

Your research should have told you how much grunt work to expect. If not, ask. Make sure this internship is mutually beneficial. Are you clear of the actual ratio of grunt work to real experience? If not, ask. Pin down *exactly* how much gofer patrol duty you'll be pulling and diplomatically ask how much time you will have to pursue your real passion, field producing for instance.

Closing Out the Interview

As we mentioned, a little healthy competition is good. Let the interviewer know that you are doing some intern shopping. Ask them if they were in your shoes, what would they do?

At the end of the interview, see if there is anything you can provide. A list of show ideas, potential news stories, or programming suggestions? Put them in a follow-up letter or the thank-you card you bought at the store earlier today. It's a definite chance to impress.

It is hard to know what kind of interview you will have. Your interviewer may have just reviewed the latest ratings, she may have just fired another intern, or she could have just been nominated for an Emmy. It's also possible that your interviewer will be pulled away right in the middle of the interview. This is why it's important to start impressing the moment the interview begins.

```
INT. OFFICE—DAWN
(PULL OUT FROM "TEEN TOWN" LOGO TO REVEAL BOB, THE EXECUTIVE
FOR THE POPULAR SHOW, WHO IS IN HIS OFFICE SITTING ACROSS FROM
HOPEFUL INTERN, BARB)


                          BOB
You made a nice impression on my assistant, Del. She says
you're doing some kind of athletic training?


                         BARB
Yes, I am a junior at Wayne State, majoring in
telecommunications. I'm also training for my college's
charity swimming marathon. We'll be swimming 15 miles across
the Detroit River next week. That is how I met Randy, who says
to say hello. Oh, and I brought you an extra copy of my resume
and a list of references.


                          BOB
Thanks. Randy is a great guy. I owe him a call. Coffee or
water? (she declines) I was a swimmer myself. What would you
like to do eventually . . . out of the water, that is?


                         BARB
I'd like to produce live events, like my swim-a-thon. I work
with our college crew when we broadcast football games. I do
```

everything from directing to running camera. Here is my highlight reel. (SHE HANDS OVER A PROFESSIONAL—LOOKING REEL, MUCH TO BOB'S DELIGHT.) I know this station does more sports than all the others combined. I really liked your use of the extra cameras this season. Tara Johnson is a great director.

BOB

Well, you've done your homework. Do you see yourself becoming a director like Tara?

BARB

Yes. I realize I won't be directing in this internship, but after I'm done with my grunt work for the day, will I get a chance to spend some time with the directors?
(BOB'S INTERCOM BUZZER SOUNDS. HE PICKS UP PHONE, FRETS, AND THEN RETURNS TO THE DISCUSSION.)

BOB

We have a large, active internship program, and we rotate a lot of responsibilities, so students get real hands-on experience. I hate to cut this short, but I have a fire to put out. Can I answer anything else?

BARB

(NOT BATTING AN EYE) No problem. Real quickly, I had a nice talk with Del about internships. Knowing that she was an intern here speaks volumes. But I mentioned to her that I also have an opportunity at ESPN. What advice do you have?

BOB

It is a good program there, but you'll have more opportunities here. I will get back to you, but I have got to dash. It was a pleasure to meet you. Tell Randy I said hi.

(FADE TO BLACK ON BOB'S QUICK EXIT)

Let's review why this meeting went well.

1. Barb already had a built-in cheerleader in Bob's assistant Del.
2. Barb had really researched her subject and his station.
3. She worked her contact, Randy, and her background into the conversation right off the top.
4. She brought a resume and had an agenda, but it came off in a natural way.
5. She worked her extracurricular activities right into her career goals.

6. Barb was unfazed when Bob had to leave; she understands pressure and deadlines.
7. She brought up another internship possibility.
8. Barb got a pledge that there would be hands-on experience and did it tactfully.

This meeting went well. If you prepare, yours could go even better.

On Your Way Out

When you leave your interview, put on your spy glasses and do some snooping. Investigate the studio surroundings and scan the intern area. Are they overwhelmed stuffing envelopes? Busy or sitting around? Do they have their own desks? Try and grab interns, even some employees, for a few comments. Trade phone numbers or e-mail addresses if you can. Even if you don't end up there, they could become important contacts or lifelong friends.

Notice what everyone is wearing. Get a fashion preview for your first day, and take notes. What about the computers? Are they IBMs or Macs? If you don't know how to use them—learn!

AFTER THE INTERVIEW

Your mind will be racing when you leave; take a deep breath and pat yourself on the back. You've zoomed in one shot closer to your dream career. While it is still fresh in your mind, write down what really worked in your interview and what didn't. This will be a great help in the future.

Next, ask yourself if you could imagine interning there. Take stock in everything you experienced that day—from the interview experience itself to your observations about the work environment. What is your gut telling you? What kind of impression do you have of the place and people? Did you trust the interviewer? Will this gig lead to a job? Hopefully you followed the advice from earlier in the channel and brought a thank-you card with you. Now is the time to fill it out. Keep it concise, but add something personal from the meeting. Say you'll call in one week, and drop it in the nearest mail box. Remember, while thank-you's are important, don't go overboard either.

"The worst internship follow-up I had was a guy who actually sent me a singing telegram the day after his interview. All I kept thinking during the musical number is that there was no way I would ever hire that person. It means much more if the person sends me a note mentioning

something very specific they may have learned in the interview than if the person tries to show me how much money they have."

—Adora English, Producer, *KTLA Morning News* in LA, and a former intern

You can also call the next day, but don't expect to talk to your interviewer. Just leave a message with your new best friend, the assistant. Thank him or her for the help; you can usually get a bit of a report card by the tone that they have with you over the phone. Keep it short. The goal is to show you are organized, polite, and hungry for an internship.

WAITING FOR THE CALL

What do you do while waiting for the callback? How long should you give it before you pick up the phone again? You've already told the executive in your thank-you note that you'll be calling in a week. Mark your calendar. Call the executive and reintroduce yourself. Don't take it personally that they forgot the specifics of your meeting. They have many other things on their TV plate. Don't be defensive or demanding.

If you call your future boss and he or she says they'll get right back to you, wait about a week and then call again. Don't expect an immediate return call. Many industry employees don't have time to phone their loved ones, so calling back an intern may be low on their priority list.

Call the assistant, remind them who you are, and ask them for their advice. Some executives welcome an intern checking in for a status report, while others hate being pestered. How do you get a good read? The assistant will usually provide this information, either directly or indirectly. This person is a godsend, so treat them accordingly.

You may get word in a day. It may be a month. Keep trying. If possible, don't leave a voice mail when you call. It is better to get a living, breathing person on the other end.

What If You Didn't Get the Internship?

Be polite. Don't get angry. Rejection happens. It will happen to you a lot in TV.

"The highs and lows of a career in TV are the most difficult paths anyone can choose. No matter how many times you are rejected and how comfortable you are with the idea that the rejection isn't about you, emotionally it is a tough experience. Just make sure to have something

else that makes you feel worthy in life . . . a partner, volunteering, etc. I think that helps keep your abilities in perspective."
—Marilyn Kagan, Radio and Television Psychotherapist

Maybe this was the ideal internship for you; maybe not. Maybe there is an even better internship out there. Can you be certain that getting rejected was a bad thing? Can you prove that this rejection won't lead you to an even better internship? If not, why get upset? It's their loss.

A key point in this industry: **Never burn a bridge.** Let the supervisor know that you really appreciated her taking the time to meet with you and that you're sorry it didn't work out. If you are a junior or a first-semester senior, ask the supervisor if you could be considered for next semester. Maybe they are aware of other programs you can research. Find out what you can do to improve your chances if you apply again.

Drop another thank-you card in the mail bin. The more the supervisor sees your name, the better. Being extra polite can only help. You never know when their needs will change, and be sure to send a note to the assistant. Assistants rarely get them. You'll vault to the top of their list.

You Got the Internship, but . . .

If you've followed the advice, you are interviewing at least three different shops. You may get an offer you don't want. Be flattered. Let them down gently. Keep the door open. Why?

1. The internship you turn down in the fall may be your dream home in spring.
2. Your other internship might not work out. A back-up plan never hurts.
3. If you keep up with your connection, this may be a possible paycheck after graduation.

Call the intern supervisor right away to say you won't be joining them. Be honest. Saying that you've been cast in *Home Boys from Outerspace* isn't necessary. They will understand that you picked another internship.

Write the executive another thank-you note. Let the internship supervisor know that you are extremely grateful for the opportunity and that you're sorry it didn't work out. This will make a big difference in how the executive sees you; chances are your paths will cross again. Once again, don't leave a voice mail, and don't write or e-mail a "Dear John" letter to the supervisor. Your live voice is what will really count. Once again, don't forget the assistant. You never know if they are going to be Aaron Spelling's assistant or the next Aaron Spelling himself.

What If You Have Several Options and Want Them All?

"Consider how each internship will look on your resume. Is it a big, prestigious company that everyone knows, or is it a little place, and you'll always have to explain what it is and why you were there."
—Carol Story, Producer, *CBS This Morning*

The bottom line: Take whatever internship is most likely going to lead you to a job in TV!

What If You Keep Interviewing, but Still Nothing?

It may be just a string of bad luck, or you may unknowingly be making a drastic error. Go to your adviser and ask them to give you a mock interview. Hopefully, they can catch your error. If that doesn't work, go to parents or your friends and ask them to check out your style. The important thing is not to give up; greatness will come your way.

YOU'VE JUST ACCEPTED YOUR PRIZE INTERNSHIP . . . NOW WHAT?

Celebrate. You've done well. You're another step closer to sharing the small screen with Katie Couric, Peter Jennings, Rosie, the Nanny, and Bill Nye, the Science Guy. Call your mom, your boyfriend, or a buddy. Then hit your favorite hangout. Be proud of your achievement. Toast your tenacity . . . but then get to work.

Thank Your Contacts

Buy stock in Hallmark greeting cards. Anyone who had anything to do with your internship search is owed a thank-you. Keep them updated on your TV career, and make them feel like they are a part of it. Your contact pool will become as important to you as water. TV executives are used to poor follow-through; be the exception.

Review Your Research Material

"What did I do before I started my internship? I read everything under the sun."
—Darnell Jones, Script Coordinator, P. J.'s, former Writer's Assistant, *Hangin' with Mr. Cooper*, and a former intern

Go back to the research files that you began in Channel 2. Review all your data on your new workplace. If you are interning on a show, learn everything you possibly can about it. When did it first go on the air? What have the ratings been? What do the trades say about it? Get your hands on any tape of the show. This book is giving you permission to become a couch potato. Does life get any better?

> *"Watch the show. Know your talent. If you don't know much about broadcasting lingo, buy a book. I did. On my first day of my news internship, they were all talking in this 'news code.' Rather than having to ask for interpretation every other sentence, I went out and taught myself. Do it before you punch in on Day One!"*
> —Shannon Keenan, Producer, Live Events, E! Entertainment Television, and a former intern

There is no limit to the amount of research you can do; catch up on the competition as well. You have a fresh set of eyes. They are in the TV fish bowl, and your insights will be welcome.

Get a Staff List
If you don't have a staff list by now, call up the assistant and get one faxed or mailed to you. Memorizing names and titles will be a lifesaver on your first day. You might be surprised to find that someone you know actually works there. You can find out where everyone lives (and size up possible rides), get a jump on extensions (you'll need to have everyone's number), and find out staff birthdays (everyone loves getting cards or presents).

Recontact Your Contacts
Since you've already thanked your contacts for intern help, they'll be more than happy to lend a hand again. If you're having trouble tracking down information on your soon-to-be office mates or other data, ask your contacts. They are bound to know something about your new office. They may call you to congratulate you on the internship. If not, give them a ring. Arm yourself with questions for them if they are in the same part of the business you are entering. Once again, keep notes and make sure all of your information is neatly filed.

Track Down Former Interns
Prior to your interview, you should have tracked down other past interns from the places you were considering. Call on them again and, if you can afford it, take them out to dinner and grill them. Which employees treated

interns well? What were the biggest mistakes they made? How would they have done the internship differently? Did the boss like candy corn or jelly beans better? If you can't afford to take your new friend out for a meal, a phone conversation will still be extremely effective. Round up as many former interns as you can. Even if you don't know any personally, it's possible that the assistant can put you in contact with them.

IMPRESSING EVEN BEFORE YOU BEGIN

"Start working out with a tripod. Bench press it a few hundred times, so you'll be prepared for hours of lugging it around on shoots."
—Claire Adamsick, Minneapolis News Intern

There is no reason to wait for your first day to begin impressing everyone. Here's a simple way to start scoring points before the game begins.

"I'd be impressed with someone who calls and says, 'Before my start day, can I just come in and observe? I'd like to get a feel for what everyone in this office is doing.' This way, the intern shows eagerness and will also have a chance to impress the staffers before the other interns even hit town."
—Jan Landis, *Sally, Home, Vicki,* and has trained more than 100 interns

If you do make a field trip into the office before you start, make sure you read the next channel before you embark on your journey. Treat your day of observation with the same mindset as you would if it were your first day of the internship.

What a Good Cup of Coffee Will Get You

From your research, you should be well aware of your internship responsibilities. Very often, you'll be responsible for making coffee. Coffee is a $2-billion-per-year business in this country. Don't take this task lightly!

"I once took 52 orders of various coffees, cappuccinos, mochaccinos, and some things I can't even pronounce, all for an entire cast and crew. I got every order correct, and each person was VERY satisfied. How cool am I?"
—Jeffrey Reingold, former intern, *The Rosie O'Donnell Show*

What will a good cup of coffee get you? Probably making the next pot of coffee. Has anyone ever been dismissed on the grounds of bad coffee? No. You may hate this chore, but look at the cup as half full, not half empty. The coffee machine has become the modern day campfire. A TV station or studio thrives on early hours and intense deadlines. Just about everyone, whether a PA, an EP, or the GM, depends on his or her morning fix. It is a great place to meet, mingle, and catch up with everyone. Why not think about bringing in your favorite hazelnut blend and brewing it sometime?

Computers, Faxes, Copiers—Befriend Them

"On my interview I was asked, 'Do you know WordPerfect?' I responded with all the self-confidence in the world, 'Do I know WordPerfect?' and the interviewer went on to the next question. Of course, I didn't know WordPerfect, but technically I didn't lie. I answered the question with a question. How difficult could it be to learn WordPerfect?"

—Rich Brandt, Post Production Supervisor, *Sightings*

The computer is the most important tool of our generation. It is impossible to make it in TV today without knowing how to use one. Hopefully, you didn't wait until the night before your internship to read this part of the book. It's no longer enough to only know how to turn a computer on and type. You must learn how to navigate the Internet. Web page design is a great area to really make your mark. Most shows have a Web page, but not many staffers know how to utilize it. Why not become the station's Web master? Take a course and learn as many skills as possible. Can you do spreadsheets? Do you know Lotus? Can you work Excel? As you'll read in Channel 6, these are great ways to compute intern success.

If you have never faxed before, you'll want to learn. Don't risk being branded incompetent if you mess up a fax early in your internship. If an employee asks you to fax something, you don't want your answer to be, "I don't know how."

You should know how to make copies; it's also to your complete advantage to understand the copy machine. If you are making copies on your first day and the paper jams, wouldn't it be much better if you could fix it yourself? Go to the office of a friend that has a copy machine like the one in your new studio or station. Learn everything you can. How do you collate or change the ink cartridge? Put simply, know copy machine first aid.

Typing skills are also keys to a good internship. If you can type fast, great. If you've only mastered the one-finger method, start practicing. You'll be surprised when you find out how many students still don't know how to type. Don't blow a great assignment!

> *"Ironically, the biggest thing that helped me in my career was the fact that I typed over 100 words per minute and could run most word processing programs. If you are good at office skills, people will be willing to believe that you would be good at other things as well. After you get your promotion, you can forget all those skills you used to get there. You don't want to be known as an executive who can type his or her own memos."*
>
> —Dan Watanabe, Director of Development, All American TV

FedEx . . . UPS. . . Get It There Tomorrow

"Can we still make FedEx?" is a chant heard around many newsrooms and production offices. "What time does UPS close?" Figuring out how to ship mail and packages for reliable overnight delivery *before* you start your internship could again make you look well prepared. Take a trip to your nearest FedEx drop and learn how to fill out one of their forms. You can also call their 800 number (1-800-GO-FEDEX); they'd be happy to explain how it works. Having this overnight insight will come in handy when it's 5:55 p.m. and your boss decides to ship some tapes to the other coast for a next-day meeting. If you are unaware that the shipping deadline is at 6 p.m., you may not be aware that the shipment needs to be your first priority.

Writing Skills

The art of writing rates big when it comes to internships. TV and film producer Alan Duncan Ross believes that the best way to prepare for an internship is to learn how to use the English language. How are your writing skills? Perhaps you should hone your grammar skills.

> *"I made myself valuable. I am a very good writer and started writing one or two stories a day, then ended up writing half the show. How could they do without me? I carved a niche for myself. They had to hire me."*
>
> —Richard Ayoub, Executive Producer, *KABC Morning News* in LA, and a former intern

Development Executive Stephanie Drachkovitch says that writing is the foundation for all communication. "If you can't write, spell, or use proper grammar, then I am not interested." Go to the bookstore and take a refresher course in English. Most people in TV are creative writers, not grammarians. A good proofreader is hard to find. Help them, and they'll make you a star!

APPEARANCE IS EVERYTHING

Office dress codes vary greatly from station to station, show to show, and coast to coast. If the recommendations were followed, you took notes during the interview of the common office attire. When the staffers get their first glimpse of you, they won't see your resume or your determination; the first thing they'll see is your wardrobe. This is not the place to try to make a bold statement or break new ground. News Executive Don Wells suggests, "Dress the part of the job you wish to have next." This is a very smart and safe way to determine your opening-day apparel.

Both men and women must remember that they are there to do a job, not to draw attention to themselves. Wearing too much makeup is not eye-catching; it is distracting. A natural look is much more appealing than an overmade face. Jewelry should be tasteful and appropriate. If you are going to wear earrings, wear one pair, not ten. As for men, although earrings may be a growing trend in the workplace, for your first few weeks, don't wear them. Being conservative is still a trend in the job world as well as in internships. After a week or so, you'll have a much stronger grasp for what is and isn't acceptable. Until then, the less attention brought to you the better. Remember, the first thing an interviewer or staff member sees is what you look like.

> *"It isn't necessary for men to wear suits or women to wear knee-length dresses, but office attire is absolutely mandatory. I have actually had to talk to a couple of interns who came into work in gangster-rap outfits. When you work at a TV network, you are in a corporate environment, and you should dress conservatively, no matter how corny it feels to you."*
>
> —John C. Zak, Supervising Producer, *The Bold and the Beautiful*, and a former intern

When it comes down to a decision between two outfits, it's usually better to go with the more conservative one. Better conservative than sorry. But if you notice the office outfitted in only jeans and T-shirts, overdressing can be equally embarrassing. MTV Vice President Brian Graden painfully recalled his first-day fashion faux pas. He wore a suit. "I was interning in a development office, and no one was wearing anything close to the standard professional attire. It was very embarrassing and earned me the nickname Poindexter."

"I was dressed to kill in a new dress, high heels, etc. Ten hours later, my dress is torn, and my feet are killing me! Part of my internship consisted of carrying 70 pounds of equipment—being a news reporter isn't as easy as it looks on TV!"

—Sheila Brummer, News Anchor, WAOW-TV, Wausau, Wisconsin, and a former intern

Finally, don't send out the wrong message with your attire. Wearing inappropriate or provocative clothing won't get you a promotion; it'll just get you labeled as unprofessional.

THE FOUR-STAR FIRST IMPRESSION—FIRST IN

The worst way to make a first impression is to make it in 10 minutes late. Come hell or high water, be punctual on your first day.

"I remember a guy who was late his first day, when he took the wrong train. He was never able to shake the image of always being late. If there was a time-sensitive project, he would never get it. Bad idea, being late."

—Jason Gurskis, Producer, Discovery Channel, and a former intern

COMMERCIAL BREAK:

"When I was an intern, I lived at home and so my family saw the way I dressed each day when I left for the office. One day, I was meeting the producer and a crew, and we were going to Jackson Prison to interview some of the lifers. I was wearing a casual jacket, and my dad stopped me at the door and asked me where was that nice new coat I'd recently bought. Well, I returned to my room and donned the pinkish spring coat. Now it wasn't anything special, but when I walked onto the prison floor, the boys behind bars knew instantly there was a female in their midst, and the cat calls nearly reduced me to tears. These were sex-starved lifers, and it was an important lesson for me in dressing for the situation."

—Barbara Koster, Field Producer, Good Morning America, and a former intern

If your commute is long and unpredictable, you may want to stay at a friend's place that is closer to the studio. If need be, get a motel room for the night. You probably know how long it takes to get to the office or studio from your now legendary first interview, but leave extra early just in case. If your interview was in a different location than where you'll be working, take a timed trip the day before. Leave nothing to chance.

The first-day ETA is actually a rarely explored golden opportunity. Here's how to take full advantage of it. Call your supervisor the workday before you begin to confirm your arrival date and time. Many interns assume that they have a 9 a.m. call time, or, if they are told a certain time, they assume they can't go in any earlier.

INT. BEDROOM—NOON
(SCENE STARTS WITH A NERVOUS INTERN PACING AROUND HIS ROOM AS HE DIALS A NUMBER ON HIS CORDLESS PHONE. A CASUAL SUIT, JUST RETURNED FROM THE CLEANERS, IS HANGING ON THE DOOR.)

                    YOU
Hello, Dan, this is Brian. Do you have a second?

                    DAN
Sure, Brian. What can I do for you?

                    YOU
What time would you like me to arrive on Monday?

                    DAN
9 a.m. will be fine.

                    YOU
Would it be okay if I came in a little earlier to begin to learn my way around the office?

                    DAN
Sure, what time do you want to come in?

                    YOU
As early as possible.

                    DAN
Great. I'll see you at 7.

(THE NERVOUS YOUNG INTERN HANGS UP THE PHONE AND MAKES CERTAIN THAT HE WILL AWAKEN ON TIME.)

Getting to the office 2 hours before everyone else will not only look ambitious, but it'll also probably land you the assignment of showing other new interns around when they arrive. It's never too soon to establish yourself as a leader. In addition, the earlier you can get some time alone with your supervisors the better. The phones aren't ringing, their heads aren't racing, and your bonding can begin.

FINALLY, RELAX—YOU'RE READY

If you've followed the preparation advice in this channel, you should be well prepared for your first day on the job. It's time to take a hot bubble bath and relax as you ponder your day tomorrow. Try to visualize it as you soak in the tub. Now hit the sack. Be sure to set at least two alarm clocks; you may even want a friend to give you a call to be sure you're up on time. You can never be too safe. Tomorrow you will be waking up to a true made-for-TV adventure.

```
. . . AND CUT!
ANNOUNCER VOICE:
```

"Coming up next: How to score big overnight ratings with the opening episode of your internship!"

```
FADE TO BLACK
ROLL "TV INTERN HALL OF FAME" PACKAGE
```

Marlaine Selip
Emmy award–winning Supervising Producer, *The Joan Rivers Show,
Donahue,* and a former intern

I was one of five children, and my television time was pretty restricted to Saturdays and Sundays. As a younger child, I loved reality, animal-based programs like *Rin Tin Tin, Fury,* and *My Friend Flicka.* I was also a big fan of the *Mickey Mouse Club,* especially on Fridays when it was rodeo day and Spin and Marty were featured. I guess I've always been a sucker for horses. In the cartoon family, irreverent and sarcastic toons like *Rocky and Bullwinkle* and the *Roadrunner* topped my hit parade. I always loved variety programs. I loved Sonny and Cher, Donny and Marie, Barbra Streisand specials, and Ed Sullivan. It's a shame they haven't resurfaced. That is an area of television I've always wanted to work in.

Being an intern makes you an insider. Every office has its secrets, most of which never leave the building. Those secrets are closely guarded within those walls . . . interns become members of that club. For better or worse, they get to see the real inner workings. Good interns generally get jobs or recommendations from grateful bosses. It is the best opportunity you will ever have to get a job. Hundreds of resumes come across bosses' desks daily. Most are filed. Friends and interns have a leg up. That's the truth. Get in that door, work hard, and you will be recognized. Don't leave early and don't complain, no matter what you are asked to do—always ask for more work. Overworked staffers will take note and put in a good word for you.

I interned on a local public affairs program at WBBM-TV in Chicago, a CBS affiliate. The program was live daily at 6:30 to 7 a.m. It was murder getting up each day but always interesting once I got to the office. Most of the guests were authors. Some stand-outs were John Kenneth Galbraith, a member of the Kennedy cabinet, a funny and irreverent guy who was very different from the stern persona he projected; Way Bandy, a famous makeup artist who was promoting a book and who taped two shows in the studio, neither of which ever aired because the tape room forgot to tape them; Dick Clark; and Bruce Jenner, fresh on the heels of his Olympic victory. They were interesting, intelligent people, and it was fun being exposed to them, if even for a brief time. Mayor Richard Daly, a long-term Chicago favorite, died during my internship, and we did a special on him. It was the first special I ever worked on—it gave me the bug for specials.

I have been blessed in my career because I've had the opportunity to work with very talented, intelligent, and in some cases, very caring hosts. I feel very proud of my time with Joan Rivers. By the time I joined Joan's morning show, she was doing a variety/celebrity–based show. That program was also live, and we would have our briefing meetings at 6:30 a.m. in Joan's office. Joan is, without a doubt, the funniest woman I have ever met. She is extremely kind, very bright, curious, dishy, and very driven. I spent three years working for her, and my strongest memories are of laughing and having a great time.

Donahue was my first job in the big leagues. He was number one in the ratings and doing interesting programs that covered a wide range of topics. He was bright, caring, and driven. I traveled to Death Row in Texas, Chernobyl, London, and on countless trips in the U.S. to cover breaking stories with Phil. I met world leaders, presidents, felons, feminists, movie stars, moguls, and ordinary, hardworking people like you and me.

There were so many wonderful moments; among the highlights were meeting Presidents Carter and Ford, Ted Koppel, Bishop Tutu, Paul Newman, Julia Roberts, Tip O'Neill, Muhammad Ali, and Joe Frazier. What stands out to me about this job was how powerful the medium can be when used to make a difference in people's lives.

Phil's audience was a powerful voice that made changes. If Donahue covered a subject, congressmen would hear from his viewers. Wrongs could be righted. I remember doing the first nationally televised show on missing POWs in Vietnam and Korea. That show had as much an impact in Washington as did the S&L scandal. One time, a man appeared on the broadcast to make an appeal for orphan diseases. His brother had died an awful and unnecessary death from a misdiagnosed orphan disease. Some time later, a program viewer wrote to say that he was diagnosed properly and that his life had been saved. I have scrapbooks full of memories of my time with Donahue. It was a time to feel proud about what you did as a producer.

channel 4

Act 1, Scene 1: The Curtain Goes Up On Your Internship

Let's make no bones about it: The first days of your internship can make or break you. This channel will focus on preparing you for the premiere. The word of the day is preparation—the essential part of any television career—and you must learn to love the process.

Unlike most things in TV Land, you can't rewrite the opening or reshoot the entire day. You are now going *live* into your internship.

THREE . . .

"Expect something completely 100 percent positive and enlightening and enjoyable. You need to plan on this being the best experience you've ever had in your life. Don't go in with fears. If you go in with fears, you're just setting yourself up for trouble."

—Chuck Lioi, Post Production Supervisor, *Sunset Beach*, and a former intern

TWO . . .

"The first week is very important because if you get on the wrong path or make the wrong impression, you're done. You're not going to get a chance to do certain things anymore. People will make an evaluation of how competent you are, how much initiative you have, and whether or not they're going to depend on you for things. If they decide it's not safe to give you tasks, then you're not going to get anything but the real perfunctory tasks to do."

—Don Wells, News Director, KGTV San Diego

ONE . . .

"Take a moment to meet as many people as you can. Introduce yourself. TV can't be done from the bleachers—you must get right in the game.

So the best advice is to jump right in and get to work. The successful interns get their hands dirty right away."

—Glenn Meehan, Managing Editor, *Entertainment Tonight*, and a former intern

AND ACTION!

BRACE YOURSELF FOR AN EMOTIONAL ROLLER COASTER

Very few people walk into their first day in any profession without a major case of butterflies in the stomach. You may be filled with confidence one minute and contemplating a break for the door the next. You're not losing it! This isn't a preamble to a nervous breakdown; it is a common feeling among interns. Let your nervous energy fuel your day instead of crippling it. Lots of people only dream about working in television. You're about to do it.

FLASHBACK

"I remember walking into Fox television the first day. Foolish enough to believe I'd be able to sleep on the plane, it had been 36 hours since I had slept. I was quickly introduced to six other interns, and my heart sank. How in the world was I going to make an impression when the others had been there for two weeks and already knew everything? I was so scared. Hoping no one would notice my knees shaking, I did my best impersonation of a confident and courageous intern. I met the executives and all the producers. I did a lot of gofer work, but toward the end of the day, a couple of the older staff members seemed to warm up to me a little. I knew I could do it; I really believed that. I now had to convince everyone else."

—Jason

"My first day at KMSP-TV was so full of information that the moment I walked out the door at the end of the day, I vomited from anxiety!"

—George Severson, LA News Producer and a former intern

"I talked too much my first day, a sure sign of nervousness. . . "

—Leeza Gibbons, Talk Show Host and former intern

"Be bright-eyed and bushy-tailed! Awake, aware, and ambitious!"

—Michelle Davis, TV Producer

Accept your anxiety while keeping your mission in mind: You are there to do a great job, learn a lot, impress as many people as possible, and start on the road to a successful television career.

IT'S YOUR FIRST DAY, NOT THEIRS

Your big day may be here, but it's business as usual for the rest of the office. When a producer is preparing for a news report, he usually doesn't have time to breathe, let alone time to meet and greet a new intern. Just stand back; you'll be able to make your impression later.

Whatever happens, don't take it personally. Everyone is extremely glad you're there, but more often than not, they are too preoccupied to express it. They perceive you as an extra hand, a motivated helper, and a blessing to a busy show or station. The golden days of Hollywood have been replaced with an environment in which projects need to be done twice as fast, on half the budget, and with one third of the staff. Once you prove yourself to the staff, you may become the office savior, but for now, don't expect a first day ovation.

Listen to what some former interns advise about the first day:

"My advice for interns on their first day . . . stay OUT of my way!"
>   —Edward Boyd, Producer/Writer, E! Entertainment Television, and a
>   former intern

"The first day: a meaningless idea. Your executive is probably so busy and so preoccupied that they won't even notice you're there. No sweat, hang in there. You're getting into this business for a twenty-year run. Get the coffee, study the people, study the papers, figure it out, then make your move sometime later."
>   —Brian Graden, Executive Vice President, MTV, Developer, *South Park*,
>   and a former intern

"I regularly put in 12- to 16-hour days. That's what it takes to oversee a department and put on a daily half-hour entertainment magazine show. It is very difficult to just drop everything and play Julie McCoy. (For those interns too young to remember, she was the cruise director on The Love Boat!*) Interns should show up on time, introduce themselves, and be alert! If it's crazy, busy, and spinning, be willing to jump in."*
>   —Brad Bessey, Coordinating Producer, *Entertainment Tonight*, and a
>   former intern

GREETING THE ASSISTANT

As we discussed in Channel 3, you should have already established a relationship with your supervisor's assistant. You will be seeking him or her out as an ally on your first day. If you've met them before, they are now your friend and glad to see you. If you haven't met them before, it's never too late to enlist them as part of your crew. Here's how you may want to introduce yourself:

```
INT. OFFICE—DAWN
(A NERVOUS BUT CONFIDENT YOUNG INTERN WHO APPROACHES THE
ASSISTANT'S DESK.)


                    YOU
Good morning. My name is Marla. I start my internship today.
I'm supposed to contact Mr. Marty Berman.


                ASSISTANT
Hi, Marla. I'll go tell Marty you're here.


                    YOU
Thank you. By the way, would you mind if I asked you some
questions later on today?


                ASSISTANT
Of course not.


                    YOU
Great. I have to confess, I'm a bit nervous. I want to learn
my responsibilities so I can really start helping out. If you
need anything taken care of, I'd love to give you a hand.
```

(GENUINELY IMPRESSED, WE SEE THE ASSISTANT GLANCE BACK AT MARLA AS SHE EXITS TO GET MARTY.)

By sharing your anxieties with the assistant, you are beginning what can be a great friendship. A little humility can go a long way, so it's better to be honest and get someone on your side than to blunder your way through a situation and risk making a noticeable mistake. Continue to be honest and helpful, and the assistant can be your greatest confidant. Nurture this relationship, since it is likely that the executive will ask his assistant for an impression of you. A positive review will put you in a great starting place.

COMMERCIAL BREAK:

"I was asked during the interview if I knew how to make coffee. I bit my tongue before I answered because, initially, I thought it was a chauvinistic thing to say. But I didn't want to come across with an attitude. I fibbed and said I did. My second day, I arrived on the job to be greeted by an empty Mr. Coffee maker. I got the coffee in okay, but when I poured the water in, I walked away and forgot to put the pot under the maker. The coffee seeped all over the machine, all over the table, went down into the carpets, and made this huge stain. I was close to tears. I was basically having a breakdown there on the carpet as I raced to clean it up before anyone arrived. Luckily, the seeping coffee was taken care of before anyone noticed the stain or my near nervous breakdown."

—*Tisi Aylward, Director, Talent, E! Entertainment Television, and a former intern*

MEETING YOUR SUPERVISOR

"I made such a big blunder on my first day. My supervisor walked in as I was eating a bagel and drinking a Coke while sitting on a script. Talk about bad first impressions."

—Patrick Jarvis, Development Executive, Tribune Entertainment, and a former intern

Your supervisor *may* give you a grand tour and introduce you to every staff member. This is not the norm, but it may happen. Your chances will increase greatly if you follow the advice in the previous channel and arrive as early as possible. If you were able to come in for a day to observe, you may be old friends with the supervisor by now. He also might be extremely busy and leave you on your own with the office pool. If this is the case, you'll have to take the initiative and establish your own presence and purpose and create your own job description. Here are some variations of what you may encounter in terms of first-day responsibilities:

1. A long shopping list of duties may be waiting for you. These tasks may range from menial to extremely creative and exciting. Advanced tasks usually don't find their way to the first-day interns, but you never know.
2. Some responsibilities may be assigned to you, but there won't be enough to keep you busy for the full day. You may be asked to go

around to the staff and see if there's any way you can be of assistance. There are always files, folders, tapes, and miscellaneous research material crying out to be organized. You will win the eternal gratitude of a producer if you volunteer to chip in.

3. The supervisor may have been unprepared for your arrival, or there just may not be any tasks that need to be tackled. Don't sit back and wait for the work to come. You're expected to self-start and fill your day with staff member requests. The right way and wrong way to do this are discussed later in this channel.

> *"If your supervisor doesn't have a plan for that first day, ask to watch tapes, straighten out files or Rolodexes (a great way to get info), or see if you can sit in on a production. Be patient, observe, and soak it all in."*
> —John Dunn, Creative Services Director, UPN affiliate

If you followed the advice from the previous channel, you already came in before your first official day to observe the office. In this case, you'll already be the head of the intern pack. Chances are the supervisor will then be asking you to show the new interns around. Remember, those fellow interns of today may be your colleagues of tomorrow, so treat these relationships respectfully as well.

Most supervisors assign interns to specific departments. You might be assigned to one particular department, you may be asked to rotate through various departments, or it may be left open ended. During your interview, you should have specified your interest to your supervisor. If your designated department doesn't match your desired career path, be sure to politely bring this up to your supervisor. Spending a summer working on field shoots won't be very beneficial if you are interested in marketing and promotion. On the other hand, you might find yourself excited about a whole new area of television you'd never even thought about. You may want to give this area a couple of weeks and see how it pans out.

DOING YOUR BEST *MAGNUM P.I.* IMPERSONATION

From your first step onto the studio floor, you must know how to be the best TV detective ever. Prepare to be exposed to an endless amount of new information. Your mission, should you choose to accept it, will be to remember all you've seen and heard plus a few things you haven't.

Here's how to do it.

Bring the Right Equipment

There's nothing worse than being given first-day instruction without having a pen and paper handy. Your place of employment will probably have all the necessary items, but don't take a chance. Supply closets often run low. Bring a pad of paper and several pens and pencils with you.

> "I was really thrown off by all of the TV lingo, packages, vo-sots, super times, etc. Taking notes really helped me in the beginning. I was thrown right into the mix of things and wasn't given any kind of intern orientation."
>
> —Claire Adamsick, Minneapolis news intern

During your interview, you may have noticed whether or not you would have a desk at your disposal. Definitely bring in some personal items for decoration. A picture of a cute dog or a cut-out from your favorite TV show can be an excellent conversation piece. A desk calendar can help keep you on schedule and advertise your productivity and ability to organize your time. Of course, only do this if you're sure you'll have your own desk. Walking in with your arms full of desk decorations when you're expected to share a small desk with thirteen other interns would be embarrassing.

The Staff List, Please

Hopefully you were able to obtain a staff list from the assistant before your internship started. If not, the assistant will probably have several copies of the staff list handy. This list will most likely have the names, positions, and extension numbers of everyone on staff and can be a lifejacket to get you through the first days. If any names on the list seem hard to pronounce, ask your new friend, the assistant, for help. Will a staff member fire you for butchering his or her name? No, but it can only look good if you're the first intern in six years to correctly pronounce a producer's last name.

> "Relax. Try not to become too overwhelmed by everything on the first day. Write things down so that it will help you remember later. Don't be afraid to ask questions. The stupidest question is the one not asked. Don't forget you are there to learn. The first day, you will meet everyone, and, if you're lucky, you will remember about half of their

names. A staff list can get you through those first days. Don't worry if you can't remember their names; you will get to it over time."

—Tim Mancinelli, Associate Director, *The Late Late Show with Tom Snyder*, and a former intern

Producers can be very impatient if an intern is introduced to them and the intern forgets their name by midday. This never has to happen! After you meet each staff member, inconspicuously place a small check next to his or her name and put down a few notes about the staff member's appearance. Something like "Tall, red hair, beauty mark on cheek" will do fine. If you can't remember a staffer's name, just check your list and you'll be home free. This roster will also allow you to know how many people are left for you to dazzle. Since you'll need this list for *at least* your first week, don't write notes about the producer's clothing. Even when producers pull all-nighters, they usually keep a change of clothing in their cars. Often, interns find themselves on the phone for at least a portion of their first day. Having a complete directory of names and titles will keep you from making any political blunders.

"I remember one of our top company executives calling down to talk with our talent. It was the intern's first day, and she was unaware of the power of the person on the other end of the phone. Thinking she was doing the talent a favor by screening her calls, the intern repeatedly asked the top executive who she was and what this was regarding. This intern aggravated the exec so much that she called the head producer and chewed her out for not letting people know how important she was. Needless to say, the intern was almost let go and never made it back to the head producer's good side."

—Chuck Lioi, Post Production Supervisor, *Sunset Beach*, and a former intern

Make a Map of the Office/Station

Throughout the day, you'll be taught where everything is, from the fax room to the rest room. If you don't want to accidentally walk into the executive producer's office when you're searching for the vending machine, create a simple map to guide you through your journey.

Draw a rough sketch of the office when you arrive and, as the information is made available, enter anything from room numbers to what can be found in the room. Make notes about off-limit areas and hard-to-find storage places. By the end of the first week, you will probably no longer need this map, but for the time being, it will be invaluable. Share it with your fellow interns.

Once you have your offices mapped out, take notes on the other shows and organizations inhabiting your building. Whether you're at a local station, a production company, or a network, you want to maximize your chances of meeting other ~~~~ ~~ building. Lifetime opportunities

Notes

own every word that flies out of ~~, it's impossible to know what get familiar with taking notes at out becoming a human dictation who scribbles down everything supervisors take it as a sign of t copy things down. "Does the important?"

on the first day? This happened . She was swamped and had to ~~~~~ ~~ facts thrown her way. Sherri is ~~~~ ~~~~~, but she forgot a large amount of the information and found herself at a major disadvantage the next day. A microcassette recorder, small enough to fit in your pocket, can be a lifesaver. Record as much as possible and transcribe when your day is complete. You will never remember as much as you think you will. But—*and this is a major point*—don't ever record someone without them knowing why you're doing it! Nobody likes to find out their conversation has been recorded after the fact.

Create a Journal

Supervisors have to train new interns as often as four times a year. And suffice it to say, this probably isn't the most enjoyable part of their job. Here is a way to give a helping hand while keeping your work on everybody's mind long after you are gone: Create an intern orientation guide.

You will end your first days with pages of notes on what to do, where to go, and how to do it. Throughout your term, continue to record as much information as possible. When your tenure is up, put all your maps and notes in a well-thought-out presentation packet with your name strategically placed on the cover. Semester after semester your supervisor will give this manual to the incoming interns. There's no better way to show your ability to create and organize while reminding your supervisor every new training period of your fabulous work.

LEARNING FROM MENIAL TASKS

Don't be offended by any task assigned to you unless it is unethical or immoral. Yes, years from now you may be running a network, but you need to prove you can run the coffee machine first. In Channels 5 and 6, you will learn how to do all tasks with 100 percent efficiency so you can graduate from menial to more creative work, but the less glamorous jobs can be a gold mine if you do them right.

> *"Anticipate the needs of your producer. Know if they take regular milk or nonfat milk in their coffee, and be sure that when they pour some in, it's not going to come out in chunks. Have a good carton in the fridge for Monday morning in case the boss comes in early before you go on your run to the market. If your job includes getting lunch for producers and writers, remember—lunch IS important. Try to get the order right on your end and make sure that the restaurant has it right on theirs. At the very least, make sure the EP's food is right, since they can fire you. The other people can just complain and not like you."*
>
> —Jeffrey Duteil, Executive Producer, *The Steve Harvey Show*, and Emmy-nominated writer, *The Golden Girls*

Consider the following seemingly menial tasks and how they can work to your advantage:

1. *Making photocopies.* When a photocopying assignment lands on your desk, this is an excellent opportunity to see what the staffers are doing and how well they do it. Memos, pitches, and proposals contain an unlimited wealth of information. As discreetly as possible—you are a *detective*, not a *spy*—feast your eyes on the work and absorb as much of the information as you can.

2. *Sending a fax.* Fax machines hold the same opportunities as photocopying. When asked to fax, guard the contents of the transmission, but by all means, read it. Learn what's going on, what's coming in, and who's working on what.

3. *Answering the telephone.* Never underestimate the power of the telephone. If you find yourself on phone duty, use the opportunity to study the office structure as well as to learn what the viewers think

about the program. Many producers don't have the time to hear the audience's opinions. Uncover all you can and look for the opportunity to share your knowledge with an inquisitive producer. Organizing and tabulating the call-in responses can be a great way to prove your analytical abilities. You'll get a course in good phone tactics in Channel 6.

4. *Being the messenger.* Delivering a memo could be the ideal way to meet an elusive executive. "Here's a memo from John Smith. My name is Jeremy. I started interning here today. If there's anything I can ever do to help, please just ask."

MEETING THE OTHER INTERNS

It's difficult to anticipate what your connection will be with your fellow interns. Your first day may be the start date for five other interns, or you may be the last one starting among a dozen interns in that particular cycle.

Regardless of your situation, do not see the other interns as your enemy. Most new interns quickly bond with one another, and veteran interns become great teachers of the office dos and don'ts. However, don't be shocked if an intern isn't helpful or friendly. If this occurs, just do your best to be as polite as possible. Staff members are aware of which interns are team players and which ones are looking for ways to quietly exterminate the rest.

> *"I think interns realize that they are the low rung on the ladder and seem to bond quickly. You really need to support one another because, at times, things can become overwhelming, and their support is invaluable to you. I actually created strong friendships with many of my fellow interns, some of which I still maintain today."*
> —Timothy P. Cavanaugh, LA Talent Agent and a former intern

During a production meeting, Geraldo once said, "I don't only look for what producer came up with a great show. It is more important to me what producer helped the other producer make a great show happen."

On the same note, establishing yourself as the intern leader through hard work can be extremely important. Later in the book we discuss the right and wrong ways to do this.

TIME TO MEET THE STAFF

There can be as many as 100 staffers on a show; therefore, this can be the most difficult part of the day. Try your best to meet the entire staff by the

COMMERCIAL BREAK:

"The first real day of work was on the second day of my internship. That was also the day I got a chance to sneak down to the Arsenio Hall set. It was so amazing to be there where it all happened. I remember looking at the interview chair and getting the chills right up my spine. So, I took a deep breath and sprinted toward the couch until I was close enough to take a flying swan dive onto it. I was no longer an Arsenio intern, I was Arsenio. I introduced the guests, I sang with the musical number. The crowd was barking; they loved me. No one was watching me, but in my mind, I was Arsenio. I did almost get fired when a security guard caught me, but how could I have possibly passed on the opportunity?"

—Darnell Jones, Script Coordinator, P. J.'s, former Writer's Assistant, *Hangin' with Mr. Cooper,* and a former intern

end of the first couple of days. You'll also want to ask the staffers if there's anything you can do to assist them. When a producer has no work for you, check back every couple of hours to see if anything new has come up. This will keep your face fresh in their mind without crossing the line from helpful to annoying. This fine line will be discussed in detail later on.

Timing is Everything

The first step to making a good impression is knowing the right and wrong time to introduce yourself. Sometimes it may seem obvious, but a poorly timed introduction can be deadly.

Whenever an office door is closed or partly shut, there is usually a reason. Sounds obvious, right? But you'd be surprised how many people think the only reason a door is shut is because it needs to be opened! A closed door means this is rarely the right time for an introduction. Reasons for a closed door can range from an important meeting or phone call to a less vital reason, like the producer cheating on his or her diet or just needing a few minutes of sacred quiet time. If the door is closed, respect it and go back a little later.

Should the door happen to be open but the producer is having an intense conversation or meeting, do not enter! If the discussion is coming to an end, you may subtly wait outside for the end of the conversation, but don't be noticeably hovering as they conduct business. Hovering is not good.

An open door with a producer typing away, pondering thoughts, or having a light-hearted conversation with a fellow staff member is a good sign of an opportune moment. Lightly knock on the door and wait for a response. Never enter without an invitation.

If you run into a producer in the halls or on stage, the same rules of etiquette apply. A restroom is usually not the best place to meet someone, but if it's your only shot, go for it. Just don't make it look obvious, and don't make it a habit.

To Speak or Not To Speak

It's nearly impossible to come up with a specific line that will make you a Super Intern. You want to appear motivated and inquisitive, but you may not be sure which type of introduction will work for a given person. Here are some rules that should be universally helpful:

1. *Whenever possible, do your homework.* Try to have done homework on the person you're about to meet. Ask your new friend, the assistant, for a quick background check. Was this person a former intern? Did he/she come from your hometown? What college did the producer graduate from? The assistant may even have staff resumes and bios you can borrow and copy.

   Information about the producer isn't always easy to come by, but it's extremely helpful when you find a connection. "Your assistant told me you also went to Brooklyn College." There's no better first conversation piece than having a common background.

2. *Don't be too confident or come on too strong.* Subtly mentioning your commitment to the career and the internship can be helpful. Most people can figure out you aren't interning just for the sheer thrill of it. And conversely, telling a producer you plan on running the network by the end of the year is going a bit far. (It may be just the job they are gunning for!) Is it possible that a producer will be drawn to an overconfident intern? Certainly, but the first day isn't the day to take the chance.

   > *"The worst thing you can do as an intern on your opening day is be too familiar. There's nothing worse than somebody who comes on too strong, somebody who wants to be your pal initially. I've had interns who have come into my office, plop down on my couch, and say, 'Hi, my name is Joe. I'm a new intern. How's it going?'*

You have to remember that these people are your superiors and your bosses, and they have earned a certain amount of respect."

—Diane Eaton, *Rescue 911*, *Wheel of Fortune*, and *The Pat Sajak Show*

3. *Show your desire to learn and assist.*

"The right way to introduce yourself—'Hi, I'm the new intern; my name is Joe. Pleased to meet you. If there's anything I can do to help you out, please let me know. And, if it's possible, I'd like to sit and observe you for a couple of hours. And then maybe I could ask some questions about the things that you do here.' "

—Diane Eaton, *Rescue 911*, *Wheel of Fortune*, and *The Pat Sajak Show*

4. *Ask questions that show off your knowledge, but make sure you have the facts.*

For example, you might offer this information: "I know we're catching up to our competition in the ratings. Do you think we'll capture the number one spot by the end of sweeps?"

5. *Be professional at all times.*

Even if the producer gets very casual with you, an initial conversation is not the time to test the producer's boundaries.

6. *Keep the conversation short and sweet, unless it is going extremely well.*

The producer is very busy and will expect you to respect their time constraints.

7. *Be humble but effective.*

Whenever you do a task, don't expect a round of applause just because you did it correctly. Even when you do a task correctly, still ask if there's any way you could have done the task better. All too often, interns get overconfident, just to find out they did the job wrong. Always play it safe. Your greatness will be recognized sooner without the attitude.

"Being humble is probably the most important thing. A lot of people have this expectation that a career should be handed to them. I probably sound like some old fogey, but I worked 18-hour days in the beginning just to try and get someone to notice that I really wanted this. Show me how badly you want this. The worst thing you can do, though, when you meet me is pitch a show or try to milk the 'connection value' of somebody in a place of power. Be genuine; it speaks volumes."

—Brian Graden, Executive Vice President, MTV; Developer, *South Park*; and a former intern

When we asked our Intern Hall of Famers about the key items for making a good impression, they offered the following advice:

"Don't make a bad impression. You have to remember that perception is reality. In the beginning of your internship, you want to try and talk to everyone alone. Everyone has a story to tell, and hearing about how other people made it in the industry or even how they got where they are is invaluable. In five minutes you can learn more about the producer than other staffers know after working with the producer for five months."

> —Adora English, Producer, *KTLA Morning News* in LA, and a former intern

"Don't expect to have your hands held because there is really very little time for that, unfortunately—that is why you have to be self-motivated and find out the answers yourself half the time. Think before you leap, and if you do need to ask questions, have a list of twelve questions instead of going in twelve times with one question. Expect the unexpected, role with the punches, and keep your sense of humor. I have worked with interns who are such whiners. If you're going to gripe, then why did you come for this internship in the first place? Be willing to go and get the coffee and make a copy of the script and then ask what more you can do. Ride in on your horse and help them."

> —Tisi Aylward, Director, Talent, E! Entertainment Television, and a former intern

Here's a sample conversation of what will ideally happen if you follow the above advice. Remember, no matter how well prepared and respectful you are, there might always be someone who doesn't respond kindly to your greeting. Don't take this to heart. The person could be having a bad day or bad life. Try your best to please everyone, but don't expect that it will happen all the time without fail.

```
INT. PRODUCER'S OFFICE—2 P.M.
(SCENE OPENS WITH A PRODUCER SITTING IN AN OPEN-DOOR OFFICE
TYPING AWAY. AN INTERN LIGHTLY KNOCKS ON THE DOOR AND AWAITS
AN INVITATION TO ENTER.)

                        YOU
Hello, Mr. Rizer. I'm _____, one of the new interns.

                        JOEL
Nice to meet you.
```

                              YOU
I'm really excited about being here. I've dreamed about
working in television since I was young. If there's anything
I can do to help you, please ask.

                              JOEL
Well, thank you.

                              YOU
Your assistant told me you started as an intern. I'd love a
chance to talk to you about your internship at some point.

                              JOEL
That would be great. Stop back.

                              YOU
Thank you. I know you're very busy, but would it be okay if I
checked back in a couple of hours to see if there's any work
I can help you with?

                              JOEL
Of course.

                              YOU
It was great meeting you.

                              JOEL
Same here.

(AS THE INTERN LEAVES THE OFFICE, WE PUSH IN ON
AN IMPRESSED EXECUTIVE WHO RETURNS TO WORK AS WE
FADE TO BLACK.)

C O M M E R C I A L   B R E A K :

"The first mistake I made was to buy three suits even though I knew the place
where I was going to intern wore casual attire. I wore one suit the first day
and never touched another suit again. So, if anyone out there is a size 10 . . .
I hate those suits."

—Adora English, Producer, KTLA Morning News *in LA, and a former intern*

LET THEM EAT LUNCH

Something as simple as how you handle your lunch hour can make a huge difference in your first week's success. Don't assume you'll be receiving a lunch *hour*. Producers don't often have time to consume a meal from morning to night. Around lunch time on the first day, ask your supervisor about the normal lunch routine. Maybe your office goes out, maybe they have it delivered, or maybe it's typical for the interns to go out and get food for the office. Asking your supervisor will avoid any meal time faux pas.

> *"My first day was dreadful. We weren't in production and there wasn't anything to do. I didn't know where to stand, how to look busy, who to—or not to—talk to, and, most important, where to eat lunch!"*
> —Gary Kordan, Writer, *The Joan Rivers Radio Show*, and a former *Joan Rivers* intern

Often, a new intern is taken out to lunch on the first day. This is not always the case, so don't be offended if it doesn't happen. If time is available but lunch is not on your supervisor's menu, take the role of intern leader and form a lunch party with your peers. Going out with other interns is a great way to bond and to get inner-office scoops, but you must remember your mission. Lunch is a great time to define your role as potential leader and do some extra office detective work, but not to gossip. By the end of the second day, you'll most likely have connected on a personal level with at least one staff member. Make it a goal to request a lunch meeting with this staffer for some time during the next week. This will give you an opportunity to learn more about them, get an unofficial evaluation of your performance, and learn from your potential mentor's success.

MAKE A FOUR-STAR IMPRESSION—LAST OUT

Being the first one in is the way to start the morning, and being the last one out is the way to end the evening.

> *"The first day, stay late. . . . You're going to make an impression on the janitor anyway, and that's the person who gossips."*
> —Bill Cosby, at Lafayette College in Easton, Pennsylvania

If there's someone in the building, there's always a reason not to go home. A bleary-eyed producer, striving to stay awake, will applaud the sight of an intern. The producer just found a helper to get him through the long night of work ahead, and the intern just proved his eagerness to learn at any hour. Plus, during the day, the producer will use a fellow producer to proof his work. If the intern is the only one left, he'll have a golden chance to prove his analytical skills.

> *"Anytime anyone is willing to stay and put in the extra hours after they've already been there 10 hours really impresses me. I know chances are the intern is exhausted and wants to go home, so when somebody is ready to pull an all-nighter, major points are scored."*
> —Don Wells, News Director, KGTV San Diego

There's no way to lose. The later you stay, the greater chance you have to learn and impress.

FINAL THOUGHTS

The first days are guaranteed to be eventful and exciting. Remember how crucial it is to establish yourself right out of the gate, but still try to cherish the journey. Try to get a good night's sleep; you have a career to produce.

```
. . . AND CUT!
CUE ANNOUNCER TEASE:
```

"And coming up next: Why it's always better to be careful than sorry, how to impress with a smile, and tips on becoming the organizational king of your office."

```
FADE TO BLACK
ROLL "TV INTERN HALL OF FAME" PACKAGE
```
....

THE TV INTERN HALL OF FAME SALUTES

Richard Ayoub
Executive Producer, *KABC-TV Morning News,*
and a former intern

Working in Los Angeles, the most competitive news market in the country—covering the funeral of Princess Diana in the first two months of being there—was the last thing on my mind when I was a teenager in El Paso.

I had always been intrigued by TV; I found it compelling, fascinating, and meaningful. Growing up in that West Texas town that Mary Robbins made famous, my only dream was to work for KDBC-TV, the number one station in El Paso. That was it. Nothing more, nothing less.

My idol was Bozo the Clown. Now, I know that sounds silly, but the man who played Bozo in El Paso was also an afternoon talk show host and the weatherman. He was always so happy, so cheerful. I wanted to be just like him. But I didn't have an announcer's voice. I thought I couldn't do it. So I didn't even try. Instead, I did what my mother always wanted me to do; I went to college to be a doctor.

In my case, I wanted to be an optometrist. I picked optometry because as a child I was always afraid of going to an optometrist. When I'd go, he'd say something like, "Does this look better, or this?" I'd say "the first one." And he'd say, "No, it doesn't." I felt I was being tested and I had failed. So I decided kids shouldn't have to put up with that; I was going to be an optometrist, and I would make everyone feel good about getting glasses or contact lenses.

Well, I took pre-optometry classes at the University of Texas at El Paso—classes like organic chemistry, microbiology, and calculus—and guess what, I was pretty good. At the same time, I found a little hobby. I was working as a disc jockey at KTEP-FM, the college radio station. I had this Saturday morning show called *Wake Up with Richard.* It was public radio, so we had to ask for pledges. My show raised more money than any other show. One woman even pulled off the freeway to a pay phone to call in a pledge.

So, it came time to apply to optometry school. I was a sophomore, competing against people with bachelor's degrees, even master's degrees. And you know, they all worked in optometrist's offices. I worked at a radio station. As you might imagine, I was rejected.

My counselor said, "Richard, don't worry about it, you'll get in next year, just hang in there." Then, that summer, I was in class looking through a microscope and thought to myself, "This is interesting, but this isn't what I want to do for the rest of my life." So I switched majors and went into broadcast journalism. Thus, microbiology, calculus, and organic chemistry all became electives. There was no music appreciation or basket weaving for me.

My senior year, I walked into the office of the chairwoman of the Department of Mass Communications and said, "I want an internship; I want to be in TV, and I want it to be at KDBC-TV." I couldn't believe I was so brave. Well, I got it.

By that time, Bozo (the weatherman), was gone. He had taken a job in Minneapolis. At first, I felt useless. I remember standing around the AP wire machine, ripping copy, feeling like I was in everyone's way.

Soon, I decided that I wasn't going to wait for someone to tell me what to do. I started taking on projects myself. I volunteered to go out on stories with photographers. I volunteered to write stories. I volunteered to help answer phones on the assignment desk. I volunteered to research stories. Then the news director, Bill Mitchell, told me. "You're a good writer, you have good news judgment. I'm going to groom you to be a producer." That led me in the right direction.

I soon became the protégé of the executive producer. It was sort of a one-sided relationship; I learned only because I forced myself on him, watched, and listened. I never understood why he was reluctant to be my teacher. Some say he was threatened by my eager, young talent.

Before my internship was over, I proved myself to be so valuable, I was hired as an associate producer. I remember the executive producer called me Pollyanna—saying I was always so cheerful. I had become my idol, Bozo.

The saddest story I ever had to cover while at KDBC-TV was the death of Bozo. My hero had committed suicide. It turns out his life wasn't as cheerful as he wanted us to believe.

Nearly ten years later, I walked into the newsroom at KCAL, in Los Angeles, as a producer. I was hired to help launch 3 hours of news during prime time at the TV station that was owned by Disney.

At one of the desks, behind one of the computers, was that old executive producer of mine. "Hi, Joe," I said. "Hi, Richard," he said in the familiar sarcastic but friendly tone. He had been hired as a writer. I was one of his bosses.

We caught up with each other. I said, "Joe, You're a lot nicer than you used to be." He said, "Richard, you're not as nice as you used to be, and I like you more."

channel 5

The Basic Steps to Getting Rave Reviews

If you followed the advice from the previous channel, the good word about you has probably already been broadcast. The next step is to develop some organizational skills and other tricks that will help you get beyond those first few days. Believe it or not, an organized individual is a rare find, and if you present yourself as one to your supervisor, you both will benefit.

THREE . . .

"Speaking from my own experience as an actor, film student, lighting director, director, and then producer, you must truly prepare yourself to start somewhere down the ladder and quietly work your way up to where you want to be, not by brownnosing or anything else phony or political, but by being organized and demonstrating professionalism, dedication, skill, a positive attitude, and perseverance. These are the things an employer will value above all others."

—John C. Zak, Supervising Producer, *The Bold and the Beautiful*, and a former intern

TWO . . .

"My internship was more valuable than my entire four years at school. It was total on-the-job training and the reason I am where I am today. My organizational skills and attitude were my focus. They are also what got me noticed, and they are the prerequisite courses for the fun, creative stuff."

—Joel Rizor, Executive-in-Charge of Production, Weller/Grossman Productions, and a former intern

ONE . . .

"By the end of your internship, you should be able to talk telepathically to the fax machine. You should at least be suffering from minor radiation burns, thanks to the copier. Sure, these tasks are boring, but

they are so important. Hey, someone's got to get copies of the script made and distributed. And how's the booking information going to get to celebrities unless someone faxes it to them? Keep in mind that these are major contributions that ensure the progress and success of a show. Always have a coffee pot within range. There's no better way to make an executive happy so quickly."

—Jeff Reingold, former intern, *The Rosie O'Donnell Show*

AND ACTION!

YOUR KEY TO ORGANIZATIONAL SUCCESS

Pretend that you were asked to write a made-for-TV movie about a star intern. What qualities would you give your main character? Obviously, your script will not open up by saying, "We see our star intern, who has just lost a phone message, searching under mountains of unorganized paper for the lost Post-It®."

FLASHBACK

"Many creative people take pride in being disorganized. It's almost a status symbol. 'My desk is messier than yours; I guess I'm more creative.' Thanks to this sense of 'disorganizational pride,' my organizational abilities were much appreciated. I quickly received the nickname 'the kid.' 'Hey, kid, where's that tape I was working on yesterday?' 'Hey, kid, where did I leave that number?' On my third day at the internship, I met two comedians who were producing a pilot the next morning. After a few hours, I offered to organize their notes, which were spread across the office floor. I worked with them until midnight and was their right-hand 'kid' the next day. Being organized is the greatest gift you can give to your office and your career."

—Jason

"The one thing that stood out was Jason's organization. He made me look SO good."

—Dan

Executive Producer Karen Stein once discovered a star intern at a sandwich shop. She walked in, ordered fifteen different salads and sandwiches, and was amazed at the response on the other side of the counter. The woman who took the order was organized and perceptive—so much so that she was hired on the spot.

"Everyone has a different working style. A different comfort level with how much 'stuff' should be on their desk at once or where it should be put. Pay attention to what your boss wants and how they organize their work. It's not the worst idea in the world to try and mimic their organization style. In doing that, you'll increase your boss's comfort level. You'll give them the impression that you're really smart because you organize your work the way they do. Some bosses will let you do your own thing; others will insist on conformity. No matter how you organize your work, make sure you can find what you need when you need it."

—Carol Story, Producer, *CBS This Morning*

As these illustrations indicate, never underestimate the power of organization. The behind-the-scenes world of TV is usually more dramatic than what's happening on-camera. Organized interns who can keep their cool in the heat of battle are immediately drafted.

Consider this: Let's say you were asked to fax a memo. About 90 percent of all interns are able to get the fax to the machine and to get the fax sent. (The other 10 percent are still trying to master the concept of walking and chewing gum.) Some of those 90 percent would fax the memo and then go on to another task without ever letting the boss know the mission was accomplished. Even fewer would call to check that the fax arrived safely. Instead of just reporting to the boss, "the fax was sent," it would be better to say, "I faxed out the memo and then called to be sure it arrived." If you never call to confirm, you can't be sure the fax made it. Chances are pretty sure that it did arrive, but why take the chance? Wouldn't you rather be certain than to answer to the boss as to why the fax never arrived at its destination? It's always better to be safe than sorry. When you're truly a control freak, you triple-check everything and never say that an assignment, no matter how small, is "mostly right." If there's even the slightest chance that you made a mistake, you don't try to hide your bones; you correct the mistake.

Laziness is our enemy. It's very easy to say, "That's probably right. I'll worry about it tomorrow." There are always going to be times when you're so tired that not only do you want to go to sleep until the end of the decade, but you also want to do so without flipping through tomorrow's director script to be sure that all the pages were copied. If you find you're so busy that you don't have time to triple-check, or even double-check, your work, lessen your load. It may seem like you're impressing a large number of staffers by taking twelve tasks at once, but no one will be impressed when you start to let details slip by. It's better to do less correctly than to do more incorrectly.

One time, on an expensive CBS soap remote being shot at a Beverly Hills mansion, the crew came to the last scene and discovered that one of the pages was left out of the script—a major goof. No one caught the error—not the director, not any of the producers, not the stage managers, not even the actors. The intern had specifically been asked to double-check all the script pages, so the blame fell on him. He was never able to recover after that. His internship quietly ended without any more important tasks being thrown his way. It would have taken him about 3 minutes to be positive that all the pages made a successful journey through the copy machine, but there isn't enough time in five semesters for him to regain the lost trust. The extra effort is always worth it.

"The most common organizational mistake is that interns don't act like professionals. They don't realize that if they drop the ball, they're not going to get a 'C,' they're going to get their walking papers."
—Tom Blomquist, Writer/Producer, *Walker, Texas Ranger*; *Christy*; *Dellaventura*

By now, you've been thoroughly convinced of the power of organization—and more importantly, the liability of being disorganized. But if organization does not come easily to you, how can you acquire these skills? Stay tuned for some tips.

GETTING YOUR ORGANIZATIONAL ACT TOGETHER

Although it's impossible to turn someone who is inherently frazzled into a detail-oriented person overnight, following some basic rules will head you in the right direction.

Cheat Sheets and Then Some

The first step to becoming an organizational superstar is having your own notebook. Yes, you can get a legal pad from the supply closet, but by the end of your internship, you'll have more pads than you can possibly keep track of. All too often, a producer has to quickly jot something down and grabs the first legal pad they can find; then, thrilled they finally received the needed information from their contact, they sprint down the hall to share the scoop. That legal pad is gone forever. Instead, buy a large five-subject notebook; it's less likely that the notebook that everyone sees constantly in your arms will end up being randomly grabbed from a desk.

Next, as we'll discuss shortly, you always want to keep all your information handy. You never know when you'll be asked to retrieve a phone message from two months prior.

Picture it, there you are in the middle of an office storm. Your news director is frantically searching everywhere for a contact who called three weeks ago. You wrote the message down for your boss, who copied the number onto the Post-It. That Post-It is now in the same place as socks that get lost in the laundry. The boss starts to panic, the boss starts to freak, but not you. You are Super Intern! You keep all your information in one book, which is surgically attached to you. As your boss is about to pop a vein in her forehead, you open up your book, quickly find the number, and save the day.

Once you purchase your five-subject bible, never write on a Post-It or a stray piece of paper again! Those papers get lost. Every assignment, every phone number, every message goes into this one book—no exceptions.

The "Double-Box" Method

At this point, you may be getting nervous about the amount of work you have to do. The thought, "Can I really do this?" may be racing around your mind. Don't panic; just think about how many times in your life you were scared to death and thought you couldn't get by.

> *"Trying to keep everything in one's head is both unnecessary and, well, stupid. Make a list in a notebook—each day, write down what you've been asked to do. Write down addresses, numbers, everything! But make a list!"*
> —Dane Hall, Writer/Producer, VH1

Whenever you are given a task to complete, a message to relay, or a thought to ponder, grab your book. Don't even think of trying to memorize the task.

> *"Write it down. Write it down. Write it down."*
> —Patrick Jarvis, Development Executive, Tribune Entertainment, and a former intern

As the producer begins to talk, you begin to write. Try to write down as much as possible, but be careful not to attempt to get every word. Unless you know shorthand, you'll end up missing the important information. Be sure you start each day with a new page, with the date at the top. Again, this will help when you need to backtrack your files.

Write down each task on a separate line; then, next to that line, put two small boxes in the margin:

☐ ☐   *Call travel agent (555-1234) and reserve airline tickets for guest.*

When you have started to attack the assignment (such as leaving a message for the travel agent), fill in half of the first box. This box should look similar to the notation for a spare in bowling. When you feel the assignment is about halfway completed (you spoke with the travel agent, and she is going to call you back), color in the first box completely. Make sure you write down what happened during the conversation

☑ ☐   *Call travel agent (555-1234) and reserve airline tickets for guest. (Agent was called, and she will get back to me with the information.)*

Once the agent gets back to you and you have completed the task, you should write down all the information. Then, you can fill in the first half of the second box. Why can't the box be filled in completely? Too often, interns complete a task and then never let the boss know the task was completed. By letting the boss know the task was completed, not only will you put their mind at ease, but you'll also be reminding them how dependable you are. The boss should never have to track you down to be sure everything has gone okay. You find them. Whatever happens, whether the world blows up or *Seinfeld* reruns are banned from TV, never forget to tell the boss when a task cannot be completed.

When you go to report a completed task, as just stated, use it as an opportunity to show off your hard work. For example, let's say you're asked to find Sara and get a pair of headsets. Don't just say, "Here you go," when the task is completed; rattle off a quick checklist of the steps you took to get the golden headsets. Don't brag; just relay the information. "I looked for Sara, but I couldn't find her, so I tracked down Jimmy. He knew where the headsets were. Just so you know, they are always in the desk drawer in the P.A. office."

What if you have tried every which way to complete a task and are coming up empty? This is yet another opportunity to shine. Let the producer know the steps you took and ask them what the next step is. "I looked for Sara in the office, had her paged, and then asked around the office, but no one has seen her. Is there another way to find her that I haven't thought of?" Make every experience a learning experience. It's okay to not have all the answers. While a boss loves a motivated, self-educated employee, he or she will still enjoy teaching you a few tricks, too.

Let's go back to the search for a flight. What if you couldn't take care of it? You can still show off your skills to your supervisor. Be specific. "I called the travel agent, and she said there were no flights at all. To be sure, I called my personal agent and another one for safe measure; they all said that the flights were fully booked. Can we consider the guest for tomorrow's show? I did reserve a flight, tomorrow just in case."

Every now and then use a completed task update as an opportunity to find out how you are doing. Assure the producer that you are giving it your all but are always looking for ways to improve. You'll earn big points!

Once you tell the boss that the task was completed, then you can fill in the second box.

☒ ☒ *Call travel agent (555-1234) and reserve airline tickets for guest. (Agent was called and she will get back to me with the information.) The reservation has been made for a flight leaving JFK at 10 a.m. and arriving in LAX at 1 p.m. Handed Tisi a memo with all the information at 3:15 p.m.*

Your double-box method can be the best organizational tool that you take out of your internship. Pass this along to other interns and execs; you'll have friends for life. By using the double-box method, you'll constantly know what work you've completed and what work you still have to do. At any point during the day, you can quickly glance at your list and be sure that no assignments were forgotten. Also, if you are asked about an assignment from weeks ago, you'll instantly be able to give the producer all the needed information. Nothing will fall through the cracks.

If a task won't be completed until the next day, make sure your boss knows this. As more tasks are thrown at you, you will easily forget which tasks have been completed and which haven't.

At the beginning of each new day, you should recopy any tasks from the previous day that have not been double-boxed yet. Some tasks will take a couple of days, and it's too easy for a task that is written on another page to be forgotten.

"A good list that you update constantly will always keep you in check. It's easy to take on a dozen tasks—then forget what you're working on.

Also, if you're not interning everyday, make a list of things you couldn't finish but that other interns could work on while you're gone. Give it to your supervisor. Not only will it show how responsible you are, it also guarantees that nothing falls through the cracks."

—Shannon Keenan, Producer, Live Events, E! Entertainment Television, and a former intern

Power Prioritizing

Whether you receive all your assignments from one supervisor or from the entire staff, you have to learn how to prioritize. If all of your work has been assigned by one person, prioritizing will be easier than if the entire staff is throwing work in your direction. Even if it is just one person's feeding frenzy you are in the middle of, you will need to put together a priority list. For example, a boss might say, "I need you to fax these three documents, FedEx this tape, and check with Connie about tonight's lead-in." In this situation, it is rare that the executive will tell you which task has to be done first or which is most important. It's assumed that all workers have the ability to read minds. If you don't have telepathic powers, you better ask.

"In being extremely anxious to help, interns often take on too many assignments, thereby spreading themselves too thin. Don't be afraid to tell a producer that you have a lot on your plate, and to do a good job, you need to finish other jobs that you have been given."

—Jason Gurskis, Producer, Discovery Channel, and a former intern

"Your boss will probably give you an idea of what needs to be done first and how long it takes to accomplish each task. If this information isn't given to you, it's your responsibility to ask for it."

—Carol Story, Producer, *CBS This Morning*

There will be times when you may not think it matters which task is attacked first, but what if the boss is assuming that you know that Connie will only be in the office for 3 more minutes? If you start with the faxing, then you'll never be able to speak with Connie. Sure, the boss should have told you that Connie was on her way out, but to be truly dependable, you must take matters into your own hands. Therefore, it's critical to ask, "Should I start with the faxing or should I immediately track down Connie?" When your boss tells you which should come first, be sure to write it down. Take the lead in the organization ring; your boss will feel more confident.

Interns who are given assignments from an array of staff members have a tougher job on their hands.

"The biggest blunder I made was taking on a task from my boss's boss without informing my superior. I just assumed that the task was more important because of the superior's position, when, in fact, the job was less urgent, causing my boss to wonder why I was wasting my time!"
— Edward Boyd, Producer/Writer, E! Entertainment Television, and a former intern

If you have ten producers heaving heavy assignments at you nonstop, it can get a bit sticky. Everyone feels his work is most important, and you can easily make enemies by playing favorites. Remember this is TV, home of the superego.

Rehearsal #1:
You're working on one producer's project, which has a deadline, when a different producer asks you to complete another rush job. What if there is no way to complete both assignments by the times requested? What should you tell the second producer?
Of course, the response, "No, I have no time to do that now," will definitely not impress the producer. An answer of, "Yes, I can definitely do that," may cause you to miss both deadlines, putting you in a very unhappy place. Here's what you can do:

```
INT. OFFICE—1 P.M.
(OPEN ON AN INTERN FIERCELY ORGANIZING SEVERAL FILES. A STACK
OF PAPERS TOPPED WITH A POST-IT READING "XEROX AND FILE"
TOWERS OVER THE DESK. A FRANTIC PRODUCER ARRIVES.)

                      FRANTIC EXEC
I need this researched and faxed by 2. Can you do it?

                          YOU
I would love to, but John has asked me to file all these charts
by 2:30, and it will take until then to finish them. Would you
like me to ask John if he can possibly extend his deadline so
I can take care of your research?

                      FRANTIC EXEC
Yes. Please do.


(WE FOLLOW THE INTERN AS HE QUICKLY RACES OUT OF
HIS CUBICLE IN SEARCH OF JOHN.)
```

You have just turned this potentially volatile situation into an opportunity to show the producer that you're willing to do as much work as possible and that you're responsible in terms of deadlines. You've just passed Juggling 101.

If John says his deadline can't be extended, you must find that frantic exec and let him or her know. If possible, find another intern who can take care of the frantic exec's assignment. "I'm sorry, but John insists that I get his work done by the given deadline; I asked the other intern, and they said they can take care of it. They'll be right up to see you." Whenever possible, don't just say "yes" or "no"; explain your situation and let the producer decide the best way to handle it. Show your drive and team spirit. Take a request to the next level. More on this approach in the following channel.

It's possible that one producer will tell you to drop everything and take care of her assignment, while another producer tells you that you better finish his assignment first. Don't try to figure out this situation on your own. First, see if the producers can settle the problem on their own: "I'm sorry, Jimmy, but Tara told me to do her assignment first, and you told me to do your assignment first. Could you please give Tara a call so I know which task should be immediately attacked?" If that doesn't help you out, tell your supervisor the situation and let her decide. This is not your battle to fight; these two producers may have a bitter history together, and you don't want to get yourself in the middle. Save your stomach for other ulcers!

"Always be realistic with projects, and if you absolutely cannot do something before a given deadline, be honest and ask for help. I would admire that more than if someone made me miss a deadline."

—Michael Seligman, Associate Producer, E! Entertainment Television, and a former intern

ALWAYS ASK QUESTIONS

Throughout this channel, we've mentioned the importance of asking questions; this point can never be made too strongly.

"Just ask."

—Charlie Cook, Supervising Producer, *Donnie and Marie*, and a former Capitol Hill intern

"Interns should listen ALL the time and ask LOTS of questions. When you're stuck photocopying something, read it. When you're stuffing

envelopes for a mailing, read the letter, and if you don't understand the purpose of what you're doing, ask. If you're lucky enough to sit in on a meeting, pay close attention, take notes, and ask your supervisor questions about those notes when the opportunity presents itself after the meeting is over."

—Craig Martinelli, Executive Director, Advertising, Publicity and Promotion, Walt Disney Television

What if you don't understand the assigned task? Ask immediately. Too many interns don't want to look stupid, so they pretend to get it. The result is major egg on their face later. The producer will be more than happy to answer questions if it will increase the chances that the task will be correctly completed. The key to success in this area can be stated in one word: anticipation! Think ahead a few steps. What problems could you possibly run into? Think about what could go wrong. Ask about potential obstacles, without questions that are obvious.

For example, you may want to ask if there's a dollar limit on the flight you may be researching. If you get a great price, should you go ahead and book it? Does the station have an account? What if you can't get the guest in for the 9 p.m. newscast; should you still try for the 10? The producer may be overwhelmed, so he'll appreciate your anticipation. Also, ask what to do if you run into trouble. "What if there's a problem? Should I find you, or is there someone else I should talk to?" You have the producer's attention, take advantage. All of these answers should be written in your book.

Remember that after a few working days, if you are still having trouble taking dictation, go and get that mini tape recorder. There is no worse feeling than having an executive entrust you with a major project and blowing it because of a missed detail.

On the same note, don't run over to the executive every time an unanticipated problem arises. Too often, interns will get a task and then go running back to the assigner the second an obstacle pops up. These interns get fewer and fewer tasks as the days go on. When possible, take each job as far as you can before you ask for help. However, if an assignment needs to be done immediately, don't spend hours trying to figure it out on your own.

Let's go back to the example of finding the headset that was mentioned earlier. Pretend that you were asked to find a production assistant and track down a pair of headsets. The attentive intern would have asked at the onset what to do if the P.A. couldn't be found. Let's suppose you didn't. What should you do?

Don't go back to the producer and say, "I can't find Sara." Put yourself in the producer's shoes; what are the possible options?

1. Ask around and see if anyone knows where the P.A. is.
2. If you still can't find the P.A., spend a few minutes looking for those headsets yourself.
3. If you don't track them down, who else might know where they are? Let your common sense kick in.

If you are still headsetless, enlist a nearby producer. They'll most likely help you out while noticing how reliable you are. You really want the producers to feel that when they give you a task, it's as good as done. This may seem like a very elementary example, but these types of activities need to be taken care of with ease. Let common sense be your guide.

HONESTY IS STILL THE BEST POLICY

You're human. Yes, you are the world's greatest intern ever, but you are still human. You are going to make mistakes.

> *"The biggest mistake . . . never lose a shot tape. A tape is like a bar of gold once it has been shot. It is the representation of all the time, money, and work that has gone into the shoot up until that moment. On our show, we value a shot tape at somewhere around $10,000. One time, we did a shoot on how the ER works. To set up the premise, we had the fire department take an old car and wrap it sideways around a tree to make it look like there had been a huge accident. Then we shot a sequence with an ambulance pulling a victim from the car crash and rushing them away. This is a pretty big setup, coordinating the fire department, location, ambulance, and the victim. So losing this tape would be a bad thing . . . and it was! I put all the tapes on my desk when I got back from the shoot. Grabbed a soda, told old war stories from the shoot, then headed back to my desk to safely stow the shot tapes. Except one was missing! I spent the next 8 hours searching everywhere twice! I 'fessed up to the missing tape. Trust me . . . it's the worst feeling ever. One good thing, it taught me the value of the shot tape, and when you mess up, 'fess up!"*
>
> —Kevin Williams, Producer, PBS's *Newton's Apple*, and a former intern

If you do make an organizational error, or any mistake for that matter, don't cover it up and don't blame it on another intern. Just let your producer know right away and then try to rectify the situation if possible. You'll probably be very nervous if you have to admit to a mistake, but the producer will understand. Everyone makes mistakes:

> *"When I was interning at KARE in Minneapolis, a photographer gave me his new light kit to carry. Well . . . it got a little heavy, and I decided to set it down on the ground. Little did I know, I had laid it down behind the wheel of someone's car. A few moments later, the driver backed up and crushed the $6,000 piece of equipment. The photographer was panic stricken for a few moments. I told him I'd take full responsibility, but he said, 'What are they going to do to you? Fire you? Take it out of your paycheck?' I guess he had a good point, but I still thought for sure I had ended my career in TV news. When we got back, we told the station the whole truth, and we all figured out a way to work out the insurance and details. I did all I could to help contact the insurance agency and fill out the paperwork. I stayed on as an intern, he kept his job, and we've been friends ever since."*
>
> —Lori Ryan, News Producer, Minneapolis and Jacksonville, and a former intern

Keep in mind that you'll get in less trouble if you make an error and let the producer know than if you are caught covering up the mistake. Sure, the mistake may not be noticed, but if it is, and you didn't let the producer know about it, you won't be trusted again. It's just not worth the risk. If you lie and you're caught, it's death to your career.

> *"Once, we had an intern forget to have a band sign release forms, a standard intern responsibility. Since the intern never admitted his error and his internship ended a few days later, it took weeks before someone else realized the mess-up. Three months later, I was still hounding these musicians to get their release forms back to me. The intern did make it through his internship without getting caught, but there's one intern who will never be offered a job."*
>
> —Jimmy Rhoades, Producer, PBS Detroit

If possible, like in Lori's situation just mentioned, do all you can to be part of the solution. Volunteer to stay as late as possible to correct the error; you may even want to ask the producer how the mistake could have been avoided. Try to turn every predicament into an opportunity.

FLASHBACK

"I walked into my office just as my boss, Carol, pushed everything from the top of my desk onto the floor. I was shocked. Papers, books, and all of my notes were falling everywhere. She said, 'Dan, you're a really great intern, but your desk is a mess. Being organized is really important, and until this desk is kept clean, I will dump your stuff on the floor once a week.' I got the message. She only had to do it twice!"

—Dan

APPEARANCE IS EVERYTHING

In the world of the small screen, perception is BIG. Getting people to notice your great attitude is key, and you can help guide people's perceptions. You may not be extraordinarily organized, but you must be perceived as organized and eager. Don't even think of saying, "I'm creative; it's in my nature to be unorganized." When you are the boss, your mess may be due to your creativity, but when you are the intern, it's due to disorganization.

What is the first step to being perceived as organized? Your desk. Keep your "home" as organized as you are. If workers pass your desk and see a pile of paper, they will be hesitant to place their assignment in your hands. What if you don't have a desk? Your large notebook will speak volumes about your organizational prowess. Don't have papers hanging out of every corner of your notebook.

DO IT ALL WITH A SMILE

Being organized and dependable is just half the battle. Picture yourself as an executive giving an urgent assignment to an intern. The intern, dressed in ripped jeans, sits slouched in the chair, scribbles down a few notes, mumbles "okay" without making eye contact with you, and then slowly walks out of the office. How much faith are you going to have that this intern will give the task the full attention it deserves? Now, let's pretend you're the same executive assigning an intern another duty. This one's sporting a shirt and a tie, sitting on the edge of the chair, leaning forward looking right at you. The intern is writing as you speak and asking questions as you go. The intern then reviews your request, asks if there is anything else he can do, and then bolts out of the office, a man on a mission. Even if both interns complete the assigned task, which one will you go to the next time you have work to assign?

"Someone I once worked with had three letters over her desk—AIE. ATTITUDE IS EVERYTHING. This is my definition of a great intern—a great attitude. That includes a positive attitude. TV is teamwork, and the interns are a major part of the team. The interns that know that will get a permanent place on that team."

—Glenn Meehan, Managing Editor, *Entertainment Tonight,* and a former intern

"A great intern is someone who is willing to learn and pitch in, no matter what the task. A great intern doesn't have an entitlement chip on her shoulder."

—Paige Wheeler, President, Creative Media Agency, Inc., and a former intern

The attitude you have while doing a task is equally as important as how well the task is completed. The last thing a TV executive with eight deadlines on her hands wants is to deal with is an intern with a negative attitude. Of course, there will be some tasks that an intern should never have to do and are probably worthy of attitude. Your legal rights will be covered in a later channel, but for now, we're going to assume that the work you are given is morally and legally acceptable.

"Too many interns don't leave their laid-back college styles home. They need to work on their people skills, the ability to write and talk clearly. Also, to know their place in the universe and seek ways to grow as individuals."

—Tom Blomquist, Writer/Producer, *Walker, Texas Ranger; Christy; Dellaventura*

If you look at each assignment as an opportunity, you have a solid chance of winning the battle of perception. When you have the right mindset, the rest comes pretty easily. It's much easier to make people think you love your job when it truly is a labor of love.

NEVER GRUNT AT GRUNT WORK

The assignment editor just asked you to pick up bagels for tomorrow morning's meeting. Were you asked to complete a task that a trained monkey could take care of? Probably. Were you also just given an opportunity to shine? Unquestionably.

COMMERCIAL BREAK:

"One day I needed to bring important videotapes down to the main studio, about 15 miles from our studio. I was driving somewhat quickly down a bumpy street in Albany. While I was in the left lane of a four-lane road, my hood flew open and crashed into my window and folded over the roof of my car. I somehow moved over to the shoulder without seeing and called back to the studio very upset. I told my boss I was sorry, but I couldn't deliver the tapes. He was shocked at my concern for the tapes. 'Forget them, are you all right?' I was so upset about not doing my job, I forgot to check. I was fine, but my car was totaled!"

—Dan Zweifler, Technical Recruiter and former news intern

"The only one who is not a gofer is the Executive Producer, so be prepared for it. Do as much gofer work as you see others do."
—Sy Tomashoff, Emmy award–winning Production Designer, *The Bold and the Beautiful*

One former intern remembers how a trip to the library was a turning point for him. The producers had asked him to gather some research on the legendary Pearl Bailey for an upcoming interview. He befriended a librarian who had a strong musical knowledge. She turned him onto some rare photos and recordings of the singer. The producers were ecstatic when he told them about the treasure he'd tracked down. After getting special permission from the library, the pictures and music were made into a wonderful opening montage. Even Pearl Bailey was impressed. But not as much as this intern's boss. The intern soon began helping producers take it to the next level. More on taking it to that next step in the following channel.

"Gofer work has always been, for me, almost an initiation and almost a test—how dedicated they are, how willing they are to give of themselves, what their attitude is, what their relationships with co-workers will be. I think gofer work is probably 90 percent of the beginning of the internship, and the more people feel comfortable around you, the more you'll get the chance to do advanced things.
—Adora English, Producer, *KTLA Morning News* in LA, and former intern

Many interns get angry when they are assigned menial tasks and think, "I'm a college student. I could do more than just get bagels! Is that all they think I'm good for?" This thought process will hurt you. Don't think of anything as a pointless task, think of everything as a test.

> *"My philosophy in dealing with interns is that I usually pick one, give him a fairly simple assignment, and, if he completes it with little thought or commitment, I simply move on to the next intern until I find one who I feel is truly going to be of some help to me. Once I find a competent intern, I go out of my way to teach him everything I can, from taking him out on shootings to bringing him into the edit room."*
>
> —Jason Raff, Producer, *Today*, and a former intern

Believe it or not, many interns never make it beyond getting the bagels. What can go wrong getting bagels? An intern could forget to pick up the bagels, may lose the directions to the bagel shop, or may not know what time the bagels are needed. The intern may not know the golden rule of always getting the managing editor a toasted egg bagel, may lose the receipt, or may have discovered a closed sign on the store door. The simple task of getting bagels is really not so simple.

Now that you see what can go wrong, let's look at what can go right. Pretend you're asked to get coffee. The first time you are given a coffee order, write down each staff member's preference. Who likes milk and sugar? Who takes it black? This way, the next time they ask you for coffee, you can say, "You like it with cream and sugar, right?" Do you want to take it to the next level? Find their favorite flavored coffees. Who loves hazelnut? Who would give their left arm for a cappuccino? Someone in the office is sure to know these answers. You're not just showing them you're a great coffee gofer, but also that you're organized and hospitable, qualities needed to be a good producer.

If you're asked to get bagels, come back and set up the most creative bagel arrangement the station has ever seen. You're not showing them that you want a career in catering; you're showing them the importance you place on detail, follow-through, and good taste.

> *"What is gofer work? I still do it. If the coffee pot is empty, I make it. I don't believe that there is such a thing as gofer work in this business—it's teamwork."*
>
> —Glenn Meehan, Managing Editor, *Entertainment Tonight*, and a former intern

Should you do cartwheels when asked to go pick up some props? Yes. Props are a range of items needed for a TV shoot and can be anything from a thumbtack to a giant plastic tree. Your shopping skills are a great way to show your reliability, judgment, and money skills. The intern with the right attitude will also go around to others in the office before the run and see if anyone needs anything picked up. Once you're on your shopping spree, compare the prices and quality of the items. Can you get a better deal for your boss? Do you see something not on your list that might be a good idea to pick up? Are there a couple of different colors you can bring back? Now, take the shopping trip to the next level. Call the office and see if they need anything else.

> *"As an intern at Good Company, a talk show in Minneapolis, it was my responsibility to fill the lunch order everyday at 11 a.m. I would go around to each of the producers' desks to get his or her order. Could they all have chosen something from the same restaurant? Of course not. I would literally run from McDonald's to Burger King to Wendy's. The things I learned most from my internship: schmoozing . . . and all the fast food locations."*

—Julie Johnson, Associate Producer, *Oprah*, and a former intern

Every time you're given a task, you must look at is as a chance to show everyone how reliable you are. Whenever you get a task, any task, you're given an opportunity to learn about the other employees, to learn about the station or show, to meet new people, and, most importantly, to prove yourself. It makes logical sense that you'll have to prove that you can effectively get bagels before you can prove you can effectively edit together a videotape package.

Try to remember that everyone has been where you are. They've all done the coffee runs and cleaned up when everyone else went out to celebrate.

IS THERE ANYTHING ELSE I CAN DO?

After you set up the bagels in the world's most breathtaking fashion, ask the most valuable phrase an intern can learn in the beginning; "Is there anything else I can do?"

This question gives the automatic impression that not only did you enjoy what you just did, but also that you want to do more of it. You're giving the boss an opportunity to think up additional assignments that you can do in an amazing fashion. You're also giving them an opportunity to think about keeping you on their staff.

AND CUT!
CUE ANNOUNCER TEASE:

"Coming up next: We'll teach you how to work the phone, and you'll be introduced to the next top-secret slogan that will lead you to TV stardom. Stay with us!"

FADE TO BLACK
ROLL "TV INTERN HALL OF FAME" PACKAGE

••

THE TV INTERN HALL OF FAME SALUTES

Shannon Keenan
Producer, Live Events, E! Entertainment Television,
and a former intern

So there I was. About to make the phone call that could change the course of my entire life . . . and I had one of those moments. You know, the kind you read about, where your whole life flashes before your eyes. I could see it all fly past in just an instant—growing up watching television with my family every Sunday night, wanting to grow up to become a meteorologist and not a ballerina or a fairy princess like the rest of my friends, rushing home to watch the news, even in high school. And of course, the day my high school drama teacher said to me, "Have you ever thought about going into television?"

And there . . . there I was. About to call a television station for the first time in my life, to ask about internships. I mean, who did I think I was, anyway? Sure, I was from Minneapolis, the home of the world's most famous (fictional) TV producer, Mary Tyler Moore. I'd seen every show so many times, I could probably draw a map of the WJM newsroom.

I was a former theater major who decided midway through to become "an anchor in a large market." (A favorite goal among college students.) So, I enrolled in the Speech Communications Department at my college. (That's right, you can succeed without a degree in journalism.) I didn't have one single contact . . . not one! I'd never set foot in a television station and had never taken a writing class, but I knew I was good at it. But could that land me a job in a real station?

I thought for sure I was kidding myself, but I wanted it so desperately. So, I put aside my fears and made the big call to the number-one station in the city. Much to my surprise, they actually wanted to speak with me. "Just bring in your resume," said the woman on the other end of the line, "and I'll see you at the station tomorrow." Tomorrow? Yikes! I didn't think it would happen that fast, on my first call. I was elated! That night, my boyfriend and I drove to the station about ten times, ten different ways . . . just to make sure I didn't get lost going to the big interview. I pressed my suit, read my resume (which had little more than a few waitressing jobs to my credit), and got ready to face the music.

Three days later, the phone rang, and I got the job. I'll never forget the fear of that first day . . . it's like the first day in a new school. Everyone else already knows each other. They know the rules. Would I fit in? I had no idea what to expect. I was the only intern working that day, which meant I didn't even have anyone on my level to show me the ropes. I was so lucky to have such a great adviser. She was so patient, even though she was really busy herself. After my initial tour, I decided to just leap in. I took a million notes, walked all around the station, introduced myself to as many people as I could find. It was a little strange, walking past people I'd grown up watching on television, trying so hard to be as professional as they were, even though I felt like the new kid on the block. I hung out with the reporters, got to watch a newscast from the control room, even answered a few phones on the assignment desk. I put in the first of many very long days . . . not calling it quits until someone finally asked if I had moved in or if I was going to go home. So, I scooped up my brand new (and virtually empty) faux-leather briefcase, all my notes, and ran home to tell my entire family about the amazing day that I had. I wonder if I will ever again feel the same pride I felt on that day. I had made it, all by myself. I walked into that intimidating environment, alone, and started making a name for myself in television.

The next day was equally as exciting. The next, even more. I put in long, hard days and went out with reporters whenever I could, but I never neglected all the busywork that is so important when you're interning. It's easy to get frustrated when you're working for free, and answering phones certainly isn't glamorous, but it didn't take long for me to figure out what separated the future TV broadcasters from the rest of the intern pack. I made a vow to learn everything about the place. I taught myself how to use computers by coming in on the overnight shift and taught myself how to edit when no one was around. I learned how to fix every printer and copier in the place. (Believe me, that's a valuable skill.) I bought every broadcasting book I could get my hands on so that I could save myself from asking too many stupid questions. I went to as many meetings as I could get myself into. I jumped at the chance to open the mail so that I could learn how to write a good press release. All the while, I was having a blast!

Toward the end of my internship, they asked me to stay another quarter. I gladly accepted, taking on even more responsibility and training the new interns. I was in my senior year of college, so I also decided to tie my thesis project into the television station somehow. I took a controversial story that had been in the news recently and asked every heavy hitter in the station if they'd do a quick on-camera interview with me. Much to my surprise, they all agreed. Not only did I get a killer 30-minute documentary on news ethics out of the deal, but I also got one-on-one time with the station manager, news director, anchors, and assistant news director and showed them that I could handle both sides of the camera. I knew there could be a job for me somewhere in that building, so before I graduated, I took yet another internship at the same station.

This time it was as a promotions intern. Granted, it took me away from news, but it kept me in the building and showed me an entirely different aspect of television. Then, about four weeks before graduation, the offer finally came. It wasn't dazzling, mind you, but in television, you can't expect your first job to be reporting for *Dateline*. So there I was, working in the dispatch shack. If you've never been in the shack, check it out sometime. If you want to start in a larger market, believe me, you'll get to know it well. I worked the weekend overnight shift for a few months, moved up to days (here's when it really starts to fly!), was promoted to production assistant, and a year later, was given a shot at assisting the executive producer on a new political show. That producer believed in me . . . so much so that she was willing to train me as a producer. So train me she did, and the rest is history. I stayed there as a producer for a few years, then decided to move on. I became the senior producer of the national magazine show *Everyday Living*. But I will never forget all of my friends at my first station . . . how their support and encouragement took me from intern to producer in only a few short years. One of my last days at the station, one of the photojournalists came up to me and told me that he remembered how green I was in my intern days. How I walked in everyday, high heels and all, ready to take on the world. He said they all thought it was kind of funny, how serious I was . . . but that they respected my determination.

And there I was, four years after that frightening first day, leaving the place that had become my home away from home. All thanks to that one phone call . . . I went from intern to producer, and I'm still going strong!

channel 6

Taking Your Internship to the Next Level

In this channel we'll show how to continue to be an effective intern while focusing your efforts on the future. This channel is the ultimate primer for the practicalities of your internship, from answering the phone to pitching your first idea. The idea is to master the basics so that you can move beyond this level—to offer some substantive input to those around you—in order to turn your internship into a job offer down the line.

• THREE . . .

"We had an intern who edited high school football highlights from a rainy, muddy night to the song 'Splish Splash.' It was so good, we aired it on our Sunday night sports show. We had another intern who couldn't understand why a video tape wouldn't fit into the machine. I then explained to him that you have to take it out of the box! Make sure you stand out in your internship in the right way."

—Matt Underwood, Sports Director, WEWS-TV, Cleveland, and a former intern

TWO . . .

"Be careful what you say, and look like you have your act together. Don't say over the phone, 'Uh, I dunno; I'm just an intern here.' This is as bad as saying that you were really hoping to intern with the news division but this was all that was available. Those kinds of comments raise big flags."

—Leeza Gibbons, Talk Show Host and a former intern

ONE . . .

"I asked for opportunities that other interns didn't even know existed."

—Lesly Goldman, News Producer and a former intern

AND ACTION!

TAKING IT TO THE NEXT LEVEL

What does it mean to take it to the next level? Let's say you're interning for a development executive who is about to go to a large conference. At this conference, your boss is going to be meeting lots of radio talent who are looking for a chance to break into television. Your boss has spoken with several of the radio personalities, but there is no way he is going to remember all the names and faces that he needs to. Your boss asks you to make up a list of all the people he is supposed to meet. Then, he wants you to contact the stations where these talents work and get some basic information on them (i.e., the format of their programs). Remember, you always want to take it to the next level. Begin by asking yourself, "What would the average intern do?" The average intern would probably make the calls, get the information, and then maybe put all the information together in a folder for the boss. However, you are the super intern, so you take a different approach.

Instead of just getting some basic information on each radio program, you hop on the Internet and see what additional information you can find. Has the show had any recent controversies? Has the show won any awards? How is the show doing in its market? Then, you'd give the station a call and see if they can send you a press packet. Your boss will love you if he has not only basic information about the radio personality, but also a picture and a bio as well. You then would put all the information in a binder for your boss. In addition to the basic information that the average intern would give, you give your boss all the information you have found. You also write down some potential topics of conversation: "I heard you guys had some show last week. What was it like having a fight break out in the studio?" The next time your boss has a task, which intern do you think he'll go to? Count on him wanting to go to your level.

Keep in mind that this is just one example of how to take it to the next level. The important thing to remember is the theory behind the steps—to consider ways to go beyond what is asked of you, to think creatively about each assignment at hand. Of course, you shouldn't try to take *every* task to the next level. Some assignments won't lend themselves to the challenge; some deadlines will be too tight for you to add your special touch, so you must use your judgement here.

Here are some specific examples of how you can take it to the next level.

Can Anyone Work This *#!!* Machine?

It's an unwritten law that when you have scripts to print at midnight, the copy machine will unquestionably break. In Channel 3, it was recommended that you master the workings of the copy machine. If you failed to do this, you are not prepared for the crisis at hand. If you were wise enough to take preventative measures and learn the mechanics of this temperamental beast of a machine, the next time you're working late with a bunch of producers and the machine breaks, guess who will be there to save the day? You'll fly in, fix the copier, save the show, and impress everyone around you. Guess which intern the producers will want with them the next time they have to stay late? In any event, prepare yourself for this situation, since it will inevitably arise on more than one occasion.

Computing Success

Normally, there's one person in the office who can fix any computer and, therefore, is constantly bothered. Hopefully, as suggested in Channel 4, you learned some basic computer programs prior to your internship run. You don't want to hound the computer genius for advice on Microsoft Word, but you do want to offer to make her life easier. "I see everyone is constantly coming to you for help. I already know many of the programs; if you could just take a few minutes to teach me how the system works and what usually has to be fixed when it doesn't, I can probably save you hours of time."

> *"I knew how to operate DOS, Windows, and Mac machines; standard word processors; and Web navigators. I also knew how to operate office machinery, write memos, answer phones, and wear nice pants. These skills were helpful."*
>
> —Dan Gepner, former Minneapolis news intern

Once you've learned the system, track down the office researcher. This person will have knowledge of Newsstar and LEXIS-NEXIS, two research programs used in many production offices to gather information on news items, and program topics or general background information. You will have struck the lottery if you learn how to master these information sources. Tell this person you'd be more than happy to take over some of his duties if he'll give you a few lessons.

It's possible you'll have to stay late or get in early to get your skills really up to par, but it will be well worth it. A few extra hours at night, for a lifetime in the industry, is a pretty cheap price to pay.

Working the Phone

In order to make it in any industry, you must have strong phone skills. The average intern is able to talk on the phone, be understood by the person on the other end, and take a semi-accurate message. You are not the average intern.

"Most college students, believe it or not, do not know how to take a decent phone message and do not know proper phone etiquette. I teach them that on day one."

—Debbi Casini, Pittsburgh TV Producer and a former intern

Hopefully, your phone anxiety was conquered when you hunted down your ideal internship; if not, there's no time like the present to conquer it. The first thing you should keep in mind is that you are not the first intern to get anxious on the telephone.

"Part of my job as a publicity intern was to answer the phones and address viewer comments regarding programming. To see how I handled such a test and to test my phone manner, my supervisor told me briefly that it was opera time at PBS and prepared me with a programming log. She then had me answer the phones cold turkey to see how I'd do. I started out fine . . . 'Good Morning, KQED,' but I lost it when the viewer asked me about programming in a language so foreign to me ('Pavara-Who?'). I had no idea who the tenors were. All I could do was panic and, speechless, pass the phone off to my boss. I literally choked. I wish I had said, 'Could you please hold while I check for you.' But I didn't. I was so green and so nervous. I got better soon enough . . . and I never was made to feel like an idiot by my supervisors. Very classy on their part."

—Jill Mullikin-Bates, Supervising Producer, *Leeza*, and a former intern

You also need to accept that it's possible you'll make a critical mistake on the phone. Most interns who are nervous around the phone are afraid that terrible things will happen if they make a mistake. This fear makes it more difficult to concentrate and, therefore, they end up making the very mistakes they were hoping to avoid. Accept that you're not perfect, and just do your best.

FLASHBACK

"Many interns literally have hang-ups when it comes to phones. Truth is, they are the nerve center to a good operation. I will never forget the day Tim saved me on *Geraldo*. It was Friday, I just had my Monday show fall through, and I had no clue what I was going to do. Tim, on a break from the switchboard, had heard about my terror in tracking down a topic. He came in and actually handed me an entire show on one scratch of paper. He had a phone message from a woman who just found out she had five siblings she

never knew existed. In 72 hours, she would be meeting them for the first time on national TV. Thanks to Tim, it was 'Shelly's Miracle Reunion' . . . on the next *Geraldo!*"
—Dan

If you have trouble talking on the phone, ask your family for help. Chances are, you're not nervous when you talk to your mom on the phone; rehearse a couple of calls with your mom first and then practice by calling some businesses to get information on products or services. Phone anxiety will not go away by itself; you must fight it by practicing and utilizing rational thought processes.

Could you possibly make it through the semester without ever answering the phone? Sure. Could you make it through your whole life without ever getting a job in the industry? Yes. Taking your phone assignments to the next level is a great opportunity you don't want to miss due to fear.

> *"As an intern, I was aggressive, really spoke up, and took advantage of the phone to set myself apart. I would volunteer to call publicists back to turn down pitches and got to know their names. I was doing real stuff, not just clerical tasks. Phone work is GREAT to do. People on the other end don't know you are an intern. You learn a lot, and you leave your internship with a solid base of professional contacts and phone manner."*
> —Marla Kell Brown, Producer, *The Arsenio Hall Show*, and a former intern

The phone is a pipeline to many people. Average interns do their phone duty and continue on with their day. As discussed earlier, the assistant could be a real asset to your career. It may be time to offer this person some assistance. Ask the assistant to train you on the phone systems. Don't just learn the basics, learn everything. Not only will you learn the system, but the assistant will also love knowing they have you as a back up.

> *"Believe it or not, phone manners are one of the most important jobs and qualities of an intern. The intern should sound interested and helpful, taking careful messages. The intern should not sound like she hates her job or can't remember to take a message."*
> —Paige Wheeler, President, Creative Media Agency, Inc., and a former intern

So, what exactly are the secrets to working the phone?

1. *Learn how the phone system works first.* Learn all there is to know about the phones. You'll be anxious enough without worrying about how to transfer a call to another extension.

2. *Gather important phone numbers and lists before manning the phones.* Viewers will often inquire about everything from hotline numbers to Bart Simpson's address. Find the staff list and any other important numbers you'll need to know. If a sheet isn't at your fingertips, make one up and pass it around.

3. *Learn the proper phone language.* Some stations are extremely particular about what to say when the phone is answered. If there is no set greeting, make up a professional one and always use it (i.e., "Good afternoon, you're talking to the *Today Show*. How can I help you?").

4. *Always be extremely friendly to every caller.* You are an ambassador for the show. If a caller gets a bad feeling from you, they may stop watching the show or even call your boss. Be polite to everyone; you never know who is on the other end.

5. *Know phone procedures ahead of time.* What should you do if a producer gets a call? Page them? Track them down? Does a GM's call to the program director automatically get put through? Do you know the name of the staff members' significant others? Who is expecting an important call, and how should it be handled? Who do you tell when someone calls in sick? What should you do with the habitual caller who seems to be badgering one of the staff members? Find out before you take the helm.

> *"Don't contact key people without consent of your producer! There's nothing worse than, as a producer, having an intern contact someone important and having no idea how to treat that person. Sometimes, an intern can be going after a prop or some small things and not understand that they are talking to someone very important to the rest of the production. Something goes wrong on the phone, the contact gets annoyed, and BOOM, the producer is in a jam."*
>
> —Kevin Williams, Producer, PBS's *Newton's Apple*, and a former intern

6. *Never give any more information than you are told to.* If a reporter calls for some gossip, be polite, be firm, and give out nothing. Never give any kind of quote to a newspaper. Never reveal personal information about the office members.

7. *Be polite, positive, clear, and concise on the phone.* Speak slowly and make sure you are understood. Here are some simple golden rules:

   —Never say, "Who is this?" Try, "May I please say who is calling?"

   —Never respond to a caller by saying, "I don't know." "I don't have that information in front of me, but I'd be more than happy to get it for you," is much better.

   —Never just put someone on hold. Ask, "Would it be okay if I put you on hold?"

   —If someone isn't in, don't just say, "He/She is not here; I'll give you his/her voice mail." Ask, "Would it be okay if I transferred you to his/her voice mail?"

   —Creative Services Director of the UPN affiliate in Minneapolis, John Dunn, warns interns to never answer the phone and only take a partial message. "Don't assume your supervisor will know who Tom is." "Tom called." "Tom who?"

   —If you normally talk at a fast pace, be very aware of your speech rate. Usually, when people get nervous, they talk faster. If you are, by nature, a fast talker, you will not be understood. Listen to yourself speak; if you sound like you're talking a little too slow, you're probably at a good pace. No one has ever complained about an intern speaking too clearly.

8. *Track down and meet your regular phone buddies.* The guard at the gate, the maintenance supervisor, the mail room clerk—these are all people you may speak with on a daily basis. Take some time to meet these people; you never know when you'll be in a jam, and people are usually more helpful to people they've actually seen.

9. *Double copy your messages.* Write down phone messages in both an office book and your personal one. You'll be the savior if the message is lost by a producer and you have it down. Plus, you'll have a long list of contacts to add to your personal collection. When taking down a phone number, always read the number back to ensure accuracy. If you're taking down an e-mail address, be sure to double-check the correct spelling. Never take a message without asking whether or not the person wants a call back, what the call is in reference to, and how urgent the call is. If your boss's husband calls and forgets to tell you that a message is important, when the boss asks you, "Was it important?" you don't want to end up staring at your boss, saying, "I don't know." You'll be the one who looks bad, not the husband.

   If you have access to a computer, type up the messages for your boss when your phone shift is over. It's a small but effective way to shine.

> *"Phone messages are a major thing—I have seen way too many interns goof up a message and have an enemy for life."*
>
> —Gary Kordan, Writer, *The Joan Rivers Radio Show*, and former *Joan Rivers Show* intern

10. *When you make a phone flub, be honest.* People can understand hanging up on someone. They won't understand your lying about it.

11. *The viewer is always right!* Often, angry viewers or clients will call. Should they take their anger out on you? No, but they may. Be kind and understanding. Give the caller your name or your boss's name if they ask. There is no advantage to a game of verbal volleyball.

12. *Avoid phone marathons!* Staying on the phone with a distressed viewer for 8 hours while the other lines go unanswered isn't right, either. Don't be rude. Try something like, "We really appreciate your call. I will pass along your comments."

13. *Know when you are in over your head on the phone.* You can handle an irate viewer, but if one is threatening to sue for punitive damages because of your report on the hazards of Spam, you may want to pass it on to your TV legal eagles.

14. *Keep a report of all the viewers who call with opinions.* Tally up your list and present it to your supervisor. This instant poll will be very appreciated by execs.

15. *No personal calls.* If you are caught once making a personal call, every time you are even near a phone, it'll be assumed it's not for business. In the same way, keep the calls you are screening professional. You are merely the messenger.

16. *Be mature when celebrities call.* Don't start screaming into the telephone just because George Clooney is on the other end. Be cordial and put him through. Of course, if you do get a bit nervous at the sound of a celebrity's voice, you won't be the first.

> *"Whoopi Goldberg was calling, and all of a sudden, the phones became difficult to handle. I hung up on her! Maybe she'd call back. Please call back. Everyone in the office asked me what was wrong. I just couldn't tell them. So she calls back, 'This is Whoopi. I was hung-up on.' I was just like, 'Hold on a minute, Whoopi,' and I successfully transferred her as if it wasn't a big deal, but I was sweating bullets."*
>
> —Darnell Jones, Script Coordinator, *P.J.'s*; former Writer's Assistant, *Hangin' With Mr. Cooper*; and a former intern

17. *Make sure that someone is covering the phone at all times!* If you have to leave the desk for any reason, even if it's just to answer nature's call, make sure you've got backup! People have been fired for leaving phones unattended.

E-mail Excellence

In today's society, e-mail has become just as important as the telephone. No longer do you hear, "Call me, we'll do lunch." Now, it's, "E-mail me, we'll make plans."

Very often, executives' e-mail boxes are filled to the brim with messages. Once you have a working relationship with a particular boss, volunteer to go through some of their e-mail. Since they probably don't want you going through any personal e-mail, tell them to forward any e-mail they want you to handle to your account.

This will give you a chance to show off your writing skills as well as meet a plethora of your boss's friends and co-workers. Keep a record of all the e-mail you respond to, and let the boss know where that file is.

If you read the trades and find out that someone you have e-mailed before won an award, write him a quick e-mail congratulating him on his success. Definitely write down the e-mail address of everyone with whom you communicate. This list will be a godsend when the job search begins.

Mail Call

"Try to have a good attitude about the mail and the phones. Twenty years ago, there were a lot more secretaries and receptionists. They're almost extinct. People don't have the support systems that they once had, so all of that has fallen on technology, like voice mail, or interns. Somebody has to run the stuff to the mail room if it has to go. Somebody has to get the FedEx."

—Jan Landis, *Sally, Home, Vicki,* and has trained more than 100 interns

Viewer mail is another slot to make your mark. Remember, ask yourself what the average intern would do and then take it at least one step further. Just like with the phone calls, keep a tally of the viewers' likes and dislikes, even if you aren't asked. Flag letters that you think the boss would like to read, and also pull letters that the talent would want to read. In soap operas, characters have been killed off by viewer mail alone. The mailbag carries a lot of weight in all areas of television. It can also offer great opportunities for you.

Make friends in the mail room. Many industry moguls got their breaks in mail rooms. Barry Manilow got his start stamping letters in the CBS mail room in New York. By volunteering to work in the mail room, the mail room workers will love you, and it's a great way to get to know people on their floors. Is there a delivery going upstairs? Ask to deliver it and you'll have a chance to make some new contacts. A mail bin can also be a great source for names and addresses—fill up your notebook with these great contacts.

If you are organizing your boss's mail, don't open up a letter that might be personal. If you accidentally do so, let the boss know. Be honest.

Viewers often pitch ideas or topics for shows; keep your eyes open. Donahue's mail included a large volume of letters written by viewers who eventually became guests. The mail is a great sampling of comments and ideas. Use it as a conversation piece to show off your knowledge. "We're getting a lot of response to the identical twin story; maybe we should do a follow up piece?" Also, track down where the mail is coming from. It could be a useful research tool for your boss. "Our fan mail seems to come largely from the South. Is there a way we could work this more to our advantage in the story line?"

When positive feedback comes in the mail about a particular news or show story, track down the recipient. Producers, reporters, and talent love hearing how their work is impacting the viewers. Also, you'll love hearing their feedback about you being so attentive.

SEE EVERY TASK AS A CHALLENGE

This is the next motto that should be tattooed on your forehead. If you follow the organizational advice from the previous channel, and you take tasks to the next level but see every task as grunt work that could be accomplished by a trained monkey, you'll be in loads of trouble. In the next channel, we'll talk about the importance of being aware of how you're attitude is being perceived. The best way to be perceived as an energetic and enthusiastic intern is to actually *be* one.

Another Photocopy—Should I Be Thrilled?

There is no way you'll be able to think of creative and ingenious ways to take assignments to the next level if you plan on assassinating your boss every time you are assigned a less-than-exciting task. The first thing to realize is that even the biggest Hollywood and New York executives started off right where you are now; some may have even had it worse.

"I had to clean up the floor of a bathroom that overflowed on a shoot. It was disgusting, but you just do it. If you don't, someone else who wants to get into TV more than you will."

—David Scott, Co-Executive Producer, *The People's Court*, and a former intern

It may not be a big thrill to make a photocopy, but it is a thrill to cover a feature story, and this is your first step to getting there. Leeza once clipped news copy for the on-air talent. Now, she is that on-air talent. Brian Graden was once listening to MTV for ideas while interning at Fox. Now, he is the President of MTV Networks. This is the life cycle of the TV world. Everyone must pay his or her dues. It makes logical sense that if you can't be trusted to fax out a memo, you're not going to be asked to research the latest political controversy.

Good Enough for a Paying Job?

Every time you're given a task, say, "This producer wants to see if I'm good enough to have a paid job with her in a few months. I'm going to show her I am." Also, be sure that you do the grunt work correctly; sometimes, even the easy tasks aren't so easy. San Francisco Producer Jill Coughlan will never forget her first days in TV. She needed to rush a note out to a producer who was in the studio. Seemed rather simple. Intent on accomplishing her mission, she ran into the studio without noticing that a bear from a previous segment on the show had made his mark on the studio floor. She went flying high as she slipped in front of the live studio audience. But the message got delivered! And Jill is not the only intern to have a wild experience. . .

"So the pig, the duck, and the goat were waiting in the prop storage area to go on camera. The pig had been in a little traveling kennel for a few hours, and needless to say, the little guy was not ready for TV at this point. So we cleaned the pig off in an industrial sink hidden in the janitor's closet. I was a bit worried and so was the pig. Do pigs bite? A nightmare, but also a dream. What producer couldn't love an intern who will ruin his pants and risk pig bites for the show?"

—Kevin Williams, Producer, PBS's *Newton's Apple*, and a former intern

TAKE YOUR GREATNESS ONE STEP FURTHER

Of course, the reason for doing all this grunt work so well is so that you can quickly move on to the more exciting assignments. It's time for the next step.

Up until this point, you've been assigned tasks and then have asked yourself, "How can I do this at least one step better then the average intern?" Now it's time to ask yourself what task has not been assigned and can be completed by super intern (that's you). Look around the office. What needs to be done? Is the tape room a mess? You're now a trusted and important part of your office. Don't just wait for tasks to come in your direction, write a list of things that you think need to be done. Patrol the office area and make a laundry list.

"Responsibility is rarely given to interns. Good interns take responsibility."

—John Dunn, Creative Services Director, UPN affiliate

Go to your supervisor and let him know your thoughts. "The tape room looks a bit unorganized. Would it be helpful if I straighten it out?" Listen around the office. Which producer is pulling out her hair in search of a subject for a story? Try to get yourself involved in something that gets good press around the office.

"The most impressive act I've seen an intern do? When I was working in Atlanta for the Olympics, I was doing a segment with Katie Couric in the Olympic Village. In the Village, I found a beauty parlor for the athletes, complete with a manicurist. I thought it would be fun if Katie went there and asked for a 'Gail Devers.' (Devers won a gold medal despite nails that are 8–10 inches long.) Well, this manicurist had no idea how to create such long nails, so I called a wonderful intern back in New York to see what she could do. Although she had never even had a manicure herself, she stayed up all night, gluing and painting these fake 8-inch nails with wild colors and decals and FedEx-ed them off to me. The athlete's manicurist simply glued the intern's creation onto Katie. After the segment ran, Newsweek magazine called because they wanted to interview the manicurist! I told them they had to talk to the intern instead!"

—Jason Raff, Producer, *Today*, and a former intern

Are there tasks that you know your boss hates doing? Make these your top priority. Maybe your boss dreads opening all the press and publicity packets that have been piling up. Offer to take that over. Does your boss complain about returning certain calls? Ask if there are any calls that you can handle. Of course, don't do anything before asking. The boss doesn't want to return from lunch to find out that you have redone the files that took him a year to get used to.

GRADUATING FROM GRUNT WORK

Every step you take away from the grunt work will be a vital one. Sure, you may still have to do some grunt work, but once you start working side by side with the producers, you'll be seen as a fellow producer who happens to still be in college, as opposed to a college student who some day wants to be a producer. One intern used to stuff recipe requests during weekend football games so he could use his on-the-job time to work on booking people for the show. One of the people he landed for the show was President Jimmy Carter! Strut your stuff.

> *"Two weeks into my internship, I overheard a group of producers talking about a painting of the White House they needed for an upcoming show. Afterwards, I told them that I was an artist and would do it for the show. After that, I was the star artist intern and did all the graphics for the show. The host asked who did the art, and before long, I was doing art for her, too."*
>
> —Gary Kordan, Writer, *The Joan Rivers Radio Show*, and former *Joan Rivers Show* intern

Now, as great as it is to go the extra mile, you have to be careful not to step over any boundaries.

Don't Overstep Your Bounds

Although it's important to establish your willingness to help and to offer your input around the office, you need to be careful to not trip over the work of paid employees. You don't want to gather enemies by doing so. Here are some possible potholes.

1. *Don't bypass your supervisor.* Respect the chain of command in your office. It's okay to walk up to a producer and offer your services, but don't walk into the vice president's office and ask to rearrange his file drawer. Your supervisor would probably get an unflattering call. Can you offer to help people above your boss on the TV ladder? Sure. Just make sure you ask your supervisor first.

2. *Make sure your daily responsibilities come first.* It is extremely rewarding to create your own assignments and impress the staff. It's far more interesting than your normal responsibilities, such as photocopying. Some interns work hard on the grunt work but feel angry when they see

the other interns not doing any menial tasks and hanging out with the staff. It seems like the intern not doing the work is having a better time and that the staff really likes him. This may be true; the staff may really like the nonworking intern, but when it comes time to hire someone, Mr. Popularity won't even be considered.

"One intern I know went about getting ahead in the wrong way. He wanted to be a news anchor after he graduated. He was interning on our local talk show, and instead of making himself look good there, he would do the minimum amount and then hang out at the newsroom. What he didn't realize was when it came time to hire people in the newsroom, they asked the producers of the talk show what they thought of him. He got a terrible review."

—Julie Johnson, Associate Producer, *Oprah*, and a former intern

3. *Never give unsolicited opinions.* Never give a review unless asked. What if it's positive? Still be hesitant. Blurting out, "That field piece was great," when everyone at the station found it extremely flawed will only show off your inexperience. If you're asked to give your opinion on something, feel free to be honest. However, "The interview with Madonna was the worst. It went about 8 hours too long," is a bit too direct. You're are not Siskel or Ebert yet. Put a more positive spin on it. "I loved the interview with Madonna, but did it possibly go a bit long?" This response will show off your instincts and your desire to learn. Even if you're wrong, the person who asked you would respect your comment and probably explain to you why it was as long as it was.

4. *Don't be part of the grapevine.* It may seem helpful to tell your boss that the office hates him, but you can get caught in the fallout. By doing so, your boss will associate you with bad news, and you'll come off as untrustworthy. If you're willing to repeat what's said in the producer's office, you'll likely repeat it to others. This is not the way to win points. Keep your mouth out of the rumor mill. Feel free to let the supervisor know if the office morale seems low, but do so diplomatically. "I just thought you might like to know that everyone seems down about the decision not to go into reruns on July 4th." Don't give names, don't give specifics, just let her know.

5. *A personal life is personal.* It's very possible you'll overhear some personal conversation. Keep your ears open but your mouth closed. Be understanding, not nosy. Never repeat what you heard, and definitely

don't offer advice. "You should dump that guy. You deserve better." Getting involved in someone's private life is again walking into murky waters.

Following are two examples that show how some interns went down the wrong road:

"There was an intern working at Entertainment Tonight *during the Oscars. She really wanted to attend the event, but was told she couldn't. She went anyway and talked her way into the show using ET as her employer. That was her last day. This is a small business. People remember."*

> —Glenn Meehan, Managing Editor, *Entertainment Tonight*, and a former intern

"Sometimes, after being in an office a while, interns will assume that they know how to do the boss's job. This is a big mistake. Chances are good that your boss makes his job look simple. That doesn't mean you can do it. I had an intern who felt that he could just sit at my desk and do my work when I wasn't around. Not good."

> —Carol Story, Producer, *CBS This Morning*

Going the Extra Mile—A Few More Tips

1. *Bring some grunt work home with you.* If you get assigned to stuff envelopes, but there's a pitch meeting you'd like to attend, ask if you can stuff the envelopes at home instead. The supervisor will be impressed with your desire to learn and your willingness to work at home to do so.

2. *Plan ahead for a special event.* Want to go on Wednesday's field shoot with Tom Cruise? Talk to your supervisor about clearing your schedule. Tell him you are more than willing to work extra hours to get everything accomplished so that you can take a day for the shoot. They will appreciate your passion and again be reminded of your area of interest.

3. *Pitch your own ideas.* When you are off duty, do some brainstorming about your own projects. Try to put together a list of assignments that you think your home away from home would benefit from. Then, at an appropriate time, try them out on your boss. If you're interning in a development office, pitch a show. In news, pitch some stories. In marketing, pitch a campaign.

Developing Perfect Pitch

Be sure not to tell a producer you are too busy to get the phone because you're writing pitches. Save that for after-hours, but definitely go for it. Here are some suggestions for putting together the perfect pitch:

1. *Find out from a producer if there's a standard way to write up pitches.* Ask to see some samples. (Make copies of these for yourself. Proposals will come in very handy down the road.) Ask the producer if you could sit in on a pitch meeting and if she'd be willing to look over your pitches before you present them.

2. *Get your pitches fully researched before you approach your supervisor.* You need to be ready to pitch at a moment's notice. They may put you on the spot right away.

3. *Ask your supervisor if you can set up a meeting to pitch your ideas.* The other option is to write them up and hand them in. However, an oral one provides a better opportunity.

4. *Keep your pitches short.* Whether in person or on paper, be quick and to the point. Type up your ideas and be sure there are no spelling or grammatical errors. Even if your pitches aren't loved, you may impress your boss with your writing. If your pitches are received well, ask if you can attend the next pitch meeting and pitch an idea there. Be understanding if they don't want to start a precedent.

THE FINE LINE BETWEEN HELPFUL AND ANNOYING

Again, appearing as if you trying to take over your supervisor's job is dangerous. Likewise, being too helpful in your internship assignments can come off as annoying. It's a fine line. The following illustrations will help you understand how far you can stretch your willingness to help.

"A great intern is somebody who has an awful lot of pep and someone who is extremely aggressive without being a constant pain. Somebody who realizes there's a fine line between being annoying and helpful. Someone who is enthusiastic about moving a waste basket from one desk to another but doesn't do it during a personal call."

—Chuck Lioi, Post Production Supervisor, *Sunset Beach*, and a former intern

"One male intern drove me crazy by always being in my face and being goofy and silly a lot of the time. He kept pestering me to do a

certain topic, and I finally relented when I realized he had a good idea. If he'd only had a different approach with me in the first place."

—Cathy Palmerino, Producer, local and national talk shows and infomercials, and a former intern

"Realize who you are working with—some people won't want to have anything to do with interns, and others love working with and teaching them. They're the ones you really want to get to know."

—Michael Keely, Associate Professor of Communication Arts, Allegheny College, Meadville, Pennsylvania, and a former intern

"Develop people radar! Learn how to read people. Producing involves so many details that, often, focus is the primary thing on a good producer's mind. Learn to sense when. Focus is really what's needed. Be available, but don't be intrusive!"

—Dane Hall, Writer/Producer, VH1

"Don't stand at my desk waiting for work. Know when to interrupt. Don't assume you're invited to every meeting. Ask. Find work to do without needing to be told. It's a fine line, but if you know how to walk it, you'll succeed. Just be sure to let your boss know where you'll be in case a story breaks."

—Shannon Keenan, Producer, Live Events, E! Entertainment Television, and a former intern

"Use common sense. Always keep a low profile and let your actions speak much louder than your words."

—Lorri Antosz Benson, former Senior Producer, *Donahue*

"If it seems people are cold to you, it may be a sign that you have become annoying. Give them some space. Do your best to read people."

—Brian Z, Children's Show Host

"Helpful is when you're doing a special with 2,000 people and an intern comes in and asks what they can do. After you tell them, 'Oh, thanks for asking. I can't think of anything right now,' the intern should say, 'I'll be sitting here at my desk; if there's anything I can do, please let me know.' When I am in show mode, I don't want to see a person sit down in my office and hang out. That's annoying."

—Jan Landis, *Sally*, *Home*, *Vicki*, and has trained over 100 interns

MEET, GREET, AND BE MERRY

In the same vein that you take your assignments to the next level, you should take your networking to the next level as well. The average intern would meet everyone he works with and probably make some solid contacts with those people. Take that idea one step further:

> *"I volunteered to stay late and help out with edit sessions. They are a great way to get to know people. You can spend a good 5 hours with producers, real quality time when the phones are not ringing. They appreciate the company and interest. Editors are great people to know, and they carry a lot of weight, too."*
>
> —Marla Kell Brown, Producer, *The Arsenio Hall Show*, and a former intern

There is no one in the station, studio, or production house whom you shouldn't know. Who is the person who comes in at midnight to listen to the scanner? Find out. Ask your supervisor if you can work with that person one night. A supervisor will appreciate someone who isn't watching the clock.

Shannon Keenan went from being a news intern to a news producer to a supervising producer, all within four years of college graduation. She says that she met everyone possible when she interned. Whether it was pulling an all-nighter so she could learn what the overnight assignment editor did or coming in on weekends to meet the weekend news crew to expand her contact base, she met everyone possible. In her own words: "Meet everyone, even the guy that works the overnight shift—even the janitor."

Another intern suggested having the executive producer of *Donahue* as a guest on his local talk show. When she came to town, he had dinner with her to go over the segment. She was so impressed with his organization, she wound up hiring him years later as a producer on her legendary talk show. Throw your net out wide when networking.

Are you working news for a station that also develops its own programming? Ask to spend one day there. See if you can put extra hours in your department so that you can spend half a day observing another. Don't do this too often; you don't want people to think you aren't happy where you are, but you never know where your first job will come from.

BE PREPARED FOR ANYTHING

Throughout this book you've heard about common intern tasks, such as faxing and copying. Depending on your internship, you may do a large amount of office work, or you may do none at all. Intern assignments vary from morning bagel runs to wearing an ape suit for a TV shoot. In either case, nothing should take you by surprise. Here are some stories of some of the best and worst assignments from the interns of days past.

"My greatest moment as an intern was as a CBS talent escort at the Daytime Emmys. My job was to stand backstage and escort presenters and winners to the pressroom as they came off stage. I got to meet a lot of people and even hang out with Oprah in the green room, until they kicked me out for not being 'talent.' "

> —Dana Sparber, Senior Marketing Analyst, ABC–New York, and a former intern

"The strangest thing I ever did as an intern? Book a lizard!"

> —Dan Gepner, former Minneapolis intern

"The worst responsibility I had was handling disgruntled viewer complaints with a smile. The best was actually getting to write press releases and getting to post my name at the top. Pretty cool!"

> —Jill Mullikin-Bates, Supervising Producer, *Leeza*, and a former intern

"I had to prepare all monologue jokes and script material for the host. Believe me, it was a heavy job. My best internship odd job was signing autographs for the host. I was the best forger they ever had."

> —Wayne Hopkins, *Later . . . with Greg Kinnear*, various *Dick Clark Specials*, *Vibe*, and a former intern

"My basic duties boiled down to five F's . . . file, fax, FedEx, fone, and food!"

> —Jason Gurskis, Producer, Discovery Channel, and a former intern

"Once I had to drive a generator truck the size of a small semi through rush-hour traffic in LA. It was a stick shift, and I didn't know how to drive one. I stalled about a dozen times on the way to the office, but the truck and I made it there in one piece. Barely!"

> —Todd Radnitz, Producer, E! Entertainment Television, and a former intern

"My internship job started pretty hideously. I had to help put up the magnetic numbers on the weather map for the anchorwoman. I

remember on one Halloween, she made me go to the supermarket and buy a witch and a pumpkin to add to the map."

—Richard Ayoub, Executive Producer, *KABC Morning News* in LA, and a former intern

"It was 110 degrees in LA, and we were working. I had completed one year at Harvard and figured I was pretty important. My boss, who insisted on doing everything on the cheap, suggested we forgo a trucking service for props. Instead, I could carry ten huge foam bowling pins (props for a show), probably 100 pounds each, into a truck and drive them into the desert in the 110 degrees of heat. It was awful, but by the end of the summer, I was wearing a headset, calling the shots, coordinating contestants . . . a happy ending and a long way from lifting huge props in the desert. Hang in there."

—Brian Graden, Executive Vice President, MTV; Developer, *South Park*; and a former intern

"As an intern at Good Company, a talk show in Minneapolis, the intern who trained me was more interested in schmoozing with the news anchors. He said, 'Julie, why don't you get started down here . . . in the kitchen.' I had to clean it . . . 4 hours and twenty loads of dishes later, I found him, feet propped up on a desk, shooting the breeze."

—Julie Johnson, Associate Producer, *Oprah*, and a former intern

Take a few moments to close your eyes and visualize about the perfect moment that you are sure to encounter during your internships. Continue reading—you can make it happen.

. . . AND CUT!
CUE ANNOUNCER:

"On deck, keeping your cool during a sea of problems and giving attitude . . . the right way. But first, it's time to hear from another one of our Hall of Fame interns."

FADE TO BLACK
ROLL "TV INTERN HALL OF FAME" PACKAGE

Jonathan C. Kilb
Coordinating Producer, New England Cable News;
Videographer, Boston Bruins/Celtics; and a former intern

Recently, my mother put together a collection of photos of me and my brother when we were younger, pictures that I had never seen. As I looked at it, one particular picture caught my eye, a picture of my best friend and me, both draped in New York Yankees clothing and Yankees hats. Although I don't remember the moment that the picture was taken, it reminded me that I have been a sports fan as far back as I can remember. I grew up watching every Yankees game that I could and listening to Phil Rizzuto's, "Holy Cow!" And once baseball season was over, it was on to football and basketball and hockey. There weren't enough games for me to watch.

It's funny how things are right there in front of us sometimes, and we don't even see them. I would have given anything to be a professional athlete, but not all of us are blessed with that ability. So, throughout my teen years, I was just resigned to being the best armchair quarterback in the country. I went to college as an undecided major, and after two years of liberal arts, I was lost. As I pondered a transfer, I realized that I needed to reach a decision on what to do with my life. As was always the case, my mother was the one with the great advice. She obviously knew my love of sports and television and suggested that I consider a career in sports broadcasting. It was so obvious to me that I couldn't believe that I never thought of it.

I transferred to the State University of New York College at Fredonia where I began my studies in communication, specializing in media management. While I enjoyed all of my classes and extracurricular work, I felt that I needed more experience. At the end of my first year at Fredonia, my third year of college, a friend told me that he was applying for an internship with a production company responsible for producing telecasts of Buffalo Bisons baseball. I decided to call and apply, too, and several weeks after returning the application, I was hired for the internship. I can remember the tremendous excitement that I felt when I realized that I would be working in sports television.

That whole summer was terrific. I went to work at a ballpark and had an important responsibility to the team. I couldn't have asked for a better start. The other interns were young and friendly, and the management treated us as regular employees. And here I was, only one step away from the major leagues. It was really a terrific opportunity, one which eventually led to my first professional job.

Over my remaining two years of college, I completed two more internships. The first was with an NBC-TV affiliate in Buffalo. In addition to my regular responsibilities, I volunteered and was allowed to attend Buffalo Bills training camp. The station did not send a reporter for morning practice, so I acted as a reporter when sound bites were needed. It was another tremendous opportunity.

My third and last internship was with a radio station in Buffalo. I chose to apply for this internship because I wanted to be more rounded and to learn the radio aspects of the broadcast industry, since all of my previous work was in television. I performed a wide variety of tasks for them, from promotions to reporting. Again, it was good experience to have when applying for jobs.

So you may be asking if all that work has paid off for me. I can say without hesitation that it certainly has. My first job in the sports industry came three months after I graduated from college. That job was as a videographer at the Fleetcenter in Boston, Massachusetts, working on the production crew for Boston Celtics and Boston Bruins games. And since then, my career in television has blossomed. At only 23 years old, I have worked at games for every professional sports team in the Boston area and also work full-time at an all-news television station. When I interviewed, it was said to me directly that my experience at these internships was a huge plus. If there is one bit of advice I can give, it is to do internships whenever possible, no matter how many or in what field. Not all internships will prove successful in the same way, but many are good for college credit, and many are good for social reasons. I hope my story has provided a bit of motivation for you.

channel 7

A Great Attitude, No Matter What

Completing a task is really only half the battle. Your attitude is the other. Some interns look like they're thrilled just to be in the TV world; others look as if they're planning the boss's demise every time a less-then-exciting task is assigned to them.

THREE . . .

"Your superiors will recognize your positive attitude by rewarding your efforts. When I was an intern at Good Morning America, I was asked to produce three segments that aired in the summer of 1994. You better believe that because my menial tasks, like filing, faxing, photocopying, and, yes, getting coffee, were completed with a zest and appreciation for even being there, I was rewarded. It lead to the trust that enabled me to be assigned to produce three segments for a nationally renowned morning show, which, in turn, helped me set higher career goals and keep a clear mind about what I want to do. Having a great attitude will never hurt you and almost always helps you get what you want."

> —Abbey LeVine, Development Coordinator, In-Finn-Ity Productions, former Assistant to the Senior Producer of *Politically Incorrect with Bill Maher*, and a former *Good Morning America* intern

TWO . . .

"If you're going to make it in TV, you're going to have to have a great and flexible attitude. Everything will change at the last minute, and you will be put in situations you never imagined. I have had to do everything from making coffee for 300 people to dealing with crabby audience members who were turned away to having to babysit the Grand Dragon of the KKK. Those were tough things, but because I handled them with grace and diplomacy, I was chosen to deal with major celebs like Lily Tomlin, Debbie Reynolds, and my girlhood crush, David Cassidy."

> —Lisa Tatum, Producer, *The Other Side*, and a former intern

ONE . . .

"Never forget that you can be replaced by the time the door hits you on your way out. There is a legion of wannabes out there who think they want your job as an entry into show business. They are not as smart as you yet. So try to maintain a pleasant attitude, despite all the grunt work you are asked to do. Rolling your eyes and/or scowling are not going to win you any fans higher up the ladder."

—Jeffrey Duteil, Executive Producer, *The Steve Harvey Show*, and Emmy-nominated writer, *The Golden Girls*

AND ACTION!

YOUR ACTIONS WILL FOLLOW YOUR THOUGHTS

The best way to be perceived as having a great attitude is to actually have one. As discussed in the previous channel, if you think about each assignment as an opportunity, you have a solid chance of winning the battle of perception. When you have the right mindset, the rest comes pretty easy; it's much easier to make people think you love your job when it truly is a labor of love.

Recall the example about the two interns who both completed the assigned task; one was energetic, well dressed, and kept solid eye contact, while the other intern wore ripped jeans, mumbled, and looked like he'd rather be anywhere else in the world. Your dress, your body language, the tone of your voice—all of these things will affect how you are perceived.

FLASHBACK

"Anytime something was needed in the office, I offered to take care of it. It didn't matter if they needed someone to sing show tunes while they worked or if they needed to someone to clean the bathroom. I wasn't 3,000 miles away from my friends and my family to be mediocre. It became the office joke. If someone said, 'I can't believe I just stained my shirt,' my shirt was offered. When John Miller, now a VP at MTV, tried a three-point shot with a tub of cream cheese, I jumped to clean the mess off the wall. No one took me up on these offers ('Kid, sit the heck down.'), but it made a definite statement. They knew I was going to make it in this industry and nothing was going to stop me."

—Jason

Your Dress

In an earlier channel we discussed dressing for intern success, but you must keep in mind that *how* you wear your clothes is as important as what you wear. There was an intern who once came into work with a wrinkled shirt and stained jeans. When questioned about his dress he replied, "How do stains on my pants affect my ability to do my job?" Welcome to the world of television and instant perceptions. Technically, the stained jeans wouldn't have affected his ability, but it would have affected people's impressions of his ability.

Producer Jason Gurskis recounts the day he made a fashion blunder when working on a network show. "I had been interning for about a week and was doing mostly phone and mail work. Everyone seemed really pleased with my abilities, and I got very comfortable there. Too comfortable." He went on to explain that since it was summer and he wasn't really working with the public, he decided to start wearing shorts to work. "The Executive Producer gave me an icy stare and told me I wasn't at college getting ready for finals." Jason learned that many bosses really want to set an office tone. Being dressed too casually makes them feel that people aren't working at full speed. You *never* want to send this message.

Your Body Language

When you talk to the executive, will you be slouching in your chair ready to fall asleep, or will you be sitting at the edge of your seat ready to take on the world? You want to always appear ready to take on any situation. Does your posture suggest power or poor self-esteem? A picture is worth a thousand words; think about how many words a 5-minute interaction is worth.

Always try to look the staff members directly in the eyes; this goes whether you're having a conversation or passing someone in the hallway. Direct eye contact shows that you have confidence in yourself and respect for your conversation partner.

There is no easier way to convey that you are getting right on an assignment than by quickly sprinting out of the office. If you are seen slowly wandering around the office, staring at the pictures on the walls as you walk, not many people are going to assume that you're doing anything all that important.

Your Voice

If you want to convince people that you can handle every situation, talking in a quick but stern tone shows you are enthusiastic and on top of the situation.

Mumbling nonstop under your breath is rarely a good thing. Try to speak in a calm but confident tone. When you make a statement, have it sound like a statement, not a question.

Remember, not only do you want to be seen as a good intern but also as an enjoyable person to be around. Think about it. If you were a producer and asked an intern how they were and they responded by looking at the floor and mumbling "fine," would you have a strong desire to spend your lunch break with this intern? Even if you love what you do, if your body language says otherwise, you're in trouble.

COOL, CALM, AND COLLECTED

Although many interns stay cool in most situations, when the office is chaotic and assignments are being blurted out by crazy producers, many interns begin to fall apart. The important thing to remember when the office has gone haywire is that the more you can remain calm, the greater asset you will become. When a producer starts throwing eighteen assignments your way, just remember to write everything down and ask questions when necessary. You might be afraid to ask the producer who has enough smoke coming out of their ears to energize all of New York City, but it's better to ask questions now than to feel their wrath later on.

> *"Find a big chaotic show to work on. If you can keep your cool, there are many more opportunities. The Late Show was a disaster for a lot of people on that show, but for me it was my biggest break. My advice, look for chaos and keep cool. You'll be a rare find."*
> —Marla Kell Brown Producer, *The Arsenio Hall Show*, and a former intern

TV people are excitement junkies and thrive on crisis. It is during the chaos that snap decisions are made about an intern and their abilities. A former intern of a late-night talk show recalls that there were times when she didn't know who was going to be hosting the show that evening, let alone who was going to be a guest. "If you can help a producer keep his head during pandemonium, you have scored big points." Going though adversity together really binds people.

Make sure you don't start speaking fast or sounding stressed; don't be nervously scribbling all over the page. Just look the executive straight in the eyes, and in your most confident voice, say, "This will be taken care of." TV execs send off a message of confidence and control, but remember that they are as insecure as the next guy. They need reassurance, and who better to give it than you?

YOU WILL GET FRUSTRATED

Interning is hard on the ego. Like *CBS This Morning*'s Producer Carol Story says, "You're at the bottom of the food chain, and when someone gets hungry, you're the one usually running to get the food." It's not easy. You'll be working for people that you know you're smarter than, and yet, you're spending your mornings ripping their scripts.

FLASHBACK

"After the first few weeks, I was getting compliment after compliment, yet I was still the one making the coffee and running errands. In one breath I was being told how valuable I was, and in the next, I was told to buy push pins. Is that all I was good for? Didn't they think I could do anything better? I already proved I was a good writer; why couldn't I help out with something important? Didn't I deserve a shot?!"
—Jason

"Jason really earned his intern stripes quickly. I knew he was ready for more responsibilities, and I tried to involve him in as many pitch meetings and shoots as I could. But there was so much less important work that needed to get done. Our office was small, and I needed to rely on Jason to take care of seemingly unimportant but actually very important details. I could sense his frustration sometimes, but I knew that he really understood that in the long haul, he was in good shape."
—Dan

There will be times when twelve different people are giving you twenty-four different assignments, and everyone will insist that they want their job done now. In the middle of all that, your boss will complain that the coffee needs exactly twenty-two more grains of sugar and that the jelly donuts have strawberry jelly instead of grape. Then, you'll finally get one task completed, just to be told by the producer that they forgot to tell you to make sure you write out all the cue cards in red marker instead of black.

One former intern was juggling many assignments and always pitching show ideas, too. He was feeling great about all that he was doing, until he overheard a producer on the phone. "I'll let my secretary get you that information. Please hold. Oh Aaron, could you get line two?" Aaron was fuming. He was an intern wearing many hats, but being called a secretary really got to him. Somehow, he swallowed what little pride he had left and cheerfully took the caller's recipe request. Six months later, Aaron was producing, and that producer was gone.

When you feel yourself getting frustrated, you need to step outside and take a few moments to read this passage:

> *"I am working toward a great career in a field I love. Right now, I am the king of the coffee; I am an intern. Many people come this far and can't deal with the frustrations. I will not let this happen to me. The office is a stressful place, but I can deal. I will make it. No one and nothing will stop me."*

One of the nicest parts of the internship will be the people you'll meet. When you feel you're going to explode, find a trusted friend and tell them your frustrations. Just getting frustrations off your chest will help you feel better. They'll understand. You're only human, and they've unquestionably felt the same way.

LEADER OF THE INTERN PACK

Your attitude toward other interns is very telling to other staff members. Many interns are great with the staff, but treat the other interns as peasants. This is bad. The staff will be well aware of how you treat your fellow interns. Being close with other interns can work to your advantage. You can share notes on producers and help each other out if one is overwhelmed. By befriending interns in other departments you may end up knowing more about the station than some of the staffers do. Share information about producers' birthdays, their favorite coffee, and their pet peeves with each other.

Here's an honest way to make yourself the intern leader:

> *"Volunteer to draw up a list of all the interns and their names and personally hand that list out to the appropriate people. Arrive an hour earlier than the other interns and go around and ask the producers what they need done first. Draw up those needs on a list and hang it in the intern area. Ask your fellow interns to please cross things off the list as they are accomplished."*
> —Dane Hall, Writer/Producer, VH1

Be careful not to get caught hanging out in the hallways with the other interns. Don't be part of this clique. It will be tempting. And what if another intern is spreading gossip or doing a bad job? Don't worry. They will cook their own goose. You won't look like a hero by reporting someone; you'll look like a trouble maker.

"We all love to gossip. It's a basic human act. But I would strongly urge all interns to steer very clear of engaging in office gossip with other interns, or producers for that matter. Save your verbal observations for your friends who DON'T work with you. I once had a staff member who loved to gossip with everyone. She lasted six months. Why? If she had time to gossip, that meant she wasn't helping others in need. Also, TV is an emotional business, and the worst thing is to have someone telling tales out of work. The bond is broken."

 —Dane Hall, Writer/Producer, VH1

ALWAYS REMEMBER THAT YOU'RE AN INTERN

Always remember your roots. One trap that interns fall into is forgetting that they are interns. For example, pretend it's late at night and you're sitting with a bunch of producers, working on a piece. Everyone, including you, is contributing ideas. You're having a blast. Then, somebody says, "I'm hungry." Many interns begin to think, "Well, I'm contributing as many ideas as anyone else; why should I get the food?" Why? Because you are the intern. Give attitude about getting food, and the next time the producers need an intern to stay late, you will not be asked. Your ego will be put to the test, but as stated before, just try to remember that everyone has been there. Development Coordinator Curt Northrup recalls being on location in an orange grove, working 20-hour days as an intern. He was asked to go pick oranges for the crew for breakfast. One minute he was helping set a shot, the next he was squeezing juice. He never flinched. You're just paying your dues like everyone else has.

"No matter how friendly you are with the staff, you are the lowest man on the totem pole—don't forget it. Don't overstep your boundaries and become too lazy or familiar with the people you work with. Above all, don't become lazy with your work."

 —Michael Seligman, Associate Producer, E! Entertainment Television,
  and a former intern

"An intern should be a model employee with never a complaint. Prompt, courteous, and cheerful. Generation X or not, there is no room for attitude or car problems when you are an intern. There is no job too big or small for anyone to do. I remember the interns who brought their lunches from home and went out for lunch for everyone else and were happy with every assignment. Great interns make cold calls to book a much-loved guest, celeb, or TV star. And when the person arrived, the

intern set the tone of pure pleasure at having this person in our studio. Unbridled enthusiasm and freshness most often generate great interviews. It is also the stuff that makes me offer jobs."

—Jane Temple, Cleveland TV Producer

SPECIAL SITUATIONS

You are bound to encounter a few personal situations while interning. Here is some quick advice:

1. *What if you are ill?* If you are physically able to make it into the office, do so. Go straight to your supervisor, let him know your situation, and he'll more than likely send you home. Why bother coming in? It shows your determination to be in the office. Before you head for home, make sure your tasks for the day are taken care of and then depart.

   If you can't make it into the office, call your supervisor. If you get the voice mail, leave a message, but keep trying to get your supervisor in person. Let him know you are too ill to make it in, and list all of the tasks that need to be done. Hopefully, this list will be a long one, thus making the supervisor realize your value.

2. *What if you have an unexpected family problem?* Your family has to come first. Don't miss a funeral just so you can intern. If there's ever a serious problem, call your supervisor and let her know immediately. Know that she has encountered every kind of situation.

   If someone in your family has unfortunately come down with an illness that won't keep you out of work but may hinder your performance, let your supervisor know. You don't want her to think that you just suddenly decided to slack off.

THE DO'S AND DON'TS OF ATTITUDE ETIQUETTE

In general, use common sense and take a great deal of pride in and responsibility for your work. Here's a quick summary of the DOs and DON'Ts of keeping a good attitude during your internship:

```
DO:     Constantly ask how you can be of more help.

DON'T:  Brag about your accomplishments. If you
        work hard, people will see it; if you do
        your task right, the producers will know
        it.
```

DO: Befriend producers. This will be a great help throughout your internship.

DON'T: Be negative, even when talking with a producer as a friend. There is always a way to put a positive spin on things. And never, never put down another employee. If you talk badly about one producer to another, the producer will assume you'll be talking badly about them when their back is turned.

DO: Let people know of your goals when asked.

DON'T: Say, "I want your job," or constantly attempt to get an on-camera audition. Your internship is not the place for this. Prove yourself as an intern, then as an anchor.

DO: Stay on top of things in the office. It's good to know a little about everything.

DON'T: Gossip or get caught in inner-office drama. Never feed the rumor mill.

DO: Look for every possible opportunity to show off your skills and be helpful.

DON'T: Try to gain by others' failures.

DO: Be confident.

DON'T: Be conceited.

DO: Give constructive criticism when asked.

DON'T: Give unsolicited opinions.

AND CUT!

FADE TO BLACK
ROLL "TV INTERN HALL OF FAME" PACKAGE

••

THE TV INTERN HALL OF FAME SALUTES

Sheila Brummer
News Anchor, WAOW-TV, Wausau, Wisconsin,
and a former intern

BIG DREAMS START SMALL!

Christmas day, twenty years ago, I found my first typewriter under the tree. Once I mastered the spelling and a bit of grammar, the *Bus 72 Review* rolled off the presses and into the hands of my bus-riding friends. The *Review* contained stories of important issues, favorite teachers, music, love interests.

A few years later, a tape recorder became the object of obsession—my sister, the object of my first interviews.

I loved every medium. Radio—I spent hours listening and hoping that someday I would be on the other side of the microphone. While my friends watched MTV, I took in *20/20, 60 Minutes,* and *Nightline.*

In college came an internship, a chance to prove what a newcomer could do. The first day was a hard one. When I walked into the newsroom, excitement rushed through my body. I dressed for the part: new suit, heels, and all. I forgot I wasn't interning for the president of a major network but for a small station ranked 147th in the nation.

The first assignment kept me busy. I learned how to use the heavy equipment. I lugged a camera, record deck, and a tripod for the reporter. At the end of the day, the reflection in the mirror showed a different girl: hideous hair, soiled suit, and ripped hose. To top it off, my feet pulsed with pain.

I tried and tried, and it finally paid off! One day, two reporters called in sick. They needed a rookie's help. You can't explain the thrill of hearing your work come to life. It wasn't just any story, but the top topic of the day. One big story doesn't make a career. It takes more. The internship ended without a job. There wasn't room for me. No problem, I turned to radio.

Radio news moves—cover all you can. A fire here, a drug bust there. A chance to do it all. I worked a 50- to 60-hour week, and then downsizing killed my nine-month run. What would I do?

Luckily, my low-on-the-totem-pole role included covering city, county, and school board meetings. Boring to some, but for me it opened another opportunity. I called a TV news director in town and sold myself as the person who could understand how the mayor operated. My intern/camera knowledge landed me on my feet. I did it all: shot, wrote, edited. Whatever needed to be done, I did it. When the producer went on vacation, I filled in. No job was too small—or too big.

The weekend anchor had the week off, and when his back-up called in sick, who was left to fill the gap? This was my perfect opportunity. The back-up experience paved the way for my current job. I anchor a morning show in a slightly bigger market and beat the streets and introduce a whole new day of stories. You never know what's going to happen, and you have to take the opportunities as they come to you.

ANNOUNCER TEASE:

"Coming up: We interrupt this book to bring you the following special report. Do you know how you would handle an employee who is making a sexual advance? And don't miss the next channel on dealing with tough personalities."

special report

Protecting
Your Rights

Authors' Note: This special report was not written to scare anyone, but to provide protection. Sexual harassment is not pervasive throughout the television business, but it is something to be aware of. Since we are admittedly not experts on the subject of sexual harassment, we advise that if you do encounter a problem, seek professional counsel. We have, however, spent a good deal of time researching the subject and speaking with interns and executives in the business. In particular, we would like to acknowledge Deborah Ann Artz, Coordinator of Applied Learning, Counseling and Career Services at the University of California, Santa Barbara, for offering her help and knowledge on the subject.

Are Interns at a Greater Risk for Being Harassed?

A recent poll conducted by Lubach and Artz states that 30 percent of communication majors who intern at local businesses and organizations reported experiencing some form of sexual harassment on the job. *Entertainment Weekly* reported that the number of incidents is highest in news divisions and almost nonexistent on daytime drama sets. One NBC News Producer says she's not surprised by the report, indicating that with all of the sexual scandals in the news, it becomes a common topic of conversation, and people begin to cross the line in the workplace.

Sexual harassment can occur when an employee sexually harasses a boss, but usually occurs when a less-powerful employee suffers harassment from a supervisor. Since interns are at the bottom of the feeding chain—and because it is known that they will be there for a short time only—they may be more susceptible to harassment. Although it's probably a situation that you will never have to deal with, it is best to be able to recognize the problem and know the reporting procedures for such behavior.

Can You Identify Sexual Harassment?

According to the U.S. Equal Employment Opportunity Commission, the following constitutes sexual harassment: "unwelcome sexual advances, requests for sexual favors, and other verbal or physical conduct of a sexual nature constitute sexual harassment when submission to or rejection of this conduct explicitly or implicitly affects an individual's work performance or creates an intimidating, hostile, or offensive environment."

When many people think of sexual harassment, they think of an employee being told that the promotion they are up for depends upon their willingness to perform a particular sexual favor. If the status of your employment is based on a sexually advanced *quid pro quo* (something for something in exchange), this constitutes sexual harassment. But this is not the only situation that falls under the sexual harassment umbrella. Any unwanted, repeated sexual attention at work is considered sexual harassment as well. It doesn't matter if the person was just joking, or says, "You're too sensitive," or, "I meant it as a compliment," unwanted, repeated sexual attention is considered sexual harassment.

Some people in the industry with whom we spoke were under the impression that a hostile work environment was not the same as sexual harassment. If someone's sexual behavior or comments cause you to feel uncomfortable at the workplace, this can be considered sexual harassment. The comments and/or behaviors don't have to be directed at you.

The following can all be considered as sexual harassment:

- Suggestive remarks or gestures
- Teasing, taunting, or telling jokes of a sexual nature
- Unwelcome physical conduct or sexual advances
- Continual use of offensive language
- Sexual bantering
- Bragging about sexual prowess
- Office or locker-room pinups and sexual graffiti
- Compliments with sexual overtones
- Asking questions about sexual conduct
- Physical interference with normal work or movement
- Requests for sexual favors
- Obscene letters and phone calls
- Inappropriate invitations
- Repeated requests for dates
- Public humiliation
- Indecent exposure

Basically, any inappropriate sexual behavior can be considered sexual harassment. It doesn't matter whether or not the perpetrator believes what he or she did is inappropriate, it is the victim's perception that counts. Any sexual comments or gestures that make you uncomfortable at work and affect your ability to do your job may be considered sexual harassment. It is also important to note that human resources professionals are reporting that sexual harassment incidents are being reported by both men and women, though women do report a larger percentage of incidents.

What to Do if It Happens to You

Having said all that, what course of action can you take if you feel you are being harassed? When sexual harassment occurs in any form, the important thing is to not sit back and let it continue, if possible. No one should feel compelled to tolerate any degrading behavior. The second you feel uncomfortable, speak up. Inform the harasser that his or her actions are unacceptable. Be direct, and make it perfectly clear that the behavior is offensive to you.

In her book *Back Off!: How to Confront and Stop Sexual Harassment and Harassers*, Martha Langelan suggests naming the specific behavior as soon as it happens. "You just made an obscene comment while placing your hand on my hip. It is 4:15 on Monday afternoon." This will not be expected, and it will show the culprit that you will not tolerate the behavior.

If this direct approach feels uncomfortable to you, Langelan suggests writing a letter to the harasser. Make sure you are specific about the time and place of the incident and the emotions you felt at the time. Send the letter by certified mail and keep a copy for yourself in a safe place.

It's important to know that quite often the culprit doesn't realize that they are making the victim feel uncomfortable. As stated in the article, "Fighting Against the Sexual Harassment of Interns," the author notes, "In the majority of cases, the confronted persons have expressed surprise and immediately changed their behavior." In this case, you still have the right to take legal action, but by communicating your feelings, you may put a quick end to the situation.

Charges of sexual harassment may be filed at any field office of the U.S. Equal Employment Opportunity Commission (EEOC). After filing a charge, the EEOC will undertake an investigation. It is important to note that charges must be filed with the EEOC within 180 days of the alleged discriminatory act. For more information on the EEOC's procedures for sexual harassment charges, visit their Web site at http://www.eeoc.gov/fact/howtofil.html.

Seek Advice

Whichever course of action you decide to take—legal or otherwise—it's important that you seek the appropriate advice. If you are unclear as to whether the offense you suffered is considered sexual harassment, consider talking to someone you trust, like a friend or a mentor, before you do anything. You don't want to make a public accusation until you're sure the behavior was legally improper.

Once you have determined the nature of the offense, however, you should not ignore it for fear of being blacklisted in the industry or losing your internship. Although it could be uncomfortable for a short while, you are bound to encounter others in the industry who have endured your plight. A recent EEOC report shows that sexual harassment complaints within the motion picture, television, and radio industries have jumped 300 percent from 1991 to 1996. This does not necessarily imply that sexual harassment is on the rise, but rather that it is being tolerated less and less within these industries.

The following are some resources available to you if you should find yourself in such a situation:

American Psychological Association
Office of Public Affairs
750 First Street, NE
Washington, DC 20002-4242
202-336-5700

National Organization for Women
1000 16th Street, NW, #700
Washington, DC 20036
202-331-0066
http://www.now.org/issues/wfw/

Women Against Sexual Harassment
102 Plymouth Park S/C, Box 181
Irving, TX 75061
http://www.pic.net/w-a-s-h

A list of state agencies that deal with sexual harassment on the job can be found at http://www.feminist.org/911/harass.html

National hotlines available to you are as follows:

- 9 to 5: National Association of Working Women 800-522-0925
- Feminist Majority Foundation—Sexual Harassment Hotline 703-533-2501
- National Job Problem Hotline 800-522-0925
- National Victim Center 703-276-5180
- National Women's Law Center 202-588-5180

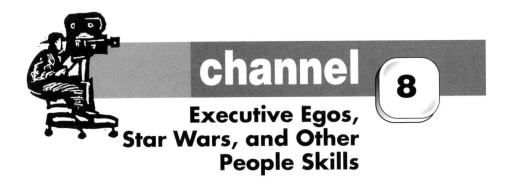

channel 8

Executive Egos, Star Wars, and Other People Skills

Imagine yourself in an idea meeting with the rest of your production staff. The executive producer, frustrated that the staff isn't getting his message, picks up a TV set and hurls it out the window. Welcome to the world of TV, land of large egos and quick tempers. In this channel, we'll look at how to handle explosive personalities, from the hyper executive and neurotic newsman to the dressing room diva.

THREE . . .

"People will try to belittle you by treating you like . . . well, like an intern. Remember, this may sound cliché, but they do it because they're insecure; they feel threatened. The ONLY way you can win is by maintaining a good attitude and doing your job. If you fight them, you'll lose. If it gets unbearable, quit. It's only a job."

—Jim Casey, Producer and President, Painless Productions; a former NBC page; and a former intern

TWO . . .

"I ended up being the driver for a particular on-air personality—driver, assistant, shopper, and confidant. One specific memory will always be etched in my brain. This host has low blood sugar and needs to have frequent nourishing snacks available during tapings. I can still feel the pain of kneeling behind the couch on the set with shredded turkey and nuts at the ready. She is also a Diet Coke fan, but after twenty or so soft drinks, she would be bouncing off the walls. I was asked by the producers to pour decaffeinated Diet Coke into regular Diet Coke bottles so she would not notice. She did."

—Jim Caruso, Talent Assistant, *Fox After Breakfast*, and Talent Liaison, *Jim J and Tammy Faye*

ONE . . .

"Executives basically act as if they need babysitters: they're immature, they lack basic coping skills, and they love to divert blame away from themselves. Granted, not all executives are like this . . . some are worse."

—Randy Polcar, LA talent agent

AND ACTION!

ATTITUDES, ATTITUDES, EVERYWHERE

You might be saying, "This attitude thing is no problem. I can handle all this, let me at 'em." If you approach it this way, great. But keep in mind, in TV land your attitude is something you can control; what you can't control, is other people's attitudes. Brace yourself for a hurricane.

"What I notice a lot as I look back at my many internships was that everyone wants proper credit for something he or she has done. In entertainment, where jobs are tough to land and you're only secure as long as your ratings are up there, there is much more interoffice competition. I learned this fast and have tried to never take things too personally in my jobs since college. Egos are BIG in this industry, and you've got to be able to work with them. Knowing this helps keep your own ego in line."

—Timothy P. Cavanaugh, LA talent agent and a former intern

Every TV person loves to tell his horror stories about various talent and bosses. Many have heard about the executive who was barred from control rooms because of his screaming matches. One day, he actually had a heart attack while arguing with the director over a shot. He had yet ANOTHER heart attack in a pitch meeting. This exec's employees were said to be singing, "Ding dong, the witch is dead," as he lay beside the copy machine grasping his heart. He survived that one and continues to thrive in TV to this day. This is a true story.

Does everyone in TV have such an attitude? No. Some people in TV are thrilled to have a job that they love and are a pleasure to work with. You just have to be prepared for any kind of ego and eccentricity. Here's a situation, based on a true story, that illustrates how things can go wrong:

On this particular day, Ron had scheduled a lunch for Helen at an Italian restaurant on Pico Boulevard. He had called the restaurant, obtained the address and cross-streets, and gave the information to Helen before she left. I returned from my lunch break around 1:10 to find Ron on the phone, wide-eyed and quivering. He looked at me and asked me where the restaurant is. He handed me the phone as I walked over. It was Helen.

Randy

This is Randy.

Helen

WHERE THE @#*!& IS IT? I want to know where this place is *right now*. Do you understand?

Randy

Okay, I'll call and get directions; hang on. (I put her on hold, quickly called the place, and got the directions, which were exactly the same as the ones Ron gave her.) Helen, it's on Pico between Beverly and . . .

Helen

I'm at Pico and Roxbury and it's NOT HERE! I'm gonna KILL RON!

Randy

Okay Helen, which direction are you going on Pico, east or west?

Helen

I don't know; he BETTER NOT BE THERE WHEN I GET BACK. DO YOU UNDERSTAND?

Randy

Okay . . .

Helen

I can't BELIEVE he screwed this up! Unbelievable, this is UNBELIEVABLE!

Randy

Okay, I have the Thomas Guide; tell me what the next cross . . .

Helen

Is this it?

Randy
```
Did you find it? Hello?
```

"I figure out that she's hung up her cell phone. In the aftermath, I figured out that she had made a wrong turn (which was, admittedly, easy to make), so when she made the next turn, she was going the wrong way. In the final analysis, Ron had gotten the correct address and directions but suffered dire consequences in her eyes anyway. The lesson to be learned here is that even though you may have done things correctly, you may get blamed for things going wrong—it's important to remain calm and focus on solutions to problems rather than causes, even if it's obvious to you that the direction of blame is unjust. By the way, Ron was let go about two weeks later (though not solely due to this incident)."

—Randy Polcar, LA talent agent

The first thing to realize is that people will have different attitudes toward interns. Some executives and talent see interns as saviors and want to make their lives as great as possible. Chances are, the caring executives have had an internship and know how hard it can be. Then, there is the other side. Some employees feel it's their personal mission to make the intern's life a living hell. Maybe they were never interns; maybe they feel that they had it hard, now you have to have it even harder. Even though those types will make you feel like you're pledging a fraternity or sorority, you still want to keep both camps happy. Some of the worst people are the ones who actually respect the interns the most. You never know.

One intern encountered a boss who asked for a soda at a city counsel meeting and then dropped the change on the floor. The intern, refusing to crawl around the floor looking for change, pulled change out of her own pocket and went to do the task. Years later, this boss told her that he was just testing her and that she passed with flying colors. She went from being an intern to an executive news producer in three years.

Expect a wide range of moods daily. Many executives set the tone of the day by the previous day's ratings. The nicest employee yesterday may be the meanest one today. Since you can't control the moods of your boss, the best you can do is try to take nothing personally and be prepared for anything so that nothing can take you by surprise.

What If an Employee Blows Up at You?

Once again, never take it personally. Look at this predicament as yet another opportunity to show off your greatness. While the employee is yelling at you, take it. Whether you are right or wrong, let them vent. Sure, it'll feel great to tell this staffer off, but what would be the benefits of such an action? You may know that everyone in that room feels exactly the same way as you and that now it is David's chance to stand up to Goliath. Don't. You will find yourself in many political potholes over the years. Maneuver around them carefully. You'll get much more sympathy and respect by taking the abuse.

More likely than not, you'll earn respect by not biting the producer's head off. The employee who blew up at you will probably track you down later to apologize. Accept the apology and try to have a quiet discussion about what provoked it. Move on. If the person doesn't approach you, go to them. How? As diplomatically as possible.

Visit the employee when he is alone. Ask him if he has a few minutes and say, "I'm sorry, I must have done something wrong earlier. Tara asked me to ask you a question, I did, and you yelled at me. I must have done something unknowingly wrong. Can you please tell me what it is so that I don't do it again. I really respect you and want to have a good working relationship with you." The employee will probably realize that you did nothing wrong and will apologize and respect you for your approach. Is this guaranteed? No. But getting into a screaming match with anyone is guaranteed to make you look bad.

What If a Particular Person Is After You?

Some people hate their lives and think that they'll feel better by making your life miserable. Chances are, your fellow employees already know how miserable this person is. This will be a tie that binds you.

"Every morning, a certain executive would come in and say, 'Everybody in my office, and YOU get me coffee and orange juice.' So he would single me out and make me go down to the truck and get him coffee and juice everyday. I would bring it to him and have to knock on the door. It was humiliating to walk into a room full of executives. Every day I went in, he would scream that this wasn't right and that he wanted it a different way. I'd have to go back every single day; it became sort of a ritual. This wasn't something they taught me about at Harvard. But having that experience was extremely humbling, and in retrospect somewhat unnecessary, but I think everyone has a story like that."

—Brian Graden, Executive Vice President, MTV; Developer, *South Park;* and a former intern

Again, the first thing to do is approach that person when he is alone. Ask him if you've done something wrong. Give specific examples of when you felt you were not treated fairly. It's possible that the person is totally unaware of how he has been treating you. In this case, he will apologize and respect you for your approach. On the same note, maybe the person won't care. If this is the case, accept it.

One intern was having a terrible time with his boss. He went and confided to another producer about the problems he was having. It turns out that this producer was in a relationship with the boss and the situation became volatile. The intern ended up leaving. Be very careful with whom you share personal information. There are many land mines in TV land.

Don't be too emotional and try not to get upset. Just inform your supervisor of the situation and ask her if she has any advice on how to handle it. At the very least, your supervisor will respect your maturity.

What If You See Two Producers Arguing?

If two producers are going at it, you stay out of it. Don't take a side, and don't join in. If there are any non–staff members in the room, such as guests or contestants, you want to escort them out of the room. If it seems overly heated, you may want to find your supervisor or another executive. Let her intervene. This is not the time for you to be a hero.

Dealing With the Dressing Room Divas

If you think dealing with executives might be bad, just wait until you have to deal with some of the talent.

FLASH BACK

"I was hired to produce the first Fox *Late Show* after Joan Rivers was fired from it. The woman who cohosted was a well-known songwriter with great celebrity connections. She was also a nightmare. She demanded all kinds of extras, including a back-up baby grand piano for her then-husband (he was performing and might not like the way the other was tuned, even though we also had a tuner on standby) and an entire crew to fly to a British island to record a celebrity greeting to her. She also decided that she wanted someone to serve drinks to her and her guests on the show. She felt that since all of these people were her friends and were served when at her home, it would be fun to have them get drinks on her show. The final straw was a phone call at 1 a.m. the night before the taping. She asked me if she could change the

waitress to a waiter for this 30-second walk on. I sarcastically told her, 'Why don't I get you both, so you can go with whatever feels right at that moment.' Happy, she hung up. There was no end to her narcissism."
    —Dan

But if you can just be yourself and don't try too hard, you will probably strike a nice professional relationship.

> *"As part of my intern duties, I had to write the cue cards for a local talk show in Detroit. Each morning before the show started, the two interns rotated days in which each had to take the cards into the dressing room of the show's cohost. This was necessary because she needed to be familiar with the copy and able to read the writing. The first time I had to do it, I was a nervous wreck. Having never worked with a celeb before, I was a bit intimidated and afraid I'd drop the cards or that she wouldn't be able to read my writing. There is a certain skill required when flipping cue cards. You've got to bring the card down as the host reads and make a very smooth transition to the next one, never interrupting the flow. That day, I couldn't do it fast enough. I started shaking, thinking she'd have me fired, but she did something I never expected. She began laughing at how personally I was taking it. She told me to relax, to take my time, and at that moment, she went from a TV star to a human being in my eyes. That was really a humbling experience."*
> —Timothy P. Cavanaugh, LA Talent Agent and a former intern

Just as with executives, some celebrities are thrilled that they have been successful and are the nicest people in the world. Others can be an intern's worst nightmare. Handle with care. Do your best to avoid showing your nerves around talent. Be cautious; being anxious will just hinder your performance. Falling apart in front of Tom Cruise is not good for your image. Look at the talent as a regular person who happens to be on television.

> *"We don't necessarily want someone to step through our doors with an awe-struck grin from ear to ear as they rub elbows with Ridge or Taylor or whomever his or her favorite soap star happens to be. We once hired a fan for a short-term entry-level position to get us through a busy period . . . big mistake; she couldn't get over talking to her idols, and everyone in the office became unnerved by her supercilious smile, which was always accompanied by incisive, probing questions like,*

'What's so and so really like?' When you land that internship or entry-level position, be cordial and professional and leave the autograph book at home!"

—John C. Zak, Supervising Producer, *The Bold and the Beautiful*, and a former intern

The first rule is: Don't ask for an autograph. The celebrity is there to perform, whether it's an anchor for the news or Jim Carrey doing an interview with Leno. Everyone on the staff may want an autograph, but the talent is not there to be bombarded. Definitely stay clear of the talent before a performance, unless you are told to take care of them. It's disturbing to the talent if in 10 minutes, ten interns ask them if they want coffee. Many shows have strict policies about interacting with celebrities; follow these policies religiously.

"Do not speak unless spoken to! Further, even though you may be the greatest fan of a celebrity, stay as far away from the celebrity and his publicist as possible, unless you have reason to be in his area. Clear any interaction with a celebrity with the talent department or the production individual responsible for the celebrity. The intern should never be the cause of any problems with a celebrity."

—Carole Chouinard, Segment Producer, *Politically Incorrect*, and Intern Coordinator, *Arsenio*

When working with celebrities, keep in mind that some will give attitude. They usually have grueling schedules, and sometimes, the first thing to go is patience. Take the abuse and turn the situation to your advantage. After dealing with the celebrity in the most mature way possible, let your boss know about the situation. He knows how temperamental some celebrities can be, and he will be impressed when you tell him how well you kept your cool.

Don't be surprised if you get some weird requests. Never question a guest's needs. If asked for lemon juice, it's not your place to ask why. Just put on a smile and put on your walking shoes. What if you spot a star doing something illegal? What if you see her doing something that could hamper her performance? Stay calm, but inform your boss. These problems are more common than you might think. Producers regularly have to contend with guests showing up in a bad state.

Having warned you about all the TV egos, your internship will give you some star stories that you will share with people for a lifetime. Here are some positive memories from our TV Intern Hall of Fame.

"At the end of my Primetime Live *run, Diane Saywer offered to take all the interns out for drinks. I couldn't believe it! Drinks with Diane Saywer!*

After all of us picked our jaws up off the floor, we headed for a city bar. None of us even thought about drinking; we were too busy hanging on Diane Saywer's every word. I couldn't believe it. Two nonstop hours of incredible stories about the places she's been and the people she's interviewed. I couldn't believe it. She was the nicest person in the world."

—Greg Kestin, former intern, *Primetime Live*

"Lamb Chop showed up for a pledge drive. It was too exciting!"

—Jill Mullikin-Bates, Supervising Producer, *Leeza*, and a former intern

"I will never forget Carol Burnett. I said, 'Hello, Miss Burnett. I've always enjoyed your work.' She was very sweet. She asked my name and where I was from. I will never forget that."

—Jack Forestell, Emmy award–winning Art Director, *The Bold and the Beautiful*, and a former TV Academy intern

"I've met plenty of celebrities, but the best are those who talk with me, not to me. The difference is that someone who talks with you finds you of interest, usually signaled by them asking you questions. The first encounter I had in this manner was when I met Frank Oz. Mr. Oz was handling the Muppet, Miss Piggy, on the Rosie O'Donnell Show. Surprisingly, not many staff members were aware of how monumental Mr. Oz has been in the industry. Let's face it, this guy started out with Jim Henson; that's colossal in itself, not to mention the countless movies he has acted in and directed. He has helped us to cherish youth and brought forth laughter in our hearts countless times. He is more than just a puppeteer, as a few of the ignorant staff members thought, I'm ashamed to say. When I introduced myself to him, he immediately shook my hand. 'To think I've just shaken the hand of the great Jedi master, Yoda,' I said with glee. He laughed. Before I could tell him about how much I admired his work, he started asking me questions, like what was my job as an intern, was I liking it, what do I plan to do in the future, etc. A passerby might have thought that I was the celebrity by the way he was questioning me. Mr. Oz showed me more respect than an intern could ever ask, and so, I'm once again indebted to him."

—Jeff Reingold, former intern, *The Rosie O'Donnell Show*

Handling Relationships with the Staff

A TV internship is as much about forming relationships as it is about learning the tricks of the trade. Make sure you don't make blunders that could cost you dearly.

Hanging Out with Producers

If you keep the smile and have the right attitude, you'll unquestionably be asked out when the staff decides to hit the town. Even if you are exhausted, you should try to go out. This is a great opportunity to learn more about the industry. Just make sure you act professionally and don't become too informal in the presence of your supervisors. You want them to respect you the next day at work.

Interoffice Dating

Some interns have found meaningful relationships through their internships; some have even found their spouses. Even so, most professionals think intern dating is just too much of a hotbed.

> *"Don't do it. Geraldo and I didn't become involved until years after my internship."*
>
> —CC Dyer, former *20/20* producer, *Geraldo* producer (and his wife)

> *"Interoffice dating is a huge no-no. It leads to conflicts of interest, potential liability for sexual harassment, wasted time, and potential discomfort when the romance breaks up. If the company is big enough, perhaps dating between divisions is okay, provided there is minimal contact between the departments. I have seen many instances of interoffice dating gone awry. Everyone always thinks his/her case will be different. It never is."*
>
> —Dan Watanabe, Director of Development, All American TV

When working in TV, you will become close to your office mates. It's almost like doing a high school play; there is a bonding that occurs. The chaotic environment . . . the long hours . . . it's a given that you'll be drawn to those with whom you have a lot in common. It's very possible you'll get a crush on someone; don't act on it. If it's true love, it will wait. Enough said.

Friendships with Your Boss

If you handle yourself well, it's unquestionable that a friendship with your boss will form. These kinships can be a great asset. You can have a great friend and a great cheerleader, but be careful about crossing that intern line.

F L A S H B A C K

"I worked about a 3-minute walk from the coffee machine. Every morning, Dan would walk in, and we'd go on our coffee walk. We'd talk about our lives, our thoughts, basically whatever was on our minds that wasn't work related. It was our personal time. Those coffee walks were short, but they were the most relaxing and enjoyable part of the day."
　　—Jason

Be sensitive when asking your boss for a work-related favor, too. You could set yourself back very far in the relationship if it is not approached in the right way.

> "Do not hand a producer a spec script to read—especially one written for the show you're working on—after two weeks on the job. He or she does not want to read it. Establish a professional and friendly relationship; then MAYBE ask the producer what his or her policy is on reading material from people working on the show. Some producers will not read material from outside writers during a production season but will read it during hiatus. Also, realize that it is very hard to be seen or appreciated as the writer you want to be and the actual P.A. you are in the minds of any of the above-the-line people you're working with on the show."
> 　　—Jeffrey Duteil, Executive Producer, *The Steve Harvey Show*, and Emmy-nominated Writer, *The Golden Girls*

Being friends with a producer doesn't mean that you should work less for her. Try twice as hard! It would be very uncomfortable for your friend to have to tell you that you're not doing a good job. Never let this happen. Double your work efforts. Also, be aware that friendships can get in the way like dating can.

> "I was the perfect intern, except I did become too good of a friend with one reporter. When we went out on stories together, we often chatted too much about personal things. This got annoying to the photographers working with us."
> 　　—George Severson, LA News Producer and a former intern

It may be tempting to let everyone know that you hung out with the boss last night, but don't. Personal lives and professional lives must be kept separate.

You want your new friend to feel comfortable with you. If he knows whatever he does will be broadcast to the office like a bad sitcom, your friendship will probably be canceled.

The goal is to be a great intern now. Plant the seeds now for some special relationships that will grow stronger after your internship is over.

> *"Throughout an internship, you should work to make personal relationships with the people who work in the company, from assistants to VPs. Make sure they know you, know your name, and know that you are smart, dependable, and a hard worker. Then, keep up those relationships when you return to school. Send notes, letting them know the project you've been doing, trips you've taken. Stop by and visit if you can, and let them know when you'll be graduating and that you're interested in a full-time position after college. Nurturing this relationship is an ongoing process."*
>
> —Michael Seligman, Associate Producer, E! Entertainment Television, and a former intern

Mentors

The most important aspect of your internship may very well be whether or not you find a mentor. This special person will take you under his or her wing and show you everything there is to know about the business. There is no selection process for gaining a mentor; it is something that happens naturally between a mentor and protégé.

FLASHBACK

> *"My life has really been shaped by the many mentors who have taken me in as a protégé, as a helper, and as a friend. In high school, Bob Gresh and Bob Herbert taught me that if I always did what I loved, everything else would be okay. In college, Loomis Irish taught me all I needed to know about the business. George Rodman, one of my closest friends today, taught me the importance of having fun with whatever I'm doing. 'Jason, you're going on a journey called life. Stop being so anxious and enjoy the ride.' Then, there was Dan Weaver. Dan taught me that you can make it in this world and still be a good person."*
>
> —Jason

> *"Finding a mentor is a blessing. Call alumni from your college; you immediately have something in common. If you're reading your local*

paper and discover that someone who went to your high school is now in TV, track them down. They will be flattered. It's so rare that somebody takes the trouble to find out who you are and where you are from. When a person graduates from college, you often lose ties. That college has four years of memories in your heart, and to help someone from your school is a real honor."

> —Adora English, Producer, *KTLA Morning News* in LA, and a former intern

"Mentoring is something that should happen naturally. I would feel uncomfortable if someone approached me, asking me about it."

> —Patrick Jarvis, Development Executive, Tribune Entertainment, and a former intern

"I guess I had many mentors. Jane Temple was the executive producer of the Morning and Afternoon Exchange *programs, two highly rated local shows. The thing that I will never forget is her faith in me. She never treated me 'like an intern,' she never talked down to me, and she encouraged me to take on jobs I was not sure I was ready for. She also has a great sense of humor, something that is extremely important in this business. I have remained friends with her, and my daughter's middle name is Jane, in her honor. She has had a profound effect on my life."*

> —Joel Rizor, Executive-in-Charge of Production, Weller/Grossman Productions, and a former intern

Your mentor will not only be your best friend but your agent as well. She is your friend and cares about your well being, giving you advice on jobs, salaries, and life. She will be the one you go to dozens of times to say you're not cut out for TV. She is also the first one you'll seek out when you've booked your first guest and written your first copy. She will be your honest answer to the question, "What are my strengths and weaknesses?"

"Recently, I returned to a former station and met a former intern who now works there. He had been my intern fifteen years earlier. We greeted each other warmly and chatted . He said, 'Carol, you gave me the advice that turned me around and got me on the right path. Without your advice, I never would be where I am today.' Naturally I was extraordinarily curious . . . what could I have possibly said that was so significant? I asked, and he replied, 'You told me to close my mouth and start breathing through my nose, that breathing through my mouth made me look stupid.' I actually remember telling this intern this. It sounds awful . . . but I was nice, and he needed to know the impression

he was making on others. He took what I said to heart and changed his behavior. I guess the moral of the story is: You never know what will make a difference in the lives of others."

—Carol Story, Producer, *CBS This Morning*

Savor this relationship, but be careful not to exploit it.

"One of the drawbacks of having a mentor is being resented by other employees who don't enjoy as close a relationship with their mentors. Try not to refer to him/her as a mentor, and avoid looking as if you are joined at the hip or being too chummy in the workplace."

—Ed Boyd, Producer/Writer, E! Entertainment Television

Here's what one internship *Hall of Famer* remembers about her mentors:

"Everyone you meet along the road can and will be a mentor to you. Life is a classroom full of teachers and students who can be both in the same moment. My life is blessed. I haven't had mentors as much as I have had cheerleaders. People who, at times, held a belief in me that transcended my own. People like my friend Tisi Aylward, who is a shining example of goodness, love, and loyalty and who has always been there for me. There have been people in my life who could be considered mentors. They have been willing to get swept up in my passion, stand by me, and take risks with me. Among these mentors, I would count Joe Sutton, who hired me three weeks into an internship; Richard S. Kline, who gave me my first job in production; Marlaine Selip and Dan Weaver, who embraced me and my talents and whose greatest gifts as leaders are in stoking the creative fires of everyone with whom they come in contact; Marta Tracy, who helped me develop as a manager at E! Entertainment TV; and, of course, Linda Bell Blue, whose role as mentor, friend, and inspiration will proudly affect my life forever."

—Brad Bessey, Coordinating Producer, *Entertainment Tonight,* and a former intern

Hopefully this channel has impressed upon you the importance of managing relationships—whether they be difficult ones or relationships that you will carry with you through your career in the television business. You will encounter poor treatment of others in the high-stress television arena, but chances are, you will be fortunate enough to find a champion of your effort, a mentor for life.

```
AND CUT!
CUE ANNOUNCER TEASE:
```

"And still to come: A do-it-yourself internship timetable;
how to never be forgotten and how to turn your boss
into a personal job recruiter."

```
FADE TO BLACK
ROLL "TV INTERN HALL OF FAME" PACKAGE
```
···

Adora English
Producer, *KTLA Morning News,* and a former intern

My mother was the one who taught me that you can accomplish your dreams, no matter how big they are. Naively, I believed every word she said. What she left out was that there would be obstacles put in my way, such as lack of money, a divorce, three colleges in four years, and what seemed like endless student loans. All I had going for me were my ambition and my dreams.

Growing up, I watched Johnny Carson on *The Tonight Show, Entertainment Tonight,* and every sitcom under the sun while thinking what a great time these people were having on TV. I wanted to be part of that. I wasn't sure what "that" entailed then, but I knew those were the people I wanted to emulate. Instead of watching the Oscars and Emmy awards on TV, I wanted to be there. How could I make the jump from suburban Philadelphia to "beautiful downtown Burbank" where Johnny was? I had no idea, but the seed had been planted.

In high school, we had a very small communication program that allowed students to get in front of or behind the camera to be part of the school's news broadcast. I learned everything about doing news, sports play-by-play, the cameras, switchers, tapes, and writing I could from our teachers, whom themselves had never worked in a TV environment. When it came to choosing a college, I wanted to go to one with the best communication program. I applied, was accepted, and felt I was on my way to Hollywood. Then I got the bill, worked three jobs while taking 18 credits, and ended up transferring to a much less expensive school after only one year. This school had a very good communication program but still turned out to be too expensive for my budget. I ended up graduating from a small state school, but I was proud to finally have a degree in communication. I wouldn't let a thing like money stand in the way of my dream.

It was from this small school that I received the best education ever. The professors stressed the importance of internships, telling us that students "would learn only 40 percent of what we truly needed to know inside the lecture halls, the other 60 percent from actually doing it." No truer words have ever been spoken. I had three internships during my years at that school and could not have begun my career in TV without them.

As an intern at a local TV station, I remember feeling that I was the last person in the world anyone wanted to talk to. But I knew I had nothing to lose and everything to gain from these people. They were the key to getting that all-important first job! After the usual filing, running for lunch, and making endless pots of coffee, I had gained the attention of a few key station members. In my mind, all I needed was someone on the inside to give me the lowdown on the station workings. That was my first goal. It turned out to be the station engineer, Bob, who had been working at this small waterfront station for thirty years, who gave me the information that I needed. Once in his graces, I soaked up everything. One opportunity I remember was a camera person calling in sick and Bob recommending that I fill in for him. What? Me? I agreed but knew nothing about how to do it. They taught me, I did it, and then went home smiling from ear to ear.

One of the best things about being an intern was being a fly on the wall. Once people were used to seeing your face, they did not care what they said in front of you. They told stories and trashed people, the company, the business—anything to get attention. I realized that everyone in this industry has an ego and a story to tell. Each was eager to take 5 minutes to tell me about their struggle to get where they were in the industry. Their stories helped tremendously in narrowing down what aspect of TV I wanted to get into. Once inside these walls, I had the chance to explore every aspect of TV without risking anything. I worked cameras, worked in sales, programming, in the executive offices, and my favorite turned out to be on the creative side with the producers. It took my going through all three internships to narrow my goal down to becoming a producer.

When I graduated with a communication degree, I saw the world as my oyster. So I headed for Hollywood! I figured that, if I could find a job within a month, I could stay. If not, I would head back home again. I was on a mission. I called every alumnus from college who was working in TV and stumbled upon the man who I consider responsible for my career. He worked at a national daytime talk show and called me to see if I wanted to interview for the position. I was there within an hour, and I started the next day. Talk about being in the right place at the right time.

I was lucky enough to work with wonderful people who taught me more than they will ever know. I was given opportunities to prove myself above and beyond the call of duty everyday. My second week on the job, I was standing backstage in the same buffet line as Bob Hope. I asked the woman next to me if she would pinch me to make sure it was real!

I have now been in the business for more than ten years and have been a producer on all kinds of national news, daytime, and late-night television shows. I've been to the Oscars, been nominated for an Emmy, met and worked with some of the biggest stars in film and television, and had my career written about in magazines.

If I left the world of TV tomorrow, I'd say it was worth every bit of sweat, humiliation, and show cancellation I have been through. I look at each intern and envy his/her ambition and determination. Some of them take their internships for granted. If one day they ask about my internships, I'll tell them it was the most important and exciting time of my career. Because when you are sitting at the Emmy awards years from now, it will never be as new and fresh as it is today. Soak up every opportunity thrown your way. Never take any experience for granted. You never know who you'll meet at the copy machine.

channel 9

Scripting Your Internship Timeline

Like every great television special, your internship needs a well-thought-out rundown. In this channel, we'll help you map out a timeline as you begin your countdown toward *actual employment* in the business. This needs to be as choreographed as a Michael Jackson routine. Put on your dancing shoes.

THREE . . .

"If an intern shows promise, usually executives will go out of their way to help. Nothing feels better than taking the next Steven Spielberg under your wing. Those of us who have been in the business more than 5 minutes know that we could be handing the intern our resume in a few years, the way the industry works these days."

— Kac Young, Vice President, Television Production and Development, Universal Studios Hollywood, and a former intern

TWO . . .

"How can an intern do better? I usually offer this: producers are, by their nature, obsessive, detail-oriented people. We assume nobody will handle the details the way we will, so, if left unchecked, we'll pretty much just do everything. It's pathetic, really. After the third 70-hour week in a row, we wonder why we're exhausted. I need people who will actively intervene on my intensity, someone who'll help take care of the boss. And I doubt I'm alone—these shows are our babies. So the interns I've valued the most are the ones who value the boss the most!"

— Jimmy Rhodes, Producer, PBS Detroit

ONE . . .

"One of the things our interns generally do is interview members of the staff and ask about what is involved with his or her job. Many interns do this, but I am surprised by the number who don't bother. Everyone in this

town has a different story, a different path to their current position, and all these people can provide clues as to how the great TV nut can be cracked."

—John C. Zak, Supervising Producer, *The Bold and the Beautiful*, and a former intern

AND ACTION!

THE FIRST-QUARTER ASSESSMENT

If you want to have a job at graduation, you must plan ahead. There's a right time and a wrong time to begin the job search, to ask for help, and to abandon ship.

FLASHBACK

"It had been two weeks since I started, and although all signs indicated that I was doing a great job, I was spending most of my savings, working 20 hours a day, and I had already graduated, so if I was mistaken about my performance, I would have been in big trouble. After a few days of trying to figure out what my boss was thinking, I came up with an ingenious idea: ask!"

—Jason

"I was surprised when Jason asked for a meeting after his first two weeks of work. Plus, why did he want to meet outside the office? Was he going to hit me up for a job? He had done such a nice job, I felt like I owed him this. At the same time, I was leery about his motivations and concerned about my time. However, looking back, I'm glad that we had this talk. I will never forget that look of sincerity in his eyes as we sat outside. No intern had ever gone to the trouble to make an appointment just to find out what he could be doing better. I looked at Jason differently from that day forward. He hooked me; if ever there was anyone who deserved to work in TV, it was he."

—Dan

As the end of your first internship quarter comes near, it's time to ask your boss for a vital meeting. This meeting will be crucial, one-on-one time with your supervisor. In addition to opening an opportunity for your boss to see how you handle direction and criticism, it is the ultimate "show and tell" of how seriously you are taking this internship. It's so easy for an intern to get lost in the crossfire of everyday work, pressures, and deadlines; this meeting can be the most important 15 minutes of your internship thus far.

How Do You Request the Meeting?

Since most interns don't ask for such meetings, your boss may be taken back a bit by your request. Simply tell your boss you would love 15 minutes to discuss how you're doing as an intern. The boss may just say, "You're doing fine," but don't accept that; assure him that it will only take a few minutes and that it would really mean a lot to you. Don't be surprised if the meeting time has to be changed a couple of times. Be flexible, but make sure that you don't let this meeting fall through the cracks.

When Should You Meet?

You should plan out the meeting about one week before you wish to have it; schedules get booked up quite quickly. When you request the meeting, use it as an opportunity to show off your scheduling skills. "I know that you have pitch meetings all day Monday and the network meeting on Tuesdays. Wednesday afternoons seem to be your most flexible days. Could we meet next Wednesday at 2?" Even if it's your boss's idea to have the meeting during his busy time, try to subtly convince him otherwise. Your boss may say that he will be able to give you his undivided attention, but more than likely, this won't happen. You want to talk to him on a day when he is less stressed and the most approachable; timing is everything.

Where to Meet

For your half-time meeting, you will ask your supervisor to lunch, but for this first-quarter meeting, an appointment at the corner coffee shop will be just fine. Basically, you want a setting that will be somewhere close to the office so that it's as convenient for the boss as possible, but you definitely want to get out of the office. Try to make the meeting as attractive to your boss as possible; do your homework before you make the request. Does the boss have a favorite spot to relax? Does she hang out at the smoker's lounge? The main thing is to keep the meeting away from the phones and distractions of the office. Even if you just go for a walk outside, it's better than sitting in the office. Try to come up with some type of personal touch for the meeting, like suggesting an appointment over his or her favorite mochas!

Meeting Preparation

You can't rehearse this production enough. To be sure you'll turn in a great performance, you may want to rehearse with a friend before the big meeting.

Give some thought about what to wear. A good rule of thumb is to dress one step up from what you would normally wear to work. If you usually wear jeans, think about a dress shirt and slacks but not a three-piece suit.

The tone of the meeting should be friendly but official, with the driving force and subtext being, "How can I help *you* better?" Point out that you really want constructive criticism so that you can perform *better.* By giving you pointers, the boss will be helping himself, and everyone loves to do that! *Don't bring up employment!* Your boss probably weeds through stacks of resumes daily and will appreciate your NOT asking for a job. If the boss brings up the "J" word, great. Otherwise, avoid that discussion. The point of this meeting is to learn how you can be a better intern.

This is just the first of four meetings, so the better this meeting is for your boss, the more receptive he will be to your future meeting requests.

What to Say

1. *Start off thanking your boss for this time.* She is extremely busy, and even 15 minutes is a large amount of time to give. You may want to begin with a sincere compliment: "I must say I am in awe of how many balls you can juggle and still be very creative. Plus, you somehow never lose your sense of humor." If you can't think of a solid compliment, don't make one up; TV people can spot a phony a mile away.

2. *Let your boss know what your future goals are.* Even if you have discussed your future dream job before, he may have forgotten. Reminding him may put your name on the top of the list when assignments in that area arise. You may even want to subtly bring up areas you'd like to work more in: "I really love the assignment desk; since I hope to be a news director someday, is there a way that I can work with Leslie more?"

> *"Mention something to your supervisor in an upbeat way. 'I just love the internship here. It has been such a great opportunity. Do you think I could go out on the next shoot or sit in on one of the idea meetings? I think that would be such a great learning experience for me.'"*
> —Julie Johnson, Associate Producer, *The Oprah Winfrey Show*, and a former intern

3. *Ask for solid feedback and make sure you write down what is said.* Be open, not defensive. If you don't take criticism well, it reflects poorly on you. As soon as you can, make sure that you implement the suggestions. Nothing is more complimentary to your boss than seeing you put his advice into action.

What If You Think the Internship Is Not Working Out?

If you have frustrations, don't be afraid to bring them up; just make sure they're not selfish ones. "I don't like making coffee," would not be a great opener. It's too soon to entertain leaving an internship; you haven't been there long enough to make a good assessment. Be careful when bringing up your unhappiness; you don't want to be pegged a whiner—or worse—a quitter.

> *"I think a good internship is composed of 65 percent real work that teaches and rewards interns and 35 percent menial tasks that are essential to the production or office. If you feel as if you are not getting anything substantial out of your internship, talk to your supervisor. Be prepared to give her some ideas of what you are interested in experiencing or working on, and let her know if you feel you have specific skills that may be helpful."*
>
> —Jill Fox, Producer, PBS, and a former intern

If, in your initial interview, you were told you'd only spend half the time on gofer work and the other half on creative work but that is not the case, ask your supervisor if you did anything wrong. It's possible that all interns spend the first few weeks with excessive gofer work. Keep it positive but honest. Make sure you are perceived as wanting to be more effective for the team, not as a complainer.

How to End the Meeting

Thank your boss once again for his time. Assure him that you will work on areas that you have discussed. Remind him again that you want to make yourself a better intern to make his life easier. Follow up the next day with a thank-you note and something personal that happened in the meeting. ("I was thrilled to hear you'd like me to try writing a promo. Thanks for your honest comments about my phone skills. I will work to slow down my delivery.") The most important thing is to leave your boss with the sense that this was productive for him. You are going to ask for three more of these meetings. Don't make him feel that this one was a wash and that he should have been planning that live report on the latest conspiracy theory instead.

Contact All Contacts Yet Again

It is important to stay in touch with the contacts who helped you get your internship gig. Now that your first big meeting is under your belt, drop them a line. Tell them about your intern highlights and keep them feeling a part of the process. Keep up with them like you would keep up with your favorite character from *All My Children*. You'll be hitting them up for a job soon!

Learning While Interning

By the time you have had your first meeting with your supervisor, you should be on pretty solid terms with at least some of the staff members. In Channel 1, you researched the duties and the lifestyle of your dream career; now it's time to take advantage of a golden opportunity to explore your career from the inside out.

Throughout the second, third, and fourth quarters you should try to set up as many minimeetings as possible. These meetings are similar to the one with the supervisor but are on a smaller scale. Starting with the production assistants (or whoever is on the lowest rung), ask one of your new friends if you can have a short meeting to find out about his or her career path. Most people love to talk about their career but are seldom asked. It's best to pick a time to meet for coffee; the morning is usually best, since lunch meetings get postponed due to the craziness of the TV existence.

To prepare for your chat, go back to your old research files about your dream career and review. When you meet with the staffer, try to confirm your research and get as much new information as possible. What does he think about the job? What does he know about the stability of the field? If he had to do it again, would he get into the same area? Tell him about your goals and ask for advice. You'll get good insight, and it's a great way to begin your network of contacts.

While you should use this time to get to know the staffer on a personal level, don't forget that you're still on camera; all the rules from the previous channels apply. Don't put people down and don't gossip, and try to show off your knowledge whenever possible. Try to find a couple of things that you have in common, and bond as much as you can. If you find out you both love to write poetry, you'll have something you can bring up whenever the time is right. This will also allow the staffer to see you as a person and not just as an intern.

After you have your first minimeeting, evaluate what went well and what didn't; then, set up a meeting with another member of the office pool. After you meet with a couple of people from the bottom of the office chain, slowly move up the line. Pace yourself so that, at the end of the internship, you'll be meeting with the big-wigs. Use the knowledge from each meeting in the next. "When I spoke with Sara, she said that the divorce rate is high among news producers. Is that your experience as well?" "Jimmy said that if

I want to be on-air, I should never take a job as an assignment editor. Tina said otherwise; what do you think?" Ask away, but try to end the meeting around the 15-minute mark; respect their time.

As you go up the TV ladder, you'll get a great diversity of information and pointers. Try to meet with every staff member possible. Why can't you just start your minimeetings with your news director? It's important to build up your knowledge and "coffee-talk" ability; the more talks you have, the better you'll be. It's better to make a mistake with a P.A. than with the big boss.

By meeting with the staff members, you are getting a huge reservoir of research, and you are showing off your people skills, your dedication, and your desires. If you meet with a producer and let her know that you like being in the field, you'll probably get an invite to the next shoot. It is another opportunity for her to take you under her wing.

Evaluations

While it is highly advisable to make a personal progress report on a weekly basis, be certain to do one after the first quarter. A weekly progress report entails finding a quiet spot and thinking about your life. This isn't meant to be a big philosophical discussion about what is the purpose for living, but more of a chance to sit down and assess how you are doing. What are your goals? Are you working toward them? Very often, we all get so busy working that we just forget what it is we're working for. Think about how you spent your time this week. Did you put too many hours toward one goal? Have you been so anxious that you haven't allowed yourself to enjoy your internship?

All too often interns get caught in the whirlwind of their internship and never have a chance to step back and see how they're doing. Take the time. If you can't find time to hit your favorite coffee shop, do the evaluation on the way to work, during lunch, or whenever you can find a moment. Taking a short moment to focus and visualize will pay off.

IT'S HALFTIME!

When you are approaching the halfway point of your internship, it's time to set up a Barbara Walters special with your boss. This is similar to the first-quarter assessment, but this time, your agenda is a bit different. Unlike your first-quarter conversation, you have now earned the right to ask for a lunch meeting. You've been interning for a good amount of time and have probably impressed the people you work with beyond their greatest expectations. It's time for the most important meal of your career thus far, where you will be getting at least 30 to 40 minutes of undivided attention.

About a week and a half before the official halfway point, ask your boss if you can take her out to lunch. Find a nice restaurant that is close and features her favorite food. Tell her that it is your treat, although she will probably pick up the tab, given that her expense account is a bit bigger than yours.

Just like the first-quarter assessment, this meeting needs to be tightly produced. You are taking your supervisor away from a lot of responsibility; once again, you don't want her to feel as if she has wasted her time.

Your Goals

In this meeting, you want to first show your boss that you still appreciate the previous meeting and that you did follow the advice and suggestions that were given. You also want to show her how much you appreciate everything you've learned thus far about the industry.

The main goal is to begin the job talks. This is when you should let your boss know your interests and enlist her as your personal job recruiter. Of course, you always want to show off your knowledge as much as possible.

How to Start the Meeting

First, thank your boss again for the internship. Despite your lack of sleep, lack of time, and lack of money, you're darned lucky to be there. Be grateful. Assure the supervisor that you are getting something out of this. Has anyone been particularly nice? Never hurts to give an unsolicited compliment.

Second, always bring it back to, "How can I help you more?" Have a list of specifics, similar to the ones you brought up in the first quarter. Reference your last meeting. "Last time, you felt that I was weak at phone skills. Have you seen any improvement? Are there any other areas that need attention? What kind of feedback have you gotten about me? Last time, you said my organizational strengths are solid. Do still feel this way?" Make her feel that you want an honest report card and not that you're fishing for compliments. Once again, remember to log your supervisor's comments. This sends a message that you are listening and that you're once again going to put the advice into action.

Don't Say, "Can I Have a Job, Please?"

It is time to bring up the most important topic of your internship: the job search. Now is the time for this legendary conversation. Pretend for a second that you're in a bar looking for a date. Running up to an attractive someone and saying, "I want to date you!" is probably not the best way to go. You want to lead your supervisor through a discussion of job opportunities without actually begging for employment.

Be sure to spend several days reviewing your notes on your chosen career before the meeting. The more research it appears you have done on your dream job, the more seriously you'll be taken. Show off this research when bringing up your job search. "I read that in broadcast news, an average entry-level salary in a small market is $20,000, and I also know that most people move several times before settling into their ideal market, but neither of those facts deters me. I was pretty sure I loved news, and this internship has really confirmed that this is a labor of love. Many people have given me advice on what the next step for me should be, but I'd really love to know you're thoughts." Don't be afraid to let your boss know that you've met with some of the other staff members. She will be impressed that you took such initiative.

Be honest about wanting a job, but don't pester your boss for a position. "I don't want you to feel that every time I see you I'm going to ask for a job, but to be honest, I really do want to work for this company. Is there something I can be doing now to increase the chances of employment here? Should I be sending resumes out to other places? Would you be willing to help me?" Nudge, but don't hold her at gun point.

The cardinal rule is never to say, "I want a job." Putting your prospective employer on the spot is not smart. "How would you go about getting a job?" is a better approach. Lead him to help you. "If you were in my shoes what would you be doing?" Ask about some of the trends you've read about in the trades. Impress your boss with your knowledge, and let him show his smarts.

If the lunch is going well and your boss doesn't have an afternoon from hell ahead of him, order some coffee and try to get to know your boss as a person. Ask him about his first TV job. There have been studies that show that the more an interviewee talks about himself during an interview, the more positive impression they have of the interviewer. While your boss talks about breaking into the business, he will associate your struggle with his.

At your meeting, be sure to come to a clear understanding about how you should follow up on job leads and your boss's help. If he says he will make some calls for you, ask, "Should I follow up with you in a week, or would you like to come to me? The last thing I want is to become a bother."

Missile a note to him the next day, underlining how much you appreciate his knowledge and advice. This note will also work as a reminder: "I really appreciate your offer to call your friends at ABC News. I can't wait to hear what they say."

What If It Still Is Not Working Out?

The first-quarter assessment meeting was not the time to bring up large numbers of problems with your internship; now it is okay to seek action and to possibly leave the internship early if necessary.

"If an intern feels it's not working out, he should immediately express his feelings to the persons who engaged him."

—Sy Tomashoff, Emmy award–winning Production Designer, *The Bold and the Beautiful*

If you were promised something in your initial interview and talking with your supervisor has not helped, you can consider leaving. Go back to your supervisor once more and let him know that you're thinking about departing. Be very clear in your explanation as to why you're upset, but don't be defensive or offensive. Your goal is to solve a problem.

"If it is not working out, the intern should have a talk with the supervisor. It's the best thing in the world to communicate and be honest. In the student's eyes, the internship may not be working, but the supervisor may be very happy. As a supervisor, I appreciate honest and open communication. If an intern is concerned about their work and cares enough to talk about it, it brings them to a different level."

—Glenn Meehan, Managing Editor, *Entertainment Tonight*, and a former intern

Be candid in a politically correct way. Once again, you should start by saying, "Have I done something wrong?" "Well, I was told at the interview and at the meeting two weeks ago that things would change, but they haven't." Be honest about your frustrations, and tell him that you are considering leaving. Ask if he sees any other options.

Really take time to decide if leaving is your best option. It's understandable if you're angry about being lied to, but you don't want to make any decisions that you'll end up regretting. Keep in mind that, even if you were told you'd be doing creative work but all you're doing is copying scripts, you still have a great opportunity to learn. You can still learn about the industry and make some great contacts. If you truly feel your time will be wasted and you have other internship possibilities, leaving may be your best bet. Keep in mind that even if you're totally in the right, you may still make some enemies for making an early departure. Definitely talk with your school's internship supervisor before implementing any decisions. Lots of times, interns do not get the experience that they were promised, but they stick with it and end up learning more then they could have ever imagined.

What If I Now Hate News?

If you have been getting the experience that you were promised but you just don't like your selected area as much as you thought, let the supervisor know this, but stick it out. You made a promise to your boss when you accepted your internship, and as long as he has held up his end of the bargain, it's only fair that you hold up yours. Be honest with your boss about your feelings; he will respect your heart and also your professionalism. Before you swear off the industry, explain your feelings. "I like everyone here, but news isn't what I thought it would be." Your boss may have had a similar experience early in his career.

"I've supervised quite a number of interns over the years. Some have continued in the business, while others have realized that this is work for which they are just not suited. I had one intern who I knew didn't like her job but still did a great job anyway. Later, after her internship, she came to me for a recommendation. While I knew her work had probably been her best shot, it's always easier to do good work when you love what you do. I saw that she was talented and ambitious, so I gave her a glowing recommendation. She is now a speech writer for a top politician."
—Paige Wheeler, President, Creative Media Agency, Inc., and a former intern

At this point, you should go back to your earlier research and revisit what led you to TV in the first place. Where did you go wrong? Come up with a new game plan that utilizes the additional knowledge you now have. At the same time, have a heart-to-heart with yourself and ask how you can make the current internship not only bearable but even fulfilling.

The Job Quandary

Hopefully, you will get a job that you love in the field you've dreamed about. What if this doesn't happen? Maybe you'll be working at a TV station in Pittsburgh as a news intern, and a production assistant job for the local talk show is offered to you. What should you do?

If you think other offers are going to come in, try to hold off as long as you can. If you have two weeks to give your decision, call around, using the offer as bargaining power. Let people know that you've been offered a job that you're planning to take unless something in your area opens up. If this is the only job offer you have, take it. Just don't sign any long-term contracts. It's easier to get a good TV job if you already have a TV job than it is if you're standing in the unemployment line.

How About Another Internship?

Sure, you would rather have a firm job offer, but be flattered nonetheless. Many interns were not asked back, while they're requesting you to give a return performance. If you haven't gotten other job offers, do the internship. Just be sure they are asking you to stay because they see a potential position in your future, not because they see you as free labor. Try to negotiate for a few things since you know they want you to stay. Is there any way you could get a minimal salary? Can they give you a new title, with additional responsibilities? Ask if you can head up training the new interns. If there is no chance to get hired there, then maybe it is time to pack up and take your intern bag of tricks elsewhere.

A Job but No Degree Yet

Can you do school and the job together? It is a full plate, but if you can handle both, go for it. Quitting school is risky; it will be difficult for you to finish school later on. On the same note, TV opportunities don't grow on trees. One student got a plum offer to work on NBC's *Law and Order* but turned it down, thinking he'd get other offers after graduation. He now works as a gardener. You may wish to find out if it's possible to work at this job on a part-time basis. Or you may be able to complete your degree on weekends, depending on how many credits you have left to earn.

Is it important to you to get your degree? In some parts of the industry, no one will ever care whether or not you have a B.A., while other sections require it. This is an important decision; talk to people whose opinions you trust, and always let your research be your guide.

What If You're Not Asked Back as an Intern?

It can be devastating for some interns to see others get offered a job when they weren't even asked to stay as an intern. First, just ask why. There is probably a perfectly good reason for why you weren't asked back. If you haven't set up the lunch meetings with your supervisor, he may not even realize that working or interning is an option for you. Remember, you are the ultimate executive producer of your career. If you leave an internship without learning why you didn't shine, it's your loss.

What If You Have to Leave Suddenly?

Maybe you just discovered that you have lost all your financial aid and don't have enough money to continue your internship. Maybe you have a big family problem that requires you to head home indefinitely. There is a chance you may have to leave the internship. Let your supervisor know right away. Believe it or not, it's not uncommon for interns to just stop showing up and never call to explain why. Be completely honest with your supervisor; they will understand. Handling this in a very professional way can only further enhance your standing. Be sure to tell your supervisor before discussing your situation with others in the office. News travels fast, and you don't want the supervisor to receive the news from someone else.

THE THIRD QUARTER COMETH

Use all the feedback that you have gained from your first two meetings with your supervisor and your minimeetings and assess your standing: What are you doing right? What are you doing wrong? How can you improve? You need to continue to consider all these questions.

Beware of Burnout

The biggest thing to be wary of during this quarter is burnout. By now, the internship is more than halfway over, and the initial novelty is long gone. You've already impressed everyone, so there's not as much thrill in being told how amazing you are. You know how to do an extremely large percentage of things around the office, and you still enjoy meeting the staff members for coffee, but it's not as exciting as it once was, and the menial tasks are now seeming more menial than ever.

The best way to avoid burnout is to set up specific goals on a weekly basis for this quarter. You should have goals dealing with the contacts you'll get in touch with, the staff members you'll meet for coffee, and the new skills you'll want to pick up. Of course, before you do any of this, take a weekend for yourself. Take a road trip, visit some friends, do what you love to do! All too often, interns get so bogged down with work that they forget to take time for themselves. This is fine for the short term, but after a while, it will affect you.

It's also time to kick off your personal job campaign. Call and update your contacts on your internship progress. It's time to put them into the game and include them in your job search. Since you've been keeping them updated on your progress thus far and thanking them every step of the way, they will probably be more than willing to help you.

Getting the Great Assignments

Remember the motto, "Try to take everything to the next level." Have you been the one who has logged the viewer mail? If so, put all this together in a binder for the whole staff to look at. If you've met everyone in your office, meet people in the other offices. Remember, don't wait for great tasks to come your way; now that the staff trusts you, they will allow you to do more, but you should be the one to think of what it is you'd like to do. If you're at a news station, now is the perfect time to really start pitching stories. "I think it would be great to do a story on all the construction they're doing near the high school. Has anyone checked to see if the students are in any danger?"

"A few weeks before the actual end of the internship, figure out if there is anything you haven't done that you'd like to do. Sit down with your boss and see if there's some way to fit it in before your departure. Don't wait until the last minute. Look at your original goals and evaluate where you are in accomplishing them. Raise the bar for yourself. See if you can increase your efficiency and accomplish more in less time."
—Carol Story, Producer, *CBS This Morning*

In addition to taking your work to the next level, try to take your relationships one step forward. Many interns feel that the staff members don't want to be their friends; this is not always the case. If you've connected at a professional level with some staffers, try to connect on a personal level as well. Many relationships could have been spawned by the minimeetings, but if this wasn't the case, make an assertive effort to get close to some staff members. People remember friends much longer than they remember their acquaintances.

Don't Neglect the Job Search

Make sure that you constantly work on your job search. If you aren't ready to graduate, then make sure you're staying on top of your internship search for next semester. You will not be having a meeting with the boss during this quarter, but you should make contact at least once a week, unless told otherwise by your boss, to ensure that you're setting yourself up once this internship is over.

The job search is not easy. Many interns feel uncomfortable when asking for favors, but it must be done. You just gave a semester of your life for free, you have every right to ask for help. All too often, interns feel that just because they did a great job as an intern, a job will fall in their lap; this is not so. Prepare to be rejected, prepare to be hurt, but most important, prepare to be strong. If needed, go back and read the earlier channels of this book. Remind yourself how scared you were when you first started calling around for internships. You were scared, but it was worth it.

THE FINAL QUARTER

Before you know it, you will have just one quarter of your internship left, and you should take advantage of the resources you have available to you. Here are three resources, in particular, that you need to maximize:

1. *The job board.* Most stations and companies have a list of open positions there and at the parent company. This list is not available to the public, and these jobs are not listed in the trade. You have the "in;" take full advantage.

2. *The fact that you're currently working in the industry.* It is much harder to get a job when the internship is over. Be discreet, but use the phone and company stationery on a regular basis. Executives are more likely to accept a phone call from Jane Doe at ABC News than from Jane Doe at Brooklyn College.

3. *The access you have to your work and the editing equipment.* If there is tape of some of the projects you were involved with (news reports, talk show segments, promos, etc.), try to get a copy of it to take with you. If you have befriended a reporter or a photographer, maybe they have even let you do a few "stand-ups" for a talent reel. A picture is worth a thousand words . . . and video is worth even more!

> *"Interns should try to make a tape before they leave. Once you depart, it's really difficult to get copies of the work you've done."*
> —Joe Dihiovanni, Minneapolis meteorologist and a former intern

The Final Meeting with Your Supervisor

You should definitely plan a final lunch with your supervisor for the last week of your internship. Prepare for this lunch like you have prepared for the other meetings. By now, your supervisor will know what to expect, and you'll already have a pretty strong relationship; this meeting will be much easier, though no less important than the others.

Carol Story of *CBS This Morning* highly recommends that interns, when asking for the final meeting, also ask for a job evaluation. This will give you something on paper about your performance, and it will also force your boss to sit down and really think about all the contributions you've made. Richard Ayoub agrees:

"When an internship is coming to a close, an intern should ask for an evaluation. Most bosses don't want to bother with it, but if you ask, they'll give you one. Ask specific questions."

—Richard Ayoub, Executive Producer, *KABC Morning News* in LA, and a former intern

Goals for This Meeting

Your goals for this meeting will really differ, depending on whether you have a job or another internship lined up.

If you have a job or internship for next semester, treat this as a thank-you meeting and a way to ensure that you will maintain this relationship. If you don't have a job or that next internship lined up, this is another vital meeting for your career. You want to make sure that this meeting is going to set the stage for future employment. The cliché, "out of sight, out of mind," is very true in this TV world; getting a letter of recommendation from your boss while you're still interning isn't too difficult; once you've gone, it becomes much harder. In the same vein that you wanted to know how to follow up after the half-time meeting, you definitely want to know how you should proceed with your job search once you depart. Can you use your boss as a reference? You should never list someone as a reference without permission.

"You should get at least three names from your boss that you can then call to set up an informational meeting, if nothing else. If you have become friendly with any of the people that regularly call, you can also ask the boss if she would mind if you called that person to solicit a job. You should not make that call on your own, without approval."

—Dan Watanabe, Creative Services Director, All American TV

Have a list of questions ready for this meeting; you don't want anything to be missed. An entire career in TV is definitely worth a few hours of preparation.

Food Glorious Food

Plan on having many breakfast, lunch, and dinner meetings these last few weeks. If you can afford it, make it your treat, as a token of your appreciation. Don't go bragging about these meetings to the other interns; otherwise, the entire staff will have dozens of interns beating down their doors for lunch. The more people you can meet with, the more connections you can make, the more you will be remembered, and the better off you will be. Express your appreciation and solidify your connections.

Keep track of all leads in your notebook. Also, hop on the phone to your contacts again. See if they have come across any openings. You would be surprised at the number of people who say, "Funny you should call. I just heard about an opening this morning. You may be perfect for it."

> *"If you want to be hired, let people know. However, there is a fine line between asking for a job and being too pushy. Remember, they owe you nothing, and you should expect only a learning experience. Anything above that is a bonus."*
>
> —Todd Radnitz, Writer/Producer, E! Entertainment TV, and a former intern

THE FINAL WEEKS

Your internship is nearly over. There are several ways to make a good impression as you say your parting words.

Smile, Please

You may want to grab a camera and begin to get photos of yourself with various staff members. Before you leave, develop these pictures, frame them, and give them as gifts to your new contacts. If they keep these framed pictures on their desks, you'll never be forgotten.

The Internship Bible

This journal was initially discussed in Channel 4, and hopefully, you took that advice to heart. By now, you should have a list of nearby restaurants, contact numbers, and anything else that could be helpful to an incoming intern. Give yourself some solid time to put this bible together; this is not just a quick, all-nighter project. This is your manual and should include everything from office maps to the closest K-Mart. Secrets to getting the copy machine to work, as well as the numbers to call when those secrets fail, should be included in this manual.

It should look as professional as possible; hit Kinko's for that professional touch. Make three copies, and make sure your name is on them so that your greatness will never be forgotten. You may want to include a disk as well, so that the bible can be updated if necessary.

At the two-week warning mark, inform your supervisor of your intentions. "I'm creating a manual for next semester's interns. Hopefully, it will be helpful to the new batch and make your life easier, too. It will have information such as a list of morning and afternoon duties, phone numbers frequently called, office policies, and how to work and fix the machines. Is there anything that you would recommend including?" Talk to the assistant about your project as well. They'll be thrilled to lend a hand.

When you are finished, definitely make a copy for your school. Make this version a bit more generic and include a job description with common responsibilities. Discuss why the internship did or didn't work for you. Future interns will petition to name a college after you.

Continue with Your Meetings and Farewells

If there's someone you want to have a minimeeting with, you'd better do it fast. The assistant is one person who is often overlooked when one is looking for knowledge; don't make this mistake. He or she has a world of information, and a minimeeting may very well be the most informative meeting of them all. Don't forget all the other key people, from your mentor to the janitor who always took care of you. If there's someone you haven't properly thanked, make sure you do so.

"Before you leave your internship, take time to meet with the producers or directors of the production company or the heads of the departments you spent time with. Let them know you are interested in what you have seen. This is the time to make an impression. Never just disappear."
—Deveney Kelly, Director/Producer, *The Bold and the Beautiful*

Resumes and Rolodex Cards

No matter what, be sure to buy a large supply of Rolodex cards. Put your name and number on each one and be sure everyone gets one when they are in their office; this way, you can be sure it makes it into their files.

Make sure everyone on staff gets a copy of your resume. It's not uncommon for a producer to get a call from a friend in desperate need of a new hire. If your resume is on file, the staffer can instantly fax a copy over to them, and the job can be yours. If the employee has to track you down and then have you fax the resume, someone may beat you to the job. Also, you want staffers to know how to contact you at all times.

Finish All Assignments

Many interns lose focus and forget basic responsibilities in the home stretch. This last week will be your boss's last impression of you. Finish ALL of your projects and give a status report. It is common to blame ex-interns for work not completed. Don't give any fuel for this fire.

> *"As your internship comes to a close, be sure to wrap up all the loose ends with the projects you are working on. If you can't complete everything, make a concise report, detailing where you left off and any important information crucial to the project. Even if you've finished everything, this will remind your supervisor and the rest of the staff of your accomplishments."*
>
> —Jill Fox, Producer, PBS, and former intern

> *"Departing interns should do the reverse of what they did at the beginning of their internship: walk around and say good-bye. I've had good and not-so-good interns say good-bye, and to the not-so-good ones, I simply wish them luck and thank them for their help. To the good ones, I'll offer continuing support. 'List me as a reference. Put my phone number down. Let me know if you need a letter.' Saying good-bye opens the door for those offers."*
>
> —Jimmy Rhoades, Producer, PBS Detroit

AFTER YOU LEAVE

As you leave your internship, another student will come through the revolving studio door, whirling with the same hopes and dreams that you had when you began. It is the intern circle of life. When you leave your internship, whether it's to start a job in the industry, to go back to school, or to stay up at night praying for a phone call from a TV employer, here are some additional suggestions for setting yourself apart:

1. *Send pizza to the office the day after you leave.* Pizza is always appreciated.
2. *Send thank-you notes to everyone after your final curtain call.* In this age of laptops, fax machines, and car phones, your handwritten note is special.
3. *Continue to write up pitches, ideas, and stories.* TV devours ideas, and yours will really be appreciated. Whenever you have an idea for a story, do some research and send it in. Every now and then, deliver them in person. Make sure that you have your name and number on anything you submit. You need all the free advertising you can get.
4. *Schedule regular lunch appointments.* Make sure that you stay in contact with a variety of people at the office. Too many great interns leave, never keep in touch, and are soon forgotten.

"One intern would constantly stop by and say, 'I had a couple of show ideas, and since I was in the neighborhood, I figured I might as well drop them by.' She was there the day someone walked out on the job, and we instantly hired her. We found out a few weeks later that she lived quite a distance from the station and that she actually traveled an hour each way, just to stop by the station. She was never 'just in the neighborhood,' but hey, it got her hired."

—Anthony Scire, Producer, Z-100 New York, and a former intern

5. *Keep up with the trades and industry news.* "Rumors persist that Channel 8 is going to go for a 3-hour news block." If you read this headline, you now know the place you want to send your resume to. Plus, if a contact of yours is mentioned in the trades, you have a perfect reason to give them a call.

6. *Send special gifts to key people.* Hopefully, you have already noted some favorite hobbies, foods, and other important items of your close contacts. Does your boss love Snickers bars? Send her a bunch. Little personal reminders show you care.

FLASHBACK

"I left my internship with the promise that my boss would try to keep a job open for me. All I had to do was finish my last term at school, graduate, and drive to my new job in Cleveland. But as good as her intentions were, my boss was swamped with work, trying to keep this position open for ten weeks. Three producers were putting 10 hours of live programming on the air each week. I heard that they might have to hire someone else. How did I find this out? A good contact and a producer on another show at the station called me with the warning. I had to do something. I called my supervisor and told her I was going to be coming to Cleveland the following week for some interviews and wanted to know if I could visit. She knew that I was keeping all my bases covered. A few hours later, she called back with an official offer of employment. I collected my diploma and bolted for Ohio. Thanks, Noreen."
—Dan

Jack Forrestel, the Emmy award–winning Art Director of *The Bold and the Beautiful,* says that no matter how busy he is, he's never too busy to take a call from a former intern. If you met ten people at your internship, six months from now, half of those people could all be at different jobs. If you've kept contact, you now have five new places of possible employment. Dana

Sparber, who now calls ABC-NY her home, says she wouldn't have received this job if she hadn't stayed in touch with her internship supervisor.

Hang in there. It's going to happen!

```
.  .  . AND CUT!
CUE ANNOUNCER TEASE:
```

"Don't touch your dial . . . stay tuned for some parting words of advice."

```
FADE TO BLACK
ROLL "TV INTERN HALL OF FAME" PACKAGE
```

••

Jim Casey
Producer and President, Painless Productions,
a former NBC page, and a former intern

While I was growing up in New Jersey, if someone claimed he worked in television, it simply meant that for 20 bucks, he'd wire your house to get free HBO. As far as we knew, no one created TV; it was just there—like air or water . . . or pizza. We tuned in on Saturday mornings and watched cartoons, never questioning how it worked. Even in college, when I discovered my fondness for writing, I considered novels my only option. I don't recall when I finally realized I could apply my passion to the little screen.

As a college junior, I eventually changed my focus from prelaw to journalism. One year later, I landed an internship at the New Jersey Bureau of ABC's *Eyewitness News*. At the time, news and dramatic writing weren't as closely related as they are today, so a kid with aspirations of writing teleplays needed an edge if he wanted to shine in the news world. As far as I could tell, I had no aptitude for news, so my only option was hard work. Since my assignment editor—a wonderful woman named Kiki Vassoler—and I were the only bodies at the bureau, finding hard work was not a problem.

My duties included browsing the wire services for good stories, researching them, pitching them to Kiki, and, if she liked them, setting up story packets for the news crew. I was 21 at the time; it would be four years before I'd know such responsibility again.

I soon discovered that being a good intern was no different than assisting my dad in repairing car engines. Like any good tool, be ready to help when you're needed, but stay out of the way so no one trips over you. I quickly learned to read people's stress levels, knowing when to speak and when to remain silent. I also tried to share information without sounding like a know-it-all. I discovered that somewhere between intense enthusiasm and invisibility is the gray area where the intern must live.

I must have done something right; at the end of the year, when Kiki left the bureau and the television industry altogether, she suggested I apply for her job. I know now I was lucky. Kiki was confident, secure, and supportive. If I had a good idea, she acknowledged it and gave me credit. She was more excited about my accomplishments than I was. But I later learned that not all employers function that way; some feel threatened by ambition, while at the same time demanding 100 percent from their employees. It's a fine line I continue to walk even today.

Immediately after graduation, I landed a job at NBC in New York as a page. Although a paying job, the wage seemed low enough to consider it an internship. But who cared? This was NBC, the number one network! I was already following in the footsteps of television icons like Johnny Carson. Unfortunately, Johnny and I took only a single step together; I quit after a month and a half. I craved a chance to prove myself, to gain hands-on experience in writing, and pointing tourists to the washroom didn't seem like the way. To this day, I am probably the only NBC page who never guided a single backstage tour.

One month later, I drove from New York to LA, where I eventually found a job as a production assistant on an ABC show called *The Home Show*. I didn't know it at the time, but this was my big break. A large part of the show's programming dealt with redecorating and refurbishing homes; since I had a working knowledge of basic construction, this became my edge. The fact that I owned a pick-up truck only increased my value to the show.

I worked hard, often seven days a week, and can't remember a day that ended in fewer than 10 hours. I ran when I could have walked. I worked when I should have slept. I smiled when I wanted to scream. But two years later, I was writing and producing segments for the show. I paid my dues.

Today, I own my own small production company. In its daily operations, I realize how much I have grown to understand: (1) You never stop paying your dues. Even network presidents work for someone. (2) Everyone, not only interns, must live in that gray area between intense enthusiasm and invisibility. (3) I still need to remember when to remain silent. (4) Despite the frustrations, I love my job . . . and that's rare.

And sometimes I am still just a little boy watching cartoons on a flickering screen and wondering how it all happens.

channel (10)

Follow This Advice . . . and You'll Never Have to Make Coffee in This Town Again

"If you want to direct film, then don't take an internship in a totally unrelated area. Start working toward your goal. If you want to direct TV, get an internship with a show that has field teams shooting around town. Offer to lug gear, anything to be around field directors. Start soaking in what you want to know. If you don't know what you want to do, then take a general internship on a show and volunteer to work in every department so you can learn what's out there."

   —Dianne Abramms Gotlieb, HBO, *Mike and Maty*, Infomercial Producer, and a former intern

"My advice to interns—don't become annoying. Make yourself useful and valuable. Think before you ask a question. Don't take the easy way out. Realize you are there to learn but that the TV station also needs to get something from you. Don't be demanding. If you're interning at a TV news department, don't tell them you want to work as an actor or in sales. They'll write you off immediately. When someone is busy, don't interrupt them. Remember, no one ever has time for interns. Make people want to make time for you."

   —Richard Ayoub, Executive Producer, *KABC Morning News* in LA, and a former intern

"The smart intern tries to get to know as many of the staff producers and directors as possible. A smart intern also offers to be on standby in case there is a last-minute need for another set of hands on the production. A smart intern learns as many jobs as possible. A smart intern asks if they can observe editing sessions or quietly sit in the control room during a studio production. Smart interns make themselves visible by being there, almost as if they were expected to be there. Inevitably, if an intern was passionately interested in breaking into the business and picked up on

some of these basic behavior and personality traits, they ended up with a paid staff position when an opening occurred."

—Sandra Bailen-Scott, Director, The Donna Reed Foundation, and a former intern

"Forget every story you've heard about the intern who was making coffee one day and producing the show six months later. There's simply a lot of tedious, unfulfilling work to do as an intern. But if you tackle it with guts, your talents will be recognized. The key is don't throw in the towel too soon. Work hard, never turn down an assignment, be patient, and look the part of a television pro."

—Bob Bates, Former Producer, E! Entertainment Television, and a former intern

"If you chase power or stardom, you'll never achieve it. Seek excellence. Recognition is a by-product of being brilliant. As a goal in and of itself, it is empty.

- *Let your vision and your values shape your job, not the other way around.*
- *Your opinion is as important as any other person's in the process. Your unique world view is one of your greatest assets.*
- *Always look for ways to go above and beyond the definition of your job.*
- *Look at everything you do as your gift to others.*
- *Let the satisfaction of knowing you've done your best be your reward.*
- *Gratitude is one of the most important qualities to possess.*
- *Become a person of integrity. Develop a reputation for honesty, fairness, dependability, loyalty, and discretion.*
- *Don't ever take a job for the money.*
- *Don't network. Build relationships.*
- *Realize that life is like a giant Nintendo game, set up for us to win. Take chances, be daring, and live your dreams with gusto. If you run a race and fail, you'll just play at that level again until you master it. Then, once you make it, you're on to the next level, with a whole new set of rules and challenges and the opportunity to master the unknown again."*

—Brad Bessey, Coordinating Producer, *Entertainment Tonight*, and a former intern

"An internship is an opportunity to get your foot in the door of television. You're able to work at places where you might not otherwise

be able to get an entry-level job because there aren't any openings. Even if you aren't being paid, you should treat your internship like a job. If you probe yourself, odds are that one of the people on that show will help you find your first paid position. Try to actively find a significant role for yourself at your internship. There is always too much work needed to be done. Recognize what pressure you would relieve and volunteer your assistance. You will probably be overqualified for most assignments, but it's your attitude and energy that are being judged as much as your execution of the task."

> —Marla Kell Brown, Producer, *The Arsenio Hall Show*, and a former intern

"Walk in with a smile on your face—soak in everything, but remember to take it one step at a time."

> —Sheila Brummer, News Anchor, WAOW-TV, Wausau, Wisconsin, and a former intern

"My final advice? Ask yourself, 'If I hired an intern, what would I expect from them?' It is just like everything else in life."

> —Jim Casey, Producer and President, Painless Productions, a former NBC page, and a former intern

"Be the most energetic professionally behaved intern you can. Never forget that most everyone you're dealing with on the staff began in a very entry-level position like an internship. Never complain about the work, because we've all done it, too. Be ready to volunteer. Never be idle—ask people if they have something for you to do. DO NOT GOSSIP, no matter what you've seen or heard in the offices. Don't try and be friends with staff members right away—impress people first with the quality of your work. If you do the work of the internship to the best of your ability, you'll spend less time at an entry-level position when you begin your paid employment. I happen to know this for a fact, because so many of my former interns were promoted very quickly from entry-level positions. Therefore, never believe that the work of an intern is menial and meaningless—it will make a difference in how you are perceived by employers."

> —Carole Chouinard, Segment Producer, *Politically Incorrect*, and Intern Coordinator, *Arsenio*

"Don't be cutthroat, just be more eager than the others and back it up with substance. Make the best of it . . . it's the start of what could be a promising career!"

> —CC Dyer, former *20/20* Producer, *Geraldo* Producer

"Pick a field you feel passionate about, learn everything you can about it, absorb information like a sponge. Always think before you act, and never bad-mouth or gossip about anyone or anything. Be responsive to advice and do not take criticism personally, as it's usually intended to improve performance. LISTEN, THINK, and ACT ACCORDINGLY."

—Gail E. Frank, Director of Primetime Programming, CNBC

"About taking risks in life: I'm conservative economically and was frightened to work without pay over one summer. But it's about the big picture. I took the job for no money, but two great things happened. My boss ended up finding me a $250-a-week stipend to help me pay for my rent (without asking). Then, at the end of the summer, I'm poor as could be. I was driving out to Malibu to take one last look at the beach, all depressed. I reach over, open my mail, and there's a surprise letter from Harvard Financial Aid . . . because I made so little in the summer, they gave me an $8,000 scholarship out of the blue from some secret fund I'd never heard of. After that, I realized that you have to take certain gambles with your time because, if you succeed, the few hundred dollars you forgo will seem irrelevant."

—Brian Graden, Executive Vice President, MTV Television Networks; Developer, *South Park*; and a former intern

"Stay out of office politics. Come ready to work. Know that people are rarely watching you, but when they do, they will make up their minds about you, so always be doing something productive."

—Patrick Jarvis, Development Executive, Tribune Entertainment, and a former intern

"Really use your internship and the people who work there to your best advantage. You're learning from people who are in the trenches. You may not get an opportunity like this again. I've been in this business ten years, and it's hard to find good people. When I come across someone really good and need a position filled, I'll track that person down."

—Julie Johnson, Associate Producer, *The Oprah Winfrey Show*, and a former intern

"Never think you're 'just an intern.' For the time you're with the show, you're an important, working member of a team! Squeeze every bit of knowledge you can out of everyone you meet, even the janitor! Take your job seriously and, above all, know that being an intern is the best

experience you will ever get. It's your time to ask questions, observe, and learn about yourself and the career you have chosen."

> —Shannon Keenan, Producer, Live Events, E! Entertainment Television, and a former intern

"Have a clear vision of what you want to do in TV. Ask questions. Be positive and interested. Make your impression before you leave the internship. These things . . . plus a good mentor, good luck, and hard work and perseverance (or a well-placed relative) and anyone can make it in the business"

> —Deveney Kelly, Producer/Director, *The Bold and the Beautiful*

"Don't be nervous; you'll find your place. If you want something, go for it. Ask to do it, volunteer to do it on extra time, and follow through with it. Don't be intimidated by athletes or celebrities. They're people just like you. And don't ask for autographs or pictures. Remain professional. No one likes a slacker."

> —Jonathan C. Kilb, Coordinating Producer, New England Cable News, Videographer, Boston Bruins/Celtics, and a former intern

"An internship is like anything in life; it's what you make it. Interns need to understand that interning is more than just making coffee and Xeroxing something on goldenrod 3-hole-punch paper. Interning is a foot in the door. What a lot of interns fail to realize is that you are given access to a lot of people you might normally have never met. Although you have your foot in the door, someone has to pull you in. No one ever finds success without the help of others. The people you meet will be vital to getting into the business. Learn everything you can and have fun."

> —Tim Mancinelli, Associate Director, *The Late Late Show with Tom Snyder*, and a former intern

"An internship is an incredible opportunity. I wish I would have had such an opportunity when I was in college. Be enthusiastic in your work, demonstrate a willingness to do whatever it takes to contribute to the group effort, and never lose sight of the fact that you are part of a team. You may not be paid, you may not be as important as some other team members, but your contribution is valuable. You have an opportunity to really make an impression—and perhaps even land yourself a job down the road—by giving your internship 110 percent."

> —Craig Martinelli, Executive Director, Advertising, Publicity and Promotion, Walt Disney Television

"Learn as much as you can while you are in the internship. Learn from the failures as well as the successes. When it's over, stay in touch. This business is all about contacts. Stay in touch with your employers; send thank-you notes. Send a resume and cover letter when you graduate."

—Glenn Meehan, Managing Editor, *Entertainment Tonight*, and a former intern

"If you are about to start an internship, go in with a great attitude, hard work ethic, and humble persona. If you are willing to pay your dues, it really does pay off in the long run. I spent many an early morning or late evening working for free . . . but now (seven years later), I'm working as a producer and making a nice living . . . so it truly does pay off. Just don't get too big for your britches too early on!"

—Loren Ruch, Producer, *Good Day LA*, and a former intern

"Be patient. Wait for the right moment to shine. Don't try to shine for the sake of shining. You will be taken advantage of; accept that going in. Show that you care about what you're doing."

—Scott St. John, former Fox Development Executive

"Don't give up. It is hard to land a paying job in TV. Only the strongest survive. If you really believe you were made to be in the entertainment business, never give up. Try again and again, and do the best you can!"

—David Scott, Co-Executive Producer, *The People's Court*, and a former intern

"When it comes to internships, I think the army said it best: 'Be all that you can be.' Look at every part of your internship as a learning experience and take as much as you can away from it. Try to develop and keep good relations with all the people you meet along the way. You never know when one of them might help you. Never burn any bridges! I've been in TV for about 2½ years, and I'm learning more every day about just how small this business really is."

—Dana Sparber, Senior Marketing Analyst, ABC-New York, and a former intern

"My final advice to interns is: Don't take things too personally in the office. I have seen employees who don't treat interns as well as they should; after all, interns are donating their time. Hang in there, do the best job you can do, ask enough questions, and if you need to research it further, do it on your own. Always follow up, always follow up, and

always, always, always follow up. Once you leave, make sure the office has your updated phone number, since students' numbers change a lot."

—Karen Stein, TV Producer and a former intern

"First, have fun. You're not the CEO of a company yet. Chances are, any mistake you make isn't going to make or break the show.

Second, try not to gossip and engage in office politics. Someone is likely to get hurt, and because you have the least amount of power in the office, that someone is probably going to be you.

Third, this actually isn't mine. It's advice from African-American author E. Lynn Harris. He says, 'When I speak to college kids today, I tell them to have big dreams, but make sure that the dreams you dream are your own.' "

—Carol Story, Producer, *CBS This Morning*

"Without sounding simple—interns must have the personal skills in place. Your professional skills will (hopefully) never be complete. You should be patient. Smile. Tell a joke. If you can succeed at having people like you, you will shine as an intern. Ten percent work, 10 percent talent, 80 percent charm. Think of this as a very cool cocktail party, not a job. Make a splash."

—Scott Storey, Emmy award–winning Hollywood Set Designer and Art Designer

"Worship the talent. Ask a lot of questions. If you don't have a lot of questions, it might look as though you know everything; in which case, why are you an intern? Learn the pecking order. All of the people above you should have your respect, and all of the people below you deserve the same. In this business, your gofer today could be your employer two years from now! Use your internship as the first step in networking. It can be an important potential employer list. Maintain contact with the people you meet, be it by phone, fax, or letter. It is true what they say: 'Out of sight, out of mind!' "

—Sy Tomashoff, Emmy award–winning Production Designer, *The Bold and the Beautiful*

"Have a goal. Try to get something tangible accomplished during your time. A mock sportscast, a stand-up and video package . . . even if you don't have on-camera aspirations, it's good to know what reporters and

anchors go through. At some point, make contact with the News Director. He's the guy who ultimately does the hiring; make sure he knows who you are."

—Matt Underwood, Sports Director, WEWS-TV, Cleveland, and a former intern.

"Treat yourself like a singer treats their voice. They tune up, they drink tea and honey with lemon, they practice, they vocalize. Interns should do the same. Consider that you are your own instrument. Train yourself to have social graces. Buy a book. Hone your people skills; learn about how to have interesting conversations. Keep conversations about yourself to a minimum. You're not interesting enough yet. Ask the other person. Read. Improve your mind. Take self-help courses to expand your interests. Finally, understand that many companies are structured on the medieval royalty model. The executive producer is the head of state, and everyone else is a minister of this or that. Kowtowing is appropriate; kissing up and making sure the monarch is properly worshipped will get you far. You think I'm kidding? Remember, play your cards right, and you'll be King one day, too."

—Kac Young, Vice President, Television Production and Development, Universal Studios Hollywood, and a former intern

"I am going to sound like an old fogy to you, 'the benefit of my experience,' . . . Wait a minute, I'm not that old, though I've seen a lot by now! Here goes: I spent several years in the faculty of UCLA, teaching television production. I noticed two distinct types of students: those who were willing to do whatever it took to make their project fly, no matter how little sleep or recognition they received, and those who sat back and expected it all to be handed to them. I even had a student who threatened me and tried to sue me for giving him a C in my class, even though he had not attended most of the meetings. What was that all about? I don't know. The television business is feast or famine. You are either sitting around pining for a job, or too exhausted to drive home after a 16-hour day. There's not a lot in between! As a prospective intern, you had better be careful what you wish for . . . you might get it. Then the real work begins!"

—John C. Zak, Supervising Producer, *The Bold and the Beautiful*, and a former intern

"Have fun and learn something. People think that interns are all about coffee and turkey sandwiches. Well, it is not all that bad. You can get a

job this way. So pay attention, laugh at the appropriate jokes, and remember: When the big boss is ticked off, blame the new guy, unless that's you!"

—Dan Zweifler, Technical Recruiter and a former Albany news intern

```
FADE TO BLACK
ROLL "TV INTERN HALL OF FAME" PACKAGE
```

• •

THE TV INTERN HALL OF FAME SALUTES

Tisi Aylward
Director of Talent, E! Entertainment Television
and a former intern

I can't stress how invaluable an internship is—in any profession. Mine just happened to be in the television industry. An internship can be an incredible learning experience and can also help you establish professional working relationships that will help you network future jobs. But it is up to you to make it happen.

How do you get a job in television? It's a question I'm often asked. My reply? I can't tell you how to get a TV job because there is no one way to do it, but I can tell you how I did it. Ask someone else, and they will have a different response.

OK, I'll admit it, I followed the Mary Tyler Moore (MTM) method. "Mare" was my idol. The patron saint of television production. Her role as a positive, nice, outgoing, honest, hard-working woman trying to make it in a male-dominated industry inspired me.

The first MTM lesson, be positive. I WAS going to get an internship. So I spent hours driving around to every TV station in the area and filled out applications. I also suggest being very nice to the receptionists. These people can be some of the most influential folks in any business. They hear all and see all.

Second important lesson? Be outgoing. During one interview, I was given a typing and translation test. I failed both miserably because I was too nervous, but I got the job anyway. When I later asked the executive producer why he hired me, his answer was, "You have a great personality." (Thanks, Mare!) No one wants to work with people who have negative or bad attitudes.

Third, be honest. I was asked if I knew how to make coffee. "Sure!" I said. (I was terrified that if I said no, I'd get the boot.) The producer asked me to have coffee made for an early meeting the next morning. So, on my first official day as an intern, I came in early to work to make it. The problem was that I didn't know how the coffee machine worked. I put the coffee in the filter, the water in the cavity, and the pot on the heated tray; however, I forgot to slide the filter basket in. Hot water sprayed all over the counter and onto the carpet and spread into a pool at my feet! If I had answered honestly and asked to be shown how, I wouldn't have been standing in a puddle of caffeine! (I managed to clean up before the producers arrived and had the coffee brewing. I'd found someone from another office to show me how to do it. Mission accomplished, lesson learned!)

Work hard. Don't be lazy. Everyday you should be learning something new, meeting someone new, or coming up with new ideas. Volunteer for extra projects. The more you can learn in an internship, the more valuable you'll be as a future employee.

One last thing I want to share with you . . . I have often heard during my long tenure in television that I was too nice to make it in this biz, that I'd have to become hardened to succeed. I have always refused to accept that notion. I've been in this biz for almost twenty years, and I've done quite well for myself. I've also made some wonderful friends in this industry who are extremely nice and very successful.

No matter what internship you land, most importantly, stay true to yourself!

Good luck. You're going to make it after all.

Appendix

TV Internships
for the Taking

Following is a list of twenty different types of internships available in the television business. For more detailed information on these organizations—and on other internship opportunities—check out the annually updated *Peterson's Internships*.

Academy of Television Arts and Sciences
5220 Lankershim Boulevard
North Hollywood, CA 91601-3109
Tel: 818-754-2830
http://www.emmys.org
E-mail: internships@emmys.org
Service and awards organization that presents the annual primetime Emmy awards, provides activities for television industry members, and fosters competition for college students in the form a paid summer internship program that places students with Los Angeles–based television stations, production companies, studios, and other television-related venues.

Broadcast News Networks
253 Fifth Avenue, 6th Floor
New York, NY 10016
Contact: Dave Goldberg
Tel: 212-779-0500; Fax: 212-532-5554
http://www.broadcastnews.com
E-mail: dave@broadcastnews.com
Television production and program development facility that produces documentaries for various cable and broadcast outlets.

CBS News, Inc.
555 West 57th Street
New York, NY 10019-2985
Contact: Eldra Rodriguez-Gillman
Tel: 212-975-5567; Fax: 212-975-8798
E-mail: eig@cbsnews.com
Television network news organization.

Children's Television Workshop
    One Lincoln Plaza
    New York, NY 10023
    Contact: Charmaine Taylor
    Fax: 212-875-6088
Not-for-profit company using media to educate children and families worldwide; sponsors programs for traditional and new media; engages in publishing, product licensing, and community outreach; producer of *Sesame Street.*

CNN America, Inc.
    820 1st Street, NE
    Washington, DC 20002
    Contact: Virginia Umrani
    Tel: 202-515-2916; Fax: 202-515-2901
    E-mail: ginny.umrani@turner.com
Cable news network offering 24 hours of news and information programming daily.

Comedy Central
    1775 Broadway, 10th Floor
    New York, NY 10019
    Contact: Mandy Preville
    Fax: 212-767-4257
    E-mail: mpreville@comcentral.com
Advertiser-supported basic cable comedy service.

C-SPAN
    400 North Capitol Street, NW
    Washington, DC 20001
    Contact: Amanda Adams
    Tel: 202-626-7968; Fax: 202-737-3323
    http://www.cspan.org
Provides audience access to live gavel-to-gavel proceedings of the U.S. House of Representatives and the U.S. Senate and to other forums where public policy is discussed.

Discovery Communications, Inc.
    7700 Wisconsin Avenue
    Bethesda, MD 20814
    Tel: 301-986-0444 Ext. 4325; Fax: 301-986-1889
A privately held, diversified media company operating the Discovery Network's channels and systems in the United States and worldwide and the Discovery Channel retail businesses.

Fox Studios East, Inc.
212 Fifth Avenue
New York, NY 10010
Contact: Rasheda M. Thomas
Tel: 212-802-4082; Fax: 212-802-4206
Cable television station.

Home Box Office
1100 Avenue of the Americas
New York, NY 10036
Contact: Kimberly Baxter
Subscriber-based cable television channel.

Jim Henson Productions
117 East 69th Street
New York, NY 10021
Independent multimedia production company; also produces children's books.

Kelly Broadcasting Company
3 Television Circle
Sacramento, CA 95814
Contact: Dave Kaylor
Tel: 916-446-3333; Fax: 916-441-4050
Commercial broadcast television station.

KQED Inc.
2601 Mariposa Street
San Francisco, CA 94110
Tel: 415-553-2307; Fax: 415-553-2380
http://www.kqed.org
E-mail: hr@kqed.org
Public broadcasting company that includes KQED-TV and KQED-FM.

The Late Show With David Letterman
1697 Broadway
New York, NY 10019
Contact: Janice Penino
Tel: 212-975-5006
A late-night television show airing weeknights on CBS.

National Association of College Broadcasters
71 George Street
Providence, RI 02912-1824
Contact: Kelley Cunningham
Tel: 401-863-2225; Fax: 401-863-2221
http://www.hofstra.edu/nacb
E-mail: nacb@brown.edu
Association that provides support services to students studying electronic media.

NBC4

30 Rockefeller Plaza, Suite 687-E1
New York, NY 10112
Contact: Millie Quiles
Tel: 212-664-4228; Fax: 212-664-6449
Television broadcasting station.

Walt Disney Pictures and Television

500 South Buena Vista Street, MIC 7376
Burbank, CA 91521-7376
Fax: 818-563-3551
Provider of family entertainment.

WHYY, Inc.

Independence Mall West
150 North Sixth Street
Philadelphia, PA 19106
Contact: Maureen Pilla
Tel: 215-351-1236; Fax: 215-351-0398
Public television and radio station.

WNYW-Fox Television

205 East 67th Street
New York, NY 10021
Contact: Iris Sierra
Tel: 212-452-5700
Television station with hands-on training program for individuals interested in
obtaining experience in various fields of TV broadcasting.

W*USA-TV

4100 Wisconsin Avenue, NW
Washington, D.C. 20016
Tel: 202-895-5810
E-mail: schang@wusatv3.gannett.com
CBS-affiliate commercial broadcast television station in Washington, D.C., offering
local news and programming.

glossary

of TV Positions

The following positions are organized according to seniority, with the most senior position leading off each section.

Broadcasting the News

General Manager
The top-of-the-ladder position at a local television station. Responsible for the overall operation and management of a TV station. *Salary:* A good six figures plus, but depends on market size and station ownership (some GM's are owners of the station).

News Director
Chief of the newsroom. Responsible for creating and maintaining a "look" for the news product, hiring all newsroom staff, overseeing budgets, and making news editorial decisions on an as-needed or required or desired basis. Reports to GM. *Salary:* depends on market size and station's rank in ratings . . . top-10 market News Directors should be bringing in low six figures per year—$100,000–$160,000.

Associate News Director
Second in command of the daily operation of the newsroom and its staff. This individual has a more hands-on relationship with the daily editorial decisions and news product. Reports to GM and/or News Director. *Salary:* varies with market size. Top-10 market: $80,000–$140,000 per year.

Executive Producer
Responsible for the producing staff and overseeing the daily presentation of the news product. Reports to News Director/Associate News Director. *Salary:* varies with market size. Top-10 market: $60,000–$120,000 per year.

Producer
Directly responsible for the creation of a specific news show. Along with the assignment desk, plans the presentation and editorial content of each minute on the air. Generally the producer is the individual in the control room during the broadcast. Reports to Executive Producer or News Director. *Salary:* again varies with market size. Top-10 market: $50,000–$100,000 per year.

Managing Editor/Assignment Desk Manager
Oversees the daily staffing of the newsroom. Responsible for reporters, photographers, editors, and other assignment desk employees. Helps coordinate and plan daily

coverage of events and breaking news. Reports to News Director/Executive Producer. *Salary:* varies with market size. Top-10 market: $55,000–$100,000 per year.

Assignment Editor/Planning Editor
Responsible for the daily arrangement of news coverage and assignment of news staff (reporters/photographers/live shot personnel). Keeps an eye open for breaking news and contacts police/fire departments and listens to emergency scanners. Usually the first person to check into a story and develop contacts and interviews. Reports to Managing Editor/Producer/Executive Producer.
Salary: varies with market size and scheduled shift (weekends, nightside or dayside weekdays). Top-10 market: $40,000–$80,000 per year.

Segment Producer
Responsible for the development and look of a specific segment of a newscast. For example, sports or entertainment or the investigative/special report segment. Reports to Executive Producer/Producer. *Salary:* varies with market size. Top-10 market: $40,000–$60,000 per year.

Associate Producer/Writer/Field Producer
Assists the show producer with the writing and scripting of the news show. Often works with reporters who are out in the field on live reports who cannot write their own story. Works with editors to get story edited visually. Reports to Producer. *Salary:* varies with market size. Top-10 market: $35,000–$50,000 per year.

Reporter
Responsible for direct news gathering and presentation of a specific story assigned to them by an assignment editor or producer. Works directly with cameraperson/photographer and video editor. Reports to Producer, Assignment Editor/Executive Producer. *Salary:* ranges with market size and on-air experience. Top-10 market: $50,000–$120,000 per year.

Photographer
Responsible for the gathering of visual elements of a story. Works directly with reporters and assignment editors on daily news gathering and presentation of live pictures. Reports to the Chief Photographer, Assignment Editor/Producer. *Salary:* varies with market size, experience, and union contracts. Top-10 market: $45,000–$90,000 per year.

Editor
Responsible for the editing or visuals of a specific story for broadcast. Works closely with writers, producers, reporters, and photographers. Reports to Chief Editor/Photographer and Assignment Editors. *Salary:* varies with market size, experience, and union contracts. Top-10 market: $40,000–$70,000 per year.

Graphics Designer
Responsible for the creation of special effects for a story for broadcast, the graphics of a newscast, and news logos. Reports to Producers/News Directors. *Salary:* varies in market size and contracts. Top-10 market: $50,000–$80,000 per year.

Director/Assistant Director
Responsible for the pacing and camera angles of a live/taped broadcast. Reports to News Director, Executive Producer. *Salary:* varies with market size. Top-10 market: $50,000–$70,000 per year.

Production Assistant
Assists Producers and Directors with script preparation and set arrangement. Reports to Director. *Salary:* $18,000–$20,000 per year.

Anchor
Last but not least . . . the talking heads. Some are very involved in the news gathering and story telling of each show they anchor . . . a few even get involved in writing scripts and some producing elements. But the majority show up a few hours before a newscast, read through their scripts and check out camera shots, go through makeup and wardrobe, and go on the air. Reports to News Directors. *Salary:* varies with experience, contracts, and market size. Top-10 main anchors: $150,000–$1,000,000 plus per year.

Behind the Soap Scenes

Executive Producer
Responsible for overall, long-term vision of the show. Works closely with writers, production staff, and casting. The Executive Producer gives the final "stamp of approval" on everything. *Salary:* $20,000 per week plus (these people can say "yes, I'll have fries with that").

Director
Responsible for blocking and pacing of an episode; they "own" the control room during production of a show; soap opera directors typically direct one to two episodes per week. Works closely with all producers. *Salary:* $3,000–$5,000 per episode. Director's Guild of America (DGA) position.

Associate Director
Assists Director in the booth; typically follows an episode into the editing process. *Salary:* $2,200 per week plus overtime; DGA position.

Supervising Producer
Reports directly to the Executive Producer. Typically known as a "booth producer"-works closely with the Director in the control room to ensure that the written word has been properly translated to tape. Supervises "look" of hair, makeup, wardrobe, sets, lighting. *Salary:* $5,000–$7,000 per week.

Coordinating Producer
Reports directly to the Executive Producer. Responsible for budgets and financing of show and staffing and scheduling; coordinates all remote location shoots. *Salary:* $3,000–$5,000 per week.

Associate Producer

Serves as a "booth producer" typically one day a week; responsible for continuity of show; coordinates press/media events, including Daytime Emmy Awards. (Susan Lucci probably is not fond of these people.) *Salary:* $1,500–$2,500 per week.

Assistant to the Producer

Serves as general assistant for all producers on staff; typically acts as office manager for production: handles office equipment and supplies, etc. Does everything from phones/faxing to assisting with remote location set-ups (the person you want to kiss up to). *Salary:* $500–$700 per week.

Production Assistant/Booth

Rotates every other day in the control room. Assists Director with paper work, etc. Responsible for the overall timing of each episode.
Salary: $800 per week plus overtime; DGA position.

Production Assistant/Office

General office slave. Phones/faxing, script distribution, messengers, lunches. (In other words, basically an intern, except paid a couple of cents more). Entry level; highly visible position. *Salary:* $500–$600 per week.

Sound Mixer

Adds all music and sound effects to show; this is typically done in postproduction. *Salary:* $2,000 per week.

Music Supervisor

Decides which music to use during an episode; works closely with sound mixer to ensure music starts/stops and fades (could probably use this power to unethically get tickets for cool concerts). *Salary:* $1,700 per week.

Script Typist

Outputs final working scripts for distribution. Incorporates all Writer and Executive Producer changes. Entry-level position (typing probably required). *Salary:* $500 per week.

The Talk Trade

Show Host

Great range of responsibilities, depending if host owns a piece of the show and has producing title. Schedule usually includes taping two shows a day, three days a week. Long hours on those days, and often they don't come in on "off days." Hosts like Rosie O'Donnell like the schedule because of the "down" weeks and long hiatus periods and the stability of not having to go on the road. *Salary:* $5,000 per week for cable gigs to several million per year on syndicated shows (rough life, huh?).

Executive Producer

Responsible for overall look of the show, liaison to network or syndicator, in charge of all key hires, including on-air talent. Directly involved in budgets, ratings, and "big picture" issues like traveling a show, key promotional tie-ins, and format changes or additions. Work hours vary greatly, but usually around 50 hours per week, with a fair number of dinners and traveling. *Salary:* $5,000–$15,000 per week, unless you own a piece of the show, which could boost it significantly. (If you can own a piece of the show, plan an early retirement.)

Executive in Charge of Production
Works directly with EP and is directly responsible for budgeting, negotiating contract for crews, craft services, editing and shooting facilities. Heavy financial skills (these are the people who never broke open their piggy banks, even when the ice cream man came around). Works out trade agreements such as free hotel rooms, airline fares, etc., in exchange for promotional consideration. Long hours, usually about 60–70 hours per week. *Salary:* $2,500–$5,000 per week.

Supervising Producer
Oversees the producing team. Responsible for show content, balancing the right topics and guests over the week (and the cycle of shows, which is usually around 200 a year). Gives input into scripts and creative direction of show, such as adding field pieces, satellite interviews, or including other guests. Long hours, usually 70 hours per week. *Salary:* $2,500–$5,000 per week.

Show Producer
Usually responsible for all elements of one complete show per week. Pitches show topics or segment ideas, tracks down and pre-interviews possible guests, and writes segment, adding elements like video tape, studio props, and "surprises" (reunions, celebrity guests, etc.). Briefs the host for the show, works the "floor" during interviews, and keeps in contact with supervising producer (usually in booth). Long hours, mostly around show days. *Salary:* $1,500–$2,000 per week.

Writer
Often takes copy written by individual Producers and gives it a universal tone and feel. "Punches up" copy, including "intros" and "outros," promotional spots, and narration for field pieces. This position can sometimes be done at home (at least part of the time) and the hours are more flexible. *Salary:* $2,000 plus per week.

Talent Executive
Responsible for booking celebrities for the show. Requires keeping up with all forms of entertainment and a great deal of extracurricular "mingling," going to previews, screenings, and talent showcases to check out various talent. Long hours due to nighttime "PR" events. *Salary:* $2,000–$4,000 per week. (Basically, you get to do lunch, have their people call your people, and act too cool to care that Tom Cruise just walked into the room.)

Associate Producer
Support person for individual Producers. Involved in researching topics, preliminary search for guests, coordinating travel arrangements, and light shopping for props. Helps in getting releases signed and guest payments. Hours vary, depending on

workload of show producer. These positions and researcher positions are great entry-level jobs for people interested in producing. *Salary:* $700–$1,000 per week.

Production Assistant and Runner
The staff "gofer" and "errand person." Usually in a car traveling to various places, picking up supplies, and delivering tapes. Hours can be insane, depending on production. It is not uncommon to have to work until 1 a.m. and be back in the office the next morning at 8 a.m., usually without overtime (in other words, basically an intern who isn't protected by the Fair Labor Act). *Salary:* $400–$600 per week.

Reality Roster

Executive Producer
Responsible for show format and design. Deals with executives who fund project, i.e., network, cable channel, syndicator, to determine show's direction and focus. Oversees staffing of producers and final production. *Salary:* $20,000–$40,000 per episode.

Supervising Producer/Show Runner
Approves everything from script to stories to hiring of personnel. Responsibilities include keeping show within its predetermined budget, approving scripts, locking down picture for final cut of show for screenings with executives. Determines the creative vision of the show and what it will eventually look like on the air. *Salary:* $10,000–$20,000 per episode.

Producer
Answers to Supervising Producer and handles the day-to-day troubleshooting of a daily production. More involved with shaping the stories and working with Directors to make sure the show gets what they had in mind from the field shoots. Also responsible for staffing. *Salary:* $2,000–$15,000 per week.

Coordinating Producer
Responsibilities include supervising research and production staff, coordinating story-finding effort, and working with segment producers to shape and troubleshoot stories during set up and on location. *Salary:* $2,500–$3,500 per week.

Director of Research
Responsibilities include supervising research staff, segment producers, and office staff. Coordinates story-finding effort and works with segment producers to help shape stories according to original break down. Communicates what is expected from stories by Producers. Deals with local footage and story sources, i.e., network affiliates. *Salary:* $1,400–$2,500 per week.

Line Producer
Hires and manages all crew, including Directors, Camermen, Audio, Grips, and Field PAs. Manages budgets for each segment. Responsible for shooting schedules. *Salary:* $1,200–$2,000 per week.

Production Coordinator

Works with line producer to assist field personnel, including travel arrangements and equipment rentals. Arranges for special needs in field, i.e., makeup, special effects, stunts, and location releases. Works closely with police for permits during shooting (both taping and gunplay). *Salary:* $550–$800 per week.

Postproduction Supervisor

Responsibilities include keeping track of field tapes and making sure they get logged and labeled and assigning stories to editors and arranging for online and sweetening mix for final show production. *Salary:* $1,200–$2,500 per week.

Editor

Screens field tapes and condenses 500+ minutes worth of footage into a 12- to 18-minute segment. (That is about as easy as finding someone in Hollywood who isn't a writer.) *Salary:* $1,500–$2,500 per week.

Assistant Editor or Logger

Works with editor, digitizes tapes for AVID, and goes through each tape to record action per reel and sound bites. (Rewind, Fast-Forward, Rewind, Fast-Forward, Rewind, Fast-Forward, Rewind, you get our drift) *Salary:* $500–$800 per week.

Writer

Works with editors to write narration for each piece. Writes wrap-around dialogue for host to intro and outro each segment and host narration when needed to move story along. *Salary:* scale varies per project.

Segment Producer

Takes written story synopsis, interviews all the participants, and arranges for field shoot of story. Works with production department to send story into field. *Salary:* $800–$1,500 per week.

Researcher

Finds and develops stories using magazines, newspapers, and television news as sources. Establishes professional contacts that pertain to the type of show you're doing. Considered entry-level, with college education as a must. *Salary:* $450–$700 per week.

Production Assistant and Receptionist

Helps out with general office needs, ordering supplies, ordering and bringing in lunch or coffee. Assists producers with any requests that arise. Answers phone and viewer mail. (Mr. Smith, your other wife called wanting to know about dinner tonight, your girlfriend called wanting to know about dinner later tonight, and I picked up that gift for that girl you started dating last week.) *Salary:* $350–$500 per week.

The Sports Lineup

Production Assistant

Responsible for providing extensive research on teams, players, and league statistics. Responsible for finding footage of teams and players that will be used in show tease, highlights, and feature stories. Responsible for logging tapes shot in the field by Segment Producer. May be expected to set up interviews and tape shoots for Segment Producer. May also be expected to oversee content of chyron and statistical information that is used during "live" broadcast. During the "live" broadcast, the Production Assistant may be expected to work alongside Show Producer in the booth preparing game statistics for the talent and providing general "runner" duties. *Salary:* Cable $12,500–$20,000 per year; Network $15,000–$25,000 per year.

Associate Producer

Responsible for providing extensive research on teams, players, and league statistics. Responsible for finding footage of teams and players that will be used in show tease, highlights, and feature stories. May be expected to set up interviews and tape shoots for Segment Producer. May also be expected to oversee content of chyron and statistical information that is used during "live" broadcast. During the "live" broadcast, may be expected to work alongside Show Producer in the booth preparing game statistics for the talent. *Salary:* Cable $20,000–$30,000 per year; Network $30,000–$50,000 per year.

Segment Producer

Works under the supervision of the Show Producer. Responsible for writing, directing, and producing taped player and team profiles that are included in the show. Responsible for producing taped show tease and highlights. Also can be expected to work with sideline reporter/talent during the game, providing him or her with up-to-the-minute statistics and procuring "live" interviews with players and coaches. May also produce highlight packages at end of "live" broadcast. *Salary:* Cable $50,000–$80,000 per year; Network: $70,000–$110,000 per year.

Producer

Responsible for content and presentation of "live" sports broadcast. Prepares show run-down, works with on-air talent preparing them for the show. Writes scripts for talent and gives them direction during the actual "live" broadcast, giving them up-to-the-minute statistics and information on players as game progresses. Producer sits in control room during the "live" sports game and works with the Director making split-second decisions as to the direction of the broadcast. *Salary:* Cable $60,000–$90,000 per year; Network $75,000–$125,000 per year.

Senior Producer

Responsible for all content and presentation of multiple "live" sports broadcasts. Oversees show run-downs and on-air. Oversees all scripts for talent and works with Show Producer as to the direction of the "live" broadcast as it's unfolding. Senior Producer may sit in control room during the live sports game and work with Show Producer and Director making split-second decisions as to the direction of the broadcast. *Salary:* Cable $75,000–$100,000 per year; Network: $100,000–$200,000 per year.

Executive Producer

Oversees a multitude of "live" broadcasts, responsible for creating show's final look (graphics, opening animation, style of taped packages, and "live" broadcast). Responsible for hiring on-air talent and all producers. Reports to head of sports division. *Salary:* Cable $80,000–$120,000; Network: $120,000–$250,000 per year.

Syndicated Show Budget

Pages	$75/day
Receptionist	$425/week
Script Coordinator	$600/week
Assistant to Hosts	$600/week
Script Supervisor	$850/week
Warm-up Person	$318/show
Production Accountant	$1,300/show
Technical Director	$450/day
Video Engineer	$350/day
Audio Engineer	$250/day
Lighting Director	$600/day
Electricians	$225/day
Camera Operators	$350/day
TelePrompTer Operator	$275/day
Set Director	$350/day
Wardrobe Designer	$1,000/week
Makeup Artist	$350/day
Studio Catering	$950/day
Editor	$2,000/week
Guest on Show	$546 per hour of appearance
Director	$3,500/show

index

LEARNING AWAITS YOU
IN EVERY PETERSON'S GUIDE

Finding the right job is never easy. Peterson's on line at the Career & Education Center at petersons.com gives you the tools and the help you need to find and win the job of your dreams.

At **petersons.com** you can
- Search for career opportunities
- Find helpf'
  steer you
- Get advic
  portfolio

14.95

And if you'
advice on f
graduate p
no further
Enrollment
at **petersor**
- Explore p
  options b
- E-mail pr
  contacts
  informati
- Best of a

791.45 W
Weaver, Dan.
Breaking into television.

WITHDRAWN

Let Pete
guide to

P

's more!➔

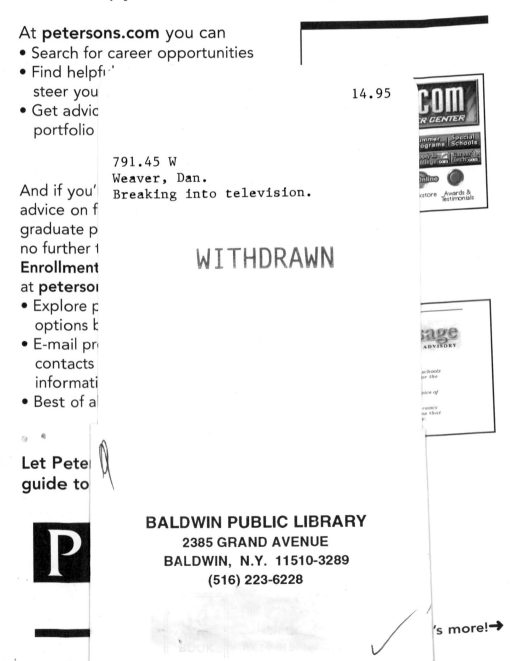